Religious Freedom in America

Recent Titles in the
CONTEMPORARY WORLD ISSUES
Series

Books in the **Contemporary World Issues** series address vital issues in today's society such as genetic engineering, pollution, and biodiversity. Written by professional writers, scholars, and nonacademic experts, these books are authoritative, clearly written, up-to-date, and objective. They provide a good starting point for research by high school and college students, scholars, and general readers as well as by legislators, businesspeople, activists, and others.

Each book, carefully organized and easy to use, contains an overview of the subject, a detailed chronology, biographical sketches, facts and data and/or documents and other primary source material, a forum of authoritative perspective essays, annotated lists of print and nonprint resources, and an index.

Readers of books in the Contemporary World Issues series will find the information they need in order to have a better understanding of the social, political, environmental, and economic issues facing the world today.

Religious Freedom in America

A REFERENCE HANDBOOK

Michael C. LeMay

ABC-CLIO™

An Imprint of ABC-CLIO, LLC
Santa Barbara, California • Denver, Colorado

Library of Congress Cataloging-in-Publication Data

Names: LeMay, Michael C., 1941– author.
Title: Religious freedom in America : a reference handbook / Michael C. LeMay.
Description: Santa Barbara : ABC-CLIO, 2018. |
  Series: Contemporary world issues | Includes bibliographical references and index. | Description based on print version record and CIP data provided by publisher; resource not viewed.
Identifiers: LCCN 2017034695 (print) | LCCN 2017042840 (ebook) | ISBN 9781440851056 (eBook) | ISBN 9781440851049 (alk. paper)
Subjects: LCSH: United States—Religion. | Freedom of religion—United States.
Classification: LCC BL2525 (ebook) | LCC BL2525 .L46 2018 (print) | DDC 323.44/20973—dc23
LC record available at https://lccn.loc.gov/2017034695

ISBN: 978-1-4408-5104-9 (print)
      978-1-4408-5105-6 (ebook)

22 21 20 19 18   1 2 3 4 5

This book is also available as an eBook.

ABC-CLIO
An Imprint of ABC-CLIO, LLC

ABC-CLIO, LLC
130 Cremona Drive, P.O. Box 1911
Santa Barbara, California 93116-1911
www.abc-clio.com

This book is printed on acid-free paper ∞

Manufactured in the United States of America

Contents

Religious freedom is a fundamental principle of the American Constitution and a guiding value for American politics. It has not, however, always been a clear principle easily understood and applied in the day-to-day life of the American polity. Just what precisely freedom of religion and freedom from religion mean, what is entailed in these two clauses of the First Amendment, have been questions engendering a perennial struggle in American politics and throughout American history. It is a cliché, but nonetheless true, that America is a nation of immigrants. The tens of millions of immigrants who came, and are still coming annually to America for permanent resettlement, brought with them a bewildering array of religious beliefs, practices, and ethno-religious organizations. The diversity of religious affiliation in the United States exceeds that of any other nation. With that diversity, however, has come a struggle to get along. Religious minority groups have often experienced prejudice and discrimination and sometimes outright suppression. Oppression and violence against minority religions, in an often futile attempt to force them to conform to the majority's religious beliefs and practices, have often occurred in America's past, are evident in its politics today, and unquestionably will be the case in the future.

The value of religious freedom is enshrined in several key founding documents: the Declaration of Independence, the

Constitution, and the First Amendment of the Bill of Rights. It is further enhanced by the Fourteenth Amendment. The two principal clauses of the Constitution—the freedom of belief or free exercise of religion and the anti–Establishment Clause or freedom from religion—have been clarified as to their meaning by subsequent legislation, by treaty, and most importantly by a host of landmark Supreme Court decisions and other court rulings.

Religious Freedom in America: A Reference Handbook offers insights into important issues and answers questions about the central meaning of the core principle of religious freedom in America in an unbiased manner, making the significant discourse on the topic accessible to high school, undergraduate students and the general reader interested in the topic. It explores the complex history of the topic, the problems raised by the practical effort to implement those two Constitutional clauses, and a considerable body of literature, which will enable the reader to further explore the topic.

Religious Freedom in America is organized into seven chapters. Chapter 1, "Background and History," introduces the reader to the diverse array of religious minorities who comprise the American body politic and discusses why so many religious groups immigrated to America or why they arose from within American society. It highlights issues for religious freedom raised by their presence within American society—at times quite knotty issues over which the political institutions struggled for some time. Its review of the discourse on the topic is comprehensive and is presented in an unbiased manner, offering the topic for the reader's consumption.

Chapter 2, "Problems, Controversies, and Solutions," outlines the most controversial events in American history related to the perennial struggle to give specific meaning to the two broad Constitutional clauses. It explores how the various religious institutions were impacted by the way in which government at all levels of American society interpreted the meaning of freedom of religion and freedom from religion over time and across the breadth of America. It divides discussion of those problems and related political controversies into two foci: problems associated with the Free Exercise Clause and problems associated with the Establishment Clause. Finally, the chapter discusses some of the proposed solutions to those problems and controversies.

Like all volumes in the Contemporary World Issues series, Chapter 3, "Perspectives," is comprised of original essays by other scholars and by activists at the grassroots level of the political struggles over the meaning of the two Constitutional clauses. These short essays offer diverse perspectives on the topic of religious freedom in America that go beyond the expertise of the author and raise additional issues for the reader to consider while exploring the topic.

Chapter 4, "Profiles," provides descriptive bio-sketches of many key individuals and organizations involved in the politics of religious freedom in America. The chapter explores persons and organizations that attempt to influence government and society on both sides of the controversies over religious freedom in America that have arisen and played out, concentrating on persons and organizations currently active in the struggle to give practical, day-to-day meaning to the two Constitutional clauses. Some are government actors involved in disputes over the meaning of the clauses. Others are nongovernmental actors who are attempting to influence government policy and court decisions to further their interests in the debate over the meaning of religious freedom in America.

Chapter 5, "Data and Documents," collects and provides summaries and a synthesis of information central to understanding the topic. It provides figures and tables that illustrate key information on the topic. It lists and discusses synopses of key documents (laws and court decisions) that have defined answers to the questions, problems, and issues raised by government policy to implement religious freedom in America. Collectively, they help inform the reader on past policy and present information for further exploration of the topic.

Chapter 6, "Resources," provides an annotated bibliography of both print and electronic resources that comprise the body of literature on the subject of religious freedom in America. It annotates books and scholarly journals from the fields of various disciplines related to the topic. It annotates feature-length films and videos that give life and a "face" to the subject. Collectively, the resources provide an extensive base for any reader wanting to further explore the topic in a scholarly way.

Chapter 7, "Chronology," offers a brief but comprehensive chronology of defining moments and events in the perennial struggle to give meaning to religious freedom in America.

The book closes with a handy glossary containing more than 80 definitions of key terms and concepts used in the discussion of the topic throughout the book and a comprehensive subject index.

Religious Freedom in America

Introduction

From colonial times to the present day, religious freedom in America has been a beacon, a contentious issue, and an evolving yet fundamental aspect of American society and its politics. This has become increasingly the case as American society developed ever more diversity in its demographic composition. The principle of religious freedom has been enshrined in the American Constitution, but throughout its history American society and American politics struggled with a tension between freedom of religion and freedom from religion, with the practice of religious freedom and a wall of separation between church and state. That struggle and that tension was largely the result of the First Amendment to the Constitution, which guaranteed the freedom of religious belief and prohibited the state's "establishment" of religion. As an increasingly diverse polity, the government and society more generally had to cope on a regular basis with the practical meaning of those two clauses and principles of the First Amendment, which are generally considered to be the most sacred of the Bill of Rights and the most important amendment ensuring our constitutional democracy.

The Pilgrim Fathers hold their first meeting for public worship in North America on January 21, 1621. Although they came for religious freedom, they were intolerant of any other religious group in their colony. (Library of Congress)

Article VI of the Constitution states one aspect of that tension when it says that "the Senators and Representatives before mentioned, and the Members of the several State Legislatures, and all executive and judicial Officers, both of the United States and of the several States, shall be bound by Oath or Affirmation, to support this Constitution, but no religious Test shall ever be required as a Qualification to any Office or public Trust under the United States."

And the First Amendment states, regarding freedom of religion, speech, and the press and the rights of assembly and petition, that "Congress shall make no law respecting an establishment of religion, or prohibiting the free exercise thereof; or abridging the freedom of speech, or of the press, or the right of the people peaceably to assemble, and to petition the Government for a redress of grievances."

America is often described as a "Christian nation." In terms of percentage of the population who self-identify their religion, this is substantiated by 70.6 percent identifying themselves as Christian, with 6.9 percent self-identifying as non-Christian faiths and 22.8 percent as religious "nones" (2010 Census, https://www.census.gov/2010census, accessed August 31, 2017; Pew Research Center's Religious Landscape Study, https://www.pewforum.org/religious-landscape-study, accessed January 26, 2017).

During colonial times, prior to independence and the adoption of the new constitution in 1789, the various colonies that were established along the eastern seaboard reflected the practice of all the European nations and principalities—namely, having an established religion. Church and state were not separate. Unquestionably, in part because of that fact, Europe convulsed with wars of religion (https://www.preceden.com/timelines/71548-european-wars, accessed January 25, 2017). For example, the Schmalkaldic Wars of 1546 to 1555 were fought largely over whether or not the various German states would be Catholic or Lutheran. The Schmalkaldic League was an alliance of Lutheran German princes who fought against

Charles V. The wars were ended in the 1555 truce, the Peace of Augsburg, which allowed the rulers of the German regions to choose between Catholicism and Lutheranism, and the people of their countries had to espouse whichever religion their prince adopted.

Similarly, the French Wars of Religion, which raged off and on between 1562 and 1598, were fierce battles between French Protestants (known as the Huguenots) and French Catholics and the French king who was trying to centralize power. It began with the St. Bartholomew's Day massacre and ended with the War of the Three Henrys. It was essentially a civil war over religious affiliation.

The Spanish Religious Wars of 1566–1648 occurred when the Dutch revolted against the Spanish king, Phillip, who tried to prevent the spread of Protestantism. The war resulted in the Union of Arras, in which the Southern Netherlands remained as part of Spain and a Catholic region of the Netherlands, while the Union of Utrecht in Northern Netherlands was protestant.

An even broader European war of religion was the Thirty Years' War, fought from 1618 to 1648. France felt surrounded by the Hapsburgs. Spain wanted to recapture the Netherlands, and the Hapsburgs wanted to establish central authority and get rid of Protestants. The war started as a religious war but ended as political and dynastic.

Finally, the English Civil War (1642–1649) occurred when King Charles wanted to put down the Scot revolt, and the Parliament Radicals won. Oliver Cromwell, leading the Protestant side, set up a military dictatorship with himself as lord protector. King Charles was executed. Throughout most of Europe, the kings or queens were both the highest political and highest religious authority of their respective kingdoms.

Established Religion in Colonial America

These wars of religion in Old World Europe were the backdrop for the movement in the New World of North America to espouse freedom of religion, which became closely tied to the ideals of American freedom and independence and the idea that church and state should be separate entities, which was beneficial to both (Kornelly 2013: 189–213). Those ideals were an evolutionary movement nearly 200 years in the making (Ahlstrom 1972; Baltzell 1996; Butler 2006; Miller 1986).

It commenced in 1620, when the Puritans fled from the religious persecution of the established Anglican Church of England to settle in the New World, seeking their promised land and a refuge to express their religious beliefs. It ended with the establishment of the new constitutional republic in 1789.

The very success of the Puritans encouraged other religious communities to do likewise. However, within each such colony, those fleeing persecution in their homelands tended to be less tolerant to outright intolerant of other religious dissenters residing within their colony. The Puritans, for example, despite fleeing from religious persecution in England, punished non-Puritans with imprisonment, whipping, exile, and even hanging. Their excesses of intolerance led to the formation of new colonies in Rhode Island and Pennsylvania. Other colonies, such as Virginia and the Carolinas, were directly sponsored by the English Crown as Royal colonies and thus had Anglicanism as their official religion. But by the early to mid-1700s, dozens of ethnic groups, each with their own religious denominations, had settled in the North American colonies. In part, the influx of so many immigrants holding different religious beliefs and denominational affiliations compelled the Founding Fathers, themselves often Deists, to establish a nation built on the premise of separation of church and state and the very notion of religious freedom as a foundational principle integral to American society (Holmes 2006; Mapp 2003; Walters 1992). European perceptions of America's religious tolerance and nearly unlimited opportunities became a pull factor drawing millions to the New World (LeMay 1987: 2).

The division between Catholic and Protestant empires reinforced ethnic and linguistic differences, leading to separate national and cultural identities in Europe. The Protestant Reformation was felt most heavily in German-speaking principalities, Scandinavia, and England. Protestant denominations—and many developed—were united in a central Christian philosophy and a distrust, even hatred, of the Roman Catholic Church, but they often had little else in common. Slight theological distinctions among Protestant groups were intensified by cultural, linguistic, and geographical barriers and caused Protestant groups to schism into distinct denominations. When they migrated to America, they settled in areas where they shared the ethnic and religious heritage of other members of that community, resulting in migration patterns reinforcing Old World ethnic divisions that helped develop regional cultures in the American colonies (Kornelly 2013: 192–194). The migration patterns led to the development of religious pluralism and religious tolerance in North America. In Pennsylvania, for example, radical Protestant groups formed small but significant alternatives to the mainline Lutheran or Reform Churches, and these groups were very diverse and totally rejected formal establishment. By the mid-17th century, Pietists challenged the tenets of mainstream Protestantism. Anabaptists (rebaptizers) and Quakers made the then radical assertion that religious practice should be separated from civil governance. As will be discussed more fully in Chapter 2, this and their strong position of pacifism caused problems with the majority culture during times of war, especially the War of 1812 and the Civil War. Schwenckfelders and Mennonites also comprised closely knit communities that followed the spiritual principles of a revered leader. The implicit political nature of such European, radical Protestant groups made them vulnerable to persecution as they defied the authority not only of the Roman Catholic Church but also of the more dominant and conservative form of Protestantism. Many of these groups migrated to North America, where they were able to reestablish their communities and forge the American frontier according to their beliefs. In the English colonies, the Anglican Church was the established religion, and conformity to the church was severely enforced against the so-called radical Protestants, such as the Quakers and Anabaptists, who held that religious beliefs and political affairs should be completely separated. As more settlements were established and more people immigrated to the colonies, attitudes toward the role of religion became more divergent (Ulrich 1991: 108). In 1649, for example, the Maryland proprietary colony granted to Cecelius Calvert, Lord Baltimore, enacted the Act of Toleration, outlining greater religious freedom than that which existed in the two Puritan colonies of Massachusetts and Connecticut (Kornelly 2013: 200). In 1639, exiles from the Massachusetts colony founded Rhode Island as their own refuge from religious intolerance. Separatist Roger Williams and Pietist Anne Hutchinson were granted the first colonial charter to explicitly grant freedom of religious conscience (Fantel 1974; Gaustad 1999). Providence became a safe haven for those who clashed with the established churches in the other New England colonies, such as the Quakers. The Rhode Island colony, however, was an idea well ahead of its time. The other colonies, such as those in Virginia, continued to have an established (Anglican) church that was government run and subsidized by local taxes. In Maryland, in 1691, King William III revoked Lord Baltimore's charter, making it a royal colony. The Anglican Church became the established church in 1702, and Maryland became the most vigilant colonial supporter of the Church of England. Similarly, in 1661, Virginia passed strict regulations against Baptists and Quakers and helped create a fertile atmosphere that led to the Great Awakening that characterized religious life in America for much of the 18th century (Kornelly 2013: 199). In the Carolinas, the Anglican Church was established in 1681, but South Carolina had a substantial number of Puritans and Baptists who had migrated there from New England, as well as French Huguenots and Quakers, and North Carolina had a growing number of German-speaking Pietist communities who had migrated there following the American Revolution.

Georgia received its charter in 1732, when King George II tasked that colony with creating a buffer between the established English colonies to the north and the territories claimed by the French and Spanish to the south. Georgia's proprietors invited persecuted protestant religious communities to settle in the colony, attracting a group of Moravian Brethren there in 1735, soon followed by Salzburg Lutherans and other Pietist communities. While officially the Anglican Church was the established one, the colony was loosely governed with respect to religion. John Wesley, who went on to develop the Methodists, and George Whitefield were among the early Anglican priests there, and they were arguably among the most significant evangelists of the Great Awakening.

Before the Revolutionary War, Virginia had many converted Baptists who were successful in evangelizing many settlers on the then frontier. The Virginia assembly passed repressive laws against nonconformists. Thomas Jefferson, then a young lawyer, witnessed their plight and advocated for their rights. That experience shaped his views, resulting in his writing of the Virginia Statute of Religious Freedom (Hening 1823: 84–86; see also Ahlstrom 1972; Butler 2006; Heimert 1966; Holmes 2006; Mapp 2003; Peterson and Vaughn 1988; Walters 1992). In later life, Jefferson was more proud of his authorship of that statute than he was of having been elected president (Jefferson 1977; see also Holmes 2006; Levy 1994; Mapp 2003; Miller 1986; Peterson and Vaughn 1988).

The mid-Atlantic region was first settled, in 1609, by the Dutch in the north and, in 1638, by Sweden to the south. They had established Dutch Reformed churches and Swedish Lutheran churches, respectively. When the English took over from the Dutch, in 1664, the royal governors had realized the economic benefits of socially liberal rule. Upstate New York became home to the Shakers in 1774. The Shakers, founded in 1770 by Quaker Ann Lee, were informally called the "Shaking Quakers" for their shaking as they danced and speaking in tongues during their services. Mother Ann Lee was viewed by her followers as the female component of Christ's spirit and represented the second appearance of Christ on earth—hence their official name was the United Society of Believers in Christ's Second Appearance. In 1774, they settled in western New York, eventually founding 18 settlements stretching from Kentucky to Maine (Portman and Bauer 2004; see also Bilhartz 1986; Butler 2006; Heimert 1966; Holmes 2006).

In New Jersey, the region became home to many Scotch-Irish Presbyterians, who left famine and unrest in Northern Ireland during the latter half of the 18th century. New Sweden's colony was founded by William Penn and a small group of fellow Quakers who founded West New Jersey in 1674. Their continued persecution in England led to more Quakers settling in the Delaware Valley, until Penn chartered the Commonwealth of Pennsylvania in 1681. Their religious tolerance attracted other persecuted groups, for instance, the Pietist community of Moravians in 1702. The colonial charter ensured freedom of religious conscience to all but Roman Catholics (Fantel 1974; see also Ahlstrom 1972; Baltzell 1996; Butler 2006; Miller 1986). Penn's sons converted to Anglicanism, and the decline in Pennsylvania's Quakerism was followed by an increase in immigrants to the colony, including the Scotch-Irish Presbyterians, who entered through the port of Philadelphia at a rate of 12,000 per year in 1740, and an estimated 120,000 German-speaking immigrants who landed between 1683 and 1820, which made them the largest non-English-speaking population in North America by 1820 (LeMay 1987: 21–22). By the turn of the 19th century, one-third of Pennsylvania's population were German immigrants or of German ancestry. Most belonged to the German Lutheran or German Reform churches, as well as small communities of German Pietists who saw Penn's "Holy Experiment" as an opportunity to establish a home in America. Soon, they came in entire groups of hundreds: Mennonites, Dunkers, Lutherans, Calvinists, and even a few Jews, arriving from such German states as Palantine, Salzburg, Wurttenburg, and Hanover (LeMay 1987: 23, 2009:

192–200; see also Boyton 1986; Driedger and Kraybill 1994; Nolt 1992).

The Mennonites are an Anabaptist sect named after Menno Simons, their prominent leader who united them with a Dutch group in 1536. The Amish split off into another sect in 1693 in Alsace, France, following the Anabaptist leader Jacob Ammann. He stressed the practice of shunning of persons excommunicated from the faith. They migrated to the United States in the 18th century. Old Order Mennonites and the Old Order Amish set up small communities of 500 or so centered in Berks County and Lancaster County, Pennsylvania. They maintained their cultural separateness by use of the *ordnung*, or understandings, which prescribed expectations for Amish and Mennonite life and practices. They became the mother settlements of both the Amish and Mennonite communities that were soon established throughout Pennsylvania and Virginia and the Carolinas (Kraybill and Nolt 1995; LeMay 2009: 193–200; Nolt 1992).

Old Order Mennonites and the Old Order Amish spoke a German dialect that came to be called "Pennsylvania Dutch," which is not the Dutch language but derived from their pronunciation of "Deutsch."

Conflict with majority society as well as between them centered on aspects of the majority culture in ways the majority deemed dangerous. Their pacifism, for example, brought persecution on them during the U.S. Civil War and led to even greater discrimination during World War I, when many Amish and Mennonite conscientious objectors refused to fight: they received verbal abuse and beatings, were forced to shave their beards (prescribed by their faith), and were occasionally even "baptized" (urinated on) in camp latrines, purposely mocking their Anabaptist beliefs (Nolt 1992; Wenger 1961).

Another conflict arose in 1955, when Congress extended Social Security to include self-employed farmers. The Amish had never taken part in Social Security, and when they refused to pay into the fund, the Internal Revenue Service collected funds through their bank accounts, foreclosed and sold several farms, and forcibly collected from 130 Amish households. In 1965, Congress finally addressed the issue by including a provision of the Medicare Act that exempted self-employed Amish from Medicare and the Social Security system (LeMay 2009: 199).

The issue that aroused the most controversy was compulsory education. Old Order Amish and Old Order Mennonite parents refused to send their children to large, consolidated elementary schools or on to high school. They had repeated run-ins in nearly every state throughout the 1950s and 1960s when they were forced to pay fines and serve jail terms. Their doctrine of educating children only enough to be able to read the Bible and their separatist culture, which made them reluctant to send their children to public school, brought them into conflict with mandatory public school laws, a conflict that was not settled until the 1972 case *Yoder v. Wisconsin* (LeMay 2009: 197–200; see also Kraybill and Olshan 1994: 162–163; Peters 2003; Urofsky 2002).

The Church of the Brethren group, more commonly called the Dunkers, were a small radical community of Pietist Anabaptists from the German Palatinate who emphasized celibacy, shared property, and practiced ancient Christian rites (e.g., triple, full-body immersion for baptism, from which their common name derived). This practice distinguished them from the sprinkling Lutherans and Methodists, or the pouring Mennonites, or the single-dunking Baptists (Holmes 2006: 3–5). They left their homeland in 1719 to help build Pennsylvania's German-speaking communities. They began in the village of Schwarzenau, Germany, along the Eder River. They originally called themselves New Baptists. They immigrated between 1719 and 1733, founding their settlements in Pennsylvania, New Jersey, Maryland, Virginia, and the Carolinas, always alongside a river that could be used for their triple-immersion baptismal rite.

The Mennonites emerged out of the Dutch Reform movement and arrived in America in 1760. Closely tied to them, the Amish pressed for more stringent observance of Mennonite practices. They left their Swiss homeland in 1727, eventually settling in central Pennsylvania, and then moved their settlements westward.

The Schwenckfelders were another insular Pietist group that followed the teachings of Kaspar Schwenckfeld von Ossig, who emphasized inner spirituality and building the true, invisible church. The founder of the Moravians, Count Nicholaus Von Zinzendorf, protected a group of Schwenckfelders from persecution in Germany and sent the first group to settle in central Pennsylvania in 1734. They were joined later by immigrants from Scandinavia. The Moravian Brethren were arguably the most vocal and prominent of the German-speaking Pietist communities to immigrate to North America. They first settled in Georgia, in 1735, but, under the guidance of the evangelical preacher George Whitefield, established a central community in Bethlehem, Pennsylvania (Kornelly 2013: 207; LeMay 2009: 192–200).

European Unitarianism flowered in Poland and Transylvania in the 16th century. Faustus Socinus was a leading theologian in a group of non-Trinitarian liberal congregations in Poland. They promoted religious liberty, reason, and tolerance, for which they were persecuted. In Transylvania, the court preacher, Ferenec David (Francis David), influenced King John Sigismund to declare the first edict of religious toleration, in 1568. In England, Joseph Priestley, the discoverer of oxygen, was a Unitarian minister who espoused a number of liberal and unpopular causes. His home, laboratory, library, and Unitarian chapel were attacked and burned. He fled to America, in 1794, at the invitation of Thomas Jefferson, and brought Unitarianism with him. Another English Universalist, John Murray, was released from debtor's prison and allowed to emigrate. His ship was grounded off the coast of New Jersey, and he went ashore landing at a farm owned by Thomas Potter, who had built a chapel and was waiting for a preacher to appear. Murray preached at his chapel, began a preaching career, and brought Universalism to the colonies. Unitarianism and Universalism took root, offering relief from the Calvinist notion of damnation. Hosea Ballou became the movement's greatest leader, and religious liberals formed their own theologies of human free will, dignity, and rationality. By the early 19th century, many Puritan Congregational churches began to call themselves Unitarian (https://www.firstunitarianportland.org/our-church/our-roots/unitarian-history, accessed January 25, 2017).

The Constitution and the First Amendment

The Reformation served as a catalyst for challenging authority (both civil and religious) and for developing grassroots religious movements. By the mid-18th century, Protestant theology in North America emphasized the conversion experience and a belief in religious freedom. The colonies became a testing ground—a "Holy Experiment"—and allowed for a diversity of attitudes toward religion and the cultivating of personal spirituality (Kornelly 2013: 209). Religious communities diverged from their counterparts in Europe as communication between the Old World and the New lapsed and parishioners experienced different pressures and resolutions to their concerns. Americans became increasingly self-sufficient. In America, the Methodist and Baptist denominations were tied to a widespread movement of evangelism as small religious communities expanded into the American frontier, which allowed for safe havens for resettlement and freedom of religious belief and practice separate from the official religious denomination of the colonial governments. The frontier was the setting for the Great Awakening, which encouraged evangelism and conversion. It coincided with the emergence of Protestant denominations, such as the Baptists and Shakers, and a brand of Pietism that did not need a church to cultivate spirituality. Spiritual revival brought about by charismatic preachers like George Whitefield and John Wesley led to a "personal rebirth in Christ." People across the colonies were united through a spiritual heritage that helped forge a collective American identity during the revolutionary era (Ahlstrom 1972; Bilhartz 1986; Butler 2006; Heimert 1966; Holmes 2006).

Churches not sponsored by the colonial governments grew into more formal institutions. As a booming metropolis in a colony that endorsed religious tolerance, Philadelphia played a key role in centralizing such Nonconformist churches. In 1790, when the United States took its first census, Philadelphia's population was 28,522, the second-largest city in America (LeMay 2013, vol. 1: 56). Philadelphia became home to the central assemblies for the Quaker, Baptist, and Presbyterian Churches and, after the Revolution, played a significant role in the development of the Protestant Episcopal Church and American Lutheranism (Baltzell 1996; Miller 1986).

At the same time as the Nonconformist denominations began to centralize, the state-sponsored churches began to disestablish. Freedom of religious choice became a rallying point for uniting the American identity, and, when the colonies became independent, the Bill of Rights provided for the separation of church and state in the federal government. In 1786, due largely to the efforts of Thomas Jefferson, Virginia became the first state to end state-sponsored churches. Written by Jefferson and secured in its adoption by James Madison, the Bill of Rights became the model for other states that began to include freedom of religion clauses or provisions in their state constitutions. By 1833, all of the states followed Virginia's model (Hening 1823; Levy 1994; Mapp 2003; Miller 1986; Peterson and Vaughn 1988; Vile 2015a, 2015b). The Virginia statute stated "that no man shall be compelled to frequent or support any religious worship, place, or ministry whatsoever, nor shall be enforced, restrained, molested, or burthened in his body or goods, nor shall otherwise suffer on account of his religious opinions or belief, but that all men shall be free to profess, and by argument to maintain, their opinion in matters of religion, and that the same shall in no wise diminish, enlarge, or affect their civil capacities" (cited in Hening 1823: 86; see also Jefferson 1977; Kornelly 2013: 211).

The idea of that separation of civil and religious authority was also recognized in one of the earliest treaties that the newly independent, constitutional government negotiated: the Treaty of Tripoli (1796). The treaty ended conflict between the U.S. Marines and pirates who had been harassing U.S. merchant ships out of Tripoli, Lebanon, a predominantly Muslim country. It was ratified unanimously by the U.S. Senate on June 7, 1787, and signed into law by President John Adams on June 10, 1797. Through Article VI of the U.S. Constitution, it became the supreme law of the land: "This Constitution, and the Laws of the United States which shall be made in Pursuance thereof, and all Treaties made, or which shall be made under the authority of the United States, shall be the supreme Law of the Land, and the Judges in every State shall be bound thereby, any Thing in the Constitution or Laws of any State to the Contrary notwithstanding." One of the treaty's opening phrases states: "As the government of the United States is not in any sense founded on the Christian religion." It is notable that the treaty was ratified by the same Senate that passed the Bill of Rights.

The impact of Deism was also notable. Deism was a movement or system of thought advocating natural religion, emphasizing morality and, in the 18th century, denying the interference of the Creator with the laws of the universe. It complicates the actual belief of the Founders. Drawing from the philosophical works of Jean-Jacques Rousseau, Isaac Newton, and John Locke, Deism argued that human experience and rationality—rather than religious dogma and mystery—determine the validity of human beliefs. Thomas Paine, a protégé of Benjamin Franklin, was the principal proponent of Deism in America (see Heimert 1966; Holmes 2006; Mapp 2003; Middlekauff 2005; Nuovo 2002).

The question of the religious faith of the Founding Fathers has generated a culture war in America. University scholars argue that the majority of the Founders were rationalists or Unitarians. Pastors and self-identified evangelicals claim most were orthodox Christians and some were born-again Christians.

By examining the terminology they used in their writings, their affiliation and attendance at church, and the testimony of those who knew them well enough to assess their personal religious beliefs, one might conclude that some of the Founders were non-Christian Deists: Thomas Paine, Ethan Allen, and James Monroe. Christian Deists included George Washington, John Adams, and Thomas Jefferson. Samuel Adams, John Jay, Elias Boudinot, and Patrick Henry were Orthodox Christians (Butler 2006; Holmes 2006; Mapp 2003; Miller 1985; Nuovo 2002; Peterson and Vaughn 1988; Walters 1992).

Benjamin Franklin noted: "When a religion is good, I conceive it will support itself, and when it does not support itself, and God does not take care to support it so that its professors are obliged to call for help of the civil power, 'tis a sign, I apprehend, of its being a bad one" (website for Americans for Religious Liberty, www.arlinc.org/about/history.html, accessed February 11, 2017).

No matter their personal faith beliefs, unquestionably, a majority of the Founding Fathers were influenced by Deism in so far as the movement opposed barriers to moral improvement and to social justice and stood for rational inquiry, skepticism about dogma and mystery, and religious tolerance. Many of its adherents favored universal education, freedom of the press, and the separation of church and state. The Founding Fathers notably embraced political ideas that were remarkably liberal for their time. These ideas informed their insistence on enacting the First Amendment in the Bill of Rights.

Following the American Revolution, the Anglicans who remained in the United States formed the Protestant Episcopal Church, in 1785. The first American-born Anglican bishop, Samuel Seabury, was consecrated in 1783 by Scottish bishops in the Anglican Church, because the English Anglican bishops refused to do so. Seabury went on to become the second presiding bishop of the Episcopal Church in America. American Episcopalians soon combined with the Swedish Lutherans in

Philadelphia and South Jersey. They retained traditional liturgy and remained closed to the charismatic evangelism of the Great Awakening (Kornelly 2013: 212).

Roman Catholics, mostly originally coming from Ireland or Germany, today number 21 million and comprise 7 percent of the population. A sizable number of Catholics were added to the U.S. population through the Louisiana Purchase of 1803.

Spain claimed ownership of the territory of Louisiana, which at the time included some 828,000 square miles, comprising all or parts of what today is 15 states between the Mississippi River and the Rocky Mountains. An earlier treaty, the Pinckney Treaty of 1795, resolved tensions between Spain and the United States, granting the United States the right to navigate the Mississippi River and for Americans to transfer their goods to ocean-going vessels at New Orleans. That situation changed when France acquired Louisiana from Spain in 1800 and took possession in 1802. Napoleon Bonaparte was anxious to revive the French empire and intended to use the territory as a base to put down a slave rebellion (on today's Haiti) and as a source of grain for his empire. The United States, and its population in the then Western region, was very apprehensive about the French control of New Orleans. President Thomas Jefferson was especially worried and sent James Monroe to France to seek to purchase New Orleans and West Florida for $10 million. A yellow fever plague decimated half of Napoleon's army on Haiti, and he decided to sell the entire territory to the United States for $15 million. Jefferson approved the deal, and Congress concurred, based on the principle of "implied powers" of the federal government. The purchase meant that the residents of the territory (many from Spain and a lesser but significant number from France) became U.S. citizens. There were suddenly many more Catholics in the population (https://www.history.state.gov/milestones/1801–1829/louisiana-purchase, accessed February 11, 2017).

Catholics also arrived in large numbers fleeing religious persecution in Ireland and in northern Germany (Prussia, particularly) in the 1840s and 1850s. Derided as "papists" by Protestant Americans, they experienced religious discrimination in the pre–Civil War era and set off a dramatic xenophobic reaction. They were easy scapegoats to blame for the social and economic problems generated by a rapidly urbanizing and industrializing country (LeMay 2009: 353). They were accused of importing crime and drunkenness. Protestant evangelizers seeking to preserve the nation's "purity" joined forces with radical nativists like the Secret Order the Star Spangled Banner (which morphed into the American party better known as the Know-Nothing Party). A wave of xenophobia led to violent attacks on churches and convents and inflammatory anti-Catholic literature, often led by a splinter group called the "Plug-Uglies." They rose up "to burn Catholic convents, churches, and homes, assault nuns, and murder Irishmen, Germans, and Negroes" (Beals 1960: 9; LeMay 1987: 32–34; see also Bailey 1976; Billington 1974). Anti-Catholic riots broke out in cities like New York, Newark, and Baltimore. The Know-Nothing movement died out by the time of the Civil War, but conflicts with Roman Catholicism over parochial schools, prayers in public schools, and which version of the Bible to be read in schools, for example, arose again in the 1870s and 1880s, when large waves of immigrants from Italy brought in a new wave of Catholics and the Ku Klux Klan espoused radical and often violent anti-Catholicism and anti-Semitism (Hofstadter and Wallace 1971; LeMay 1987: 44).

The absorption of large numbers of Catholics by treaty rights happened again in 1848. The Treaty of Guadalupe-Hidalgo (February 2, 1848) was the peace treaty ending the Mexican-American War (1846–1848), fought largely over the annexation of Texas by the United States. The treaty added 525,000 square miles to U.S. territory, comprising all or parts of present-day Arizona, California, Colorado, Nevada, New Mexico, Utah, and Wyoming. Mexicans living in the newly acquired territory were made U.S. citizens unless they opted out. The treaty instantly added a large population of Roman

Catholics to the national population. Acquisition of the new territory also fueled the slave state versus free state controversy and conflict that ultimately led to the Civil War.

The Rise of Homegrown Minority Religions

Not all religious groups comprising the rich and complex diversity of religion in the United States came as immigrants. There arose some significant "home-grown" minority religions in American history, each of which had a profound impact on American politics, laws, and court cases that shaped the debates and conflicts over religious freedom in America. This section will discuss four such minority religions: the Mormons, who arise in 1823; the Seventh-day Adventists, who appear in 1844; the Jehovah's Witnesses, who surface in 1844; and the Nation of Islam (better known as the Black Muslims), who develop in Detroit in the 1930s.

The Church of Jesus Christ of Latter-day Saints: The Mormons

Today, the Mormon Church is clearly mainstream, with more than seven million adherents in the United States (Davies 2000: 243). It is one of the fastest-growing world religions. Its historical significance is that it was a new religious tradition founded in 19th-century America and exhibited a complex, embattled relationship to the society from which it emerged and to the evangelicalism that was such a dominant force in American society at the time it was founded (https://national humanitiescenter.org/tserve/nineteen/nkeyinfo/nmormon.htm, accessed February 11, 2017).

Joseph Smith Jr. (1806–1844), its founder, was born in Vermont, and his family moved to Palmyra, New York, in 1816. There, Smith claims he received his first revelation from God and his first visit from an angel, Moroni, in 1823 (LeMay 2009: 173, http://nationalhumanitiescenter.org/tserve/nineteen/nkeyinfo/nmormon.htm).

In 1827, Moroni gave him tablets, which he and a few trusted associates translated over the next two years, before returning the plates to Moroni. The translated text became known as *The Book of Mormon*, and in 1830, he and six of his followers established the Church of Jesus Christ of Latter-day Saints. For Mormon believers, *The Book of Mormon* possessed the same canonical standing as the Old and New Testaments do for Protestants and Catholics. They saw Smith as a new prophet and the book as God's third and final revelation of scriptural truth: the "sealed" book described in the Book of Isaiah, signaling the coming of the "end-times" as predicted in the Book of Revelation. The faithful identify themselves as saints, the new Israelites called out from the Gentiles to usher in the millennium, to establish the Godly kingdom on earth to prepare the way for Christ's Second Coming (Abanes 2002; Arrington and Bitton 1992; Bushman and Bushman 2001; The Church of Jesus Christ of Latter-day Saints 1989; Davies 2000; Mauss 1994; McConkie 1966; Tanner 1976).

Almost immediately, they experienced intense discrimination. They moved to Kirtland, Ohio, and Independence, Missouri. In 1836, they built an elaborate temple, and like other communitarian groups (e.g., the Shakers or the Amish and Mennonites), they set up cohesive, economically self-sufficient and largely self-governing settlements, marking themselves not only as a group of worshipers but also as a people set apart. Discrimination developed early and led to expulsion through the use of violence, as well as applied the force of law to pressure them to change their tenets to be more acceptable to the views of the majority society. In part, this was a reaction to their dogmatism and to the "theocracy" of their communities (Hardy 1992; LeMay 2009: 173).

The tenet of their faith that caused the most trouble for the majority society was polygamy, or the plural marriage principle, and "celestial marriage," defined in Mormon doctrine as "marriages performed in the temples for time and eternity," which remains a central doctrine of Mormonism

(McConkie 1966: 117). They stressed speaking in tongues and faith healing. Their dogmatism aroused animosity similar to anti-Catholicism so prevalent at the time. Every adult male adhering to the faith was considered a priest, and Mormons developed a group of Melchizedek priests (the Council of Seventies), considered as militant as the Roman Catholic Jesuits. In the words of Stanley Hirshson (1969: 18–19), "As much as a church, moreover, the Saints created a society. In specifically designed communities they gathered and became in every sense a people. Often migrating in groups, they proved a new society following the same model could even be moved physically from one part of the world to another." Mounting tensions with their Gentile neighbors escalated into armed conflict, forcing the Mormons to flee once again. In 1821–1833, a virtual war broke out, involving some 1,200 Mormons in pitched battles. Mormon homes were burned down, and on October 25, 1838, the Battle of Crooked River took place, becoming known as the Mormon Rebellion. Missouri governor Boggs issued an extermination order. He was shot and severely wounded in 1842, an act broadly held to have been ordered by Joseph Smith (LeMay 2009: 174).

In 1839, 15,000 Mormons crossed into Illinois, where they bought the town of Commerce and renamed it Nauvoo. It had a charter, with Smith as its mayor, making it an independent municipality with its own court system, militia, and political party (the Mormon's People's Party). The merging of the religious, the military, and the secular political structure created a virtual theocracy. It quickly became the largest city in the state. They developed a doctrinally complex and elaborate hierarchical religious structure, embracing a Hebraic model or organization. They had deacons, elders, priests, and bishops, with Smith as "First Presidency" and a high counsel, a special Quorum of Seventy, a Council of Twelve Apostles, and a patriarch—Joseph Smith I (Abanes 2002, http://nationalhu manitiescenter.org/tserve/nineteen/nkeyinfo/nmormon.htm, accessed January 28, 2017).

In 1840, Brigham Young and several others were sent to serve as missionaries in England. Their first year there yielded 9,000 converts, many of whom emigrated to New Zion when Young returned there in July 1841 (LeMay 2009: 174).

Mormons voted as a bloc following directions from the pulpit. In 1844, Smith revealed a plan for organizing the kingdom of God on earth, with himself as king, and he declared his candidacy for president of the United States (on the Mormon People's Party ticket). On June 27, 1844, Smith and his brother, Hyrum, were arrested and later dragged from jail and murdered by a group of militia called out to protect the state from a feared Mormon uprising. Their martyrdom led to the last great migration of the Mormons, to Utah, begun in February 1846, after the Nauvoo charter was revoked.

Following the Smiths' murder, the Mormons splintered. The largest group was led by Brigham Young, the successor to Joseph Smith. Young led a group of about 4,000 as they began their "great trek" westward. They first wintered in what is now Omaha, Nebraska. Then, in April 1847, Young led a party of 148 in 73 wagons, and on July 21, 1847, they entered Salt Lake Valley, stopping on July 23 at the site that became Salt Lake City. A second group of about 500 joined them, settling in the Utah territory, where they established a virtual Mormon kingdom, centered in Salt Lake City, which they called the State of Deseret.

Joseph Smith's death led to a crisis in the movement's leadership and to the first of several schisms. The splintering is not surprising given that the movement arose in a crisis of authority. Mormonism was a divisive and ringing dissent from the existing churches and theologies of the time, and its early attempts to develop a communal utopia under theocratic control in the 1830s and 1840s led to dissenters within. Joseph Smith's death created the major split in the summer of 1844. The main line followed Brigham Young westward, and a minor line stayed in the Midwest, espousing a different doctrine as well as leadership. The Midwest line, the Reorganized Church of Jesus Christ of Latter Day Saints, rejected the plural marriage tenet and practice completely (Abanes 2002; Launius and Thatcher 1994; Tanner 1976). Other schisms resulted in the Strangites and the Cutterites. The Strangites remained in Wisconsin and Michigan. Sidney Rigdon led the Church of Christ, which lasted from 1845 through his death in 1876, located mostly in Pennsylvania and Iowa. The Reorganized Church of Jesus Christ of Latter Day Saints was headquartered in Independence, Missouri, and headed for some 40 years by Joseph Smith III, the son of founder Joseph Smith II. His mother, Joseph Smith II's first wife, stayed with him (Launius and Thatcher 1994; LeMay 2009: 176–177; Young 1972).

In Utah, Young commenced a long period of leadership (1847–1877), during which the Mormon leadership elaborated on the precepts of plural marriage and patriarchal governance promulgated by founder Joseph Smith. The Utah Mormons, with an influx of converts from England and elsewhere in Europe, soon numbered close to 150,000, and the Great Basin Kingdom remained largely intact into the 1880s, despite military occupation of the territory during 1858–1860 (Arrington and Bitton 1992: 169). Brigham Young died in 1877 and the practice of polygamy began to whither somewhat. Congress declared the practice of polygamy illegal in 1882, and under great pressure (a number of Mormon leaders were arrested), the president of the Church of Jesus Christ of Latter-day Saints, Wilford Woodruff, in exchange for granting statehood to the Utah territory, agreed to halt the *practice* of plural marriage (though maintaining the *doctrine* of celestial marriage) and to dissolve the separate Mormon political party (Abanes 2002; Launius and Thatcher 1994; LeMay 2009: 175–176; Tanner 1976).

Two U.S. Supreme Court rulings upheld the acts of Congress against polygamy. The first, *Reynolds v. United States* (1879), was written for a unanimous court by Chief Justice Waite, in which he expounded the "wall of separation" doctrine with regard to church and state relations. The case ruled that religious *beliefs* did not justify polygamy as a *practice.* The final case, *LDS v. United States* (1890), upheld the validity of an 1887 act of Congress that annulled the charter of the Mormons and declared all Church property forfeit save for a small portion used exclusively for worship. That case was necessitated because the Mormons ignored the earlier ruling and continued to practice polygamy despite the law. That ruling led to the Mormon Manifesto of 1890, promulgated by Mormon president Woodruff (LeMay 2009: 177).

The manifesto led to some schisms and further splinter groups that broke away from the main body to continue the practice of plural marriage. Even in the main body, polygamous marriages continued after the manifesto of 1890, with the consent of general authorities (Abanes 2002). Within the main body, however, the practice increasingly withered under the pressures of the dominant society and adverse testimony of Mormon "apostates" (Young 1972).

The tendency toward schism has continued within the Mormon movement. The Aaronic Order, a Levite sect, emerged in the 1930s and formally organized in 1940, whose leaders considered it a "revitalization." It has a high priesthood and maintains polygamous marriage. They are similar to Amish and Mennonites in wearing distinctive garb or uniform dress, even using a woman's cap modeled after the Mennonite cap (Baer 1988).

Since that split, the main Mormon Church has become increasingly incorporated into American politics and society, perhaps best exemplified by the candidacy for president of the United States by Republican nominee Mitt Romney in 2007 (LeMay 2009: 181–182).

The Seventh-day Adventists

The Seventh-day Adventists emerged from the religious revival in the northeastern United States known as the Second Great Awakening, specifically from a millennial movement led by a

Baptist preacher, William Miller (Bilhartz 1986, http://chris tianity.about.com/od/seventhdayadventists/a/7thdayadventist, accessed January 28, 2017). Millennial movements can be religious, political, social, or a combination of those types. It typically refers to a long period of time (hence, millennial or a thousand years) and involves belief in a prophecy of a major event associated, in religious terms, with the end of times (Ahlstrom 1972; Casey 1918; Fenn 1997; Kaplan 1997; Landes 2000, 2011; Wessinger 2000, 2011; Wojcik 1997). Its members typically feel they are under attack by a "they" group bent on destroying their way of life. In the Christian tradition, they identify themselves with the oppression and deliverance of the Israelites of the Old Testament. Given their vision of the future, they are often referred to as revitalization movements. Millennial ethno-religious movements are often perceived as cults and sects. *Cults* are often small groups that hold a system of religious worship or ritual, often living in a colony, and led by charismatic leaders. *Sects* are typically religious bodies that form in small- to medium-sized groups that break away from an established orthodoxy or church. They have a common leadership and hold a strong set of opinions, philosophical doctrines, religious principles and practices, and often associated political principles. A member of a sect—a sectarian—is a person who is rather blindly and narrow mindedly devoted to the sect. Examples of groups considered sects by the orthodox and mainline denominations would include Mormons, Jehovah's Witnesses, the Unification Church (more commonly known as Moonies after their founder, Sun Myung Moon), New Age, Christian Science Church, Church of Scientology, Worldwide Church of God, Unitarian/Universalists, and Socinianism. Historically, other Christian cults, considered heresies, were the Gnosticism, Neo-Gnosticism, and Agnosticism (Ammerman 1997; LeMay 2009: 243–244).

The Seventh-day Adventist Church take its name from its holding Saturday as the Sabbath Day—it believes that other Christian denominations moving celebration of the Sabbath to Sunday, the day of Christ's resurrection, is unbiblical. According to the Seventh-day Adventist Church, the end of the times would begin the 1,000-year reign of Christ and his saints when Christ and the Holy City would descend from heaven to earth and the redeemed would live eternally on the New Earth, when God would dwell with his people and the condemned would be consumed by fire and be annihilated (http://chris tianity.about.com/id/seventhdayadventists/a/ythdayadventist, accessed January 27, 2017).

Miller preached that Jesus Christ was coming back on October 22, 1843. Most Americans at the time were surprised not only by the fact that he had set a date but also by the very notion that Christ was literally returning—in itself a radical idea at the time (https://www.adventist.org/en/infor mation/history/article/go/-seventh-day-adventistbeliefs.htm, accessed January 27, 2017).

As of 2008, Seventh-day Adventists claimed about 15.9 million members worldwide, and in the American Religious Identification Survey (ARIS) in 2001, 724,200 self-identified as Seventh-day Adventists. In a 1990 survey, they ranked among the top 20 churches in 39 states and were among the top 10 in 6 states ("Largest Religious Groups in the United States of America," http://www.adherents.com/rel_USA.html, accessed January 31, 2017). While they hold many of the same doctrines as mainstream Christian denominations, they differ on some issues. Adventists baptize by immersion. They hold scripture as divinely inspired by the Holy Spirit and that the Bible contains all the knowledge necessary for salvation. Their communion service involves foot washing as a spirit of humility and a symbol of service to others. Unlike most other Christian denominations, they hold that the dead do not go directly to heaven or hell, but enter a period of "soul sleep" in which they are unconscious until their resurrection and final judgment. Many members are vegetarian, and they prohibit drinking alcohol or using tobacco or illegal drugs. There is no racial discrimination in the church, although women cannot be ordained as pastors, and the church currently is undergoing debate about whether homosexuality must be condemned as sin.

The Second Great Awakening (1798–1820s), was a revival movement in the United States that stimulated many Bible societies and a reform movement that sought to remedy the evils of society before the anticipated Second Coming of Jesus Christ. The Seventh-day Adventist Church formed out of one of the Second Great Awakening movements, known as the Millerites. Based on the Old Testament scripture of Daniel 8:14, Miller had calculated that the Second Coming would occur between March 1843 and March 1844 and gathered a following that included Baptist, Methodist, Presbyterian, and Christian Connection Church members. Miller had calculated the event would occur in 1843, and when it did not come to pass, Samuel Snow recalculated it would occur in 1844. They linked the cleansing of the sanctuary in Daniel with the Jewish Day of Atonement, believed to be October 22, 1844. Some 100,000 people awaited the Second Coming, and when it passed without their expectations being fulfilled, the event became known as the Great Disappointment.

After the Great Disappointment, many left the church, and Miller withdrew from its leadership and died in 1849. Ellen and James White, Joseph Bates, J. N. Andrews, Hiram Edson, and other Adventists formed a group of several hundreds in Washington, New Hampshire, on the farm of Hiram Edson, which became the Seventh-day Adventist Church in 1863. The Church is best known for its Saturday Sabbath. Helen White (1827–1915) is considered by the faithful to be a prophet as well as one of the Church founders. The Adventist practice of Baptism is performed on believers at the age of accountability and by full immersion. Communion is an ordinance, not a sacrament, and is performed quarterly in the sanctuary, sharing unleavened bread and unfermented grape juice as a memorial to the Lord's Supper. Their worship service consists of music, a Bible-based sermon, and prayer, similar to evangelical Protestant services. Adventists see themselves as heirs of earlier outcast believers and Protestant Reformers like the Anabaptists, English and Scottish Puritans, and 18th-century evangelicals like the Methodists, Seventh Day Baptists, and other sects or denominations that rejected the established church traditions. In 1874, J. N. Andrews became the first official missionary, traveling to Switzerland, and from then on the Church spread worldwide.

Evangelicals consider Adventists to be "premillennial" in their teachings and post-tribulation premillennialists who accept the biblical teaching on a literal 1,000 years in Revelation 20, which immediately follows a literal Second Coming of Christ, as described in Revelation 19. Instead of a 1,000-year reign of Christ on earth, Adventists teach that there is only a desolated earth for 1,000 years, during which time the saints are in heaven with Christ (http://christianity.about.com/od/seventhdayadventists/a/7thdayadventistsbeliefs.htm, accessed January 27, 2017).

While holding no official role, Ellen White was a dominant personality who moved the Adventists to concentrate on missionary and medical work, which continues to be a central role into the 21st century. The concentration on missionary work and the holding of revivals saw the membership triple to 16,000 by 1880 and to 75,000 members in 1901. The Church by then operated two colleges, a medical school, a dozen academies, 27 hospitals, and 13 publishing houses. The Church was heavily involved in the temperance movement of the late 1800s and promoted religious liberty. Given their doctrine that the Sabbath Day should be Saturday, the Adventists were opposed to Sunday laws, common in many states, and fought establishment of a National Day of Worship. Many of its members were arrested for working on Sunday. As Sabbatarians, they had to fight for their liberty to worship on that day, and soon they were fighting for religious liberty on a far broader basis.

Jehovah's Witnesses

Jehovah's Witnesses began in 1872, started by Charles Taze Russell (http://carm.org/jehovahs-witnesses-history, accessed

January 28, 2017; Bowman 1992; Penton 1997). Russell struggled with the doctrine of heaven and hell, and his studies led him to reject not only eternal punishment but also the Trinity, the deity of Christ, and the Holy Spirit.

According to the ARIS, in 2004, 1,878,431, or 0.6 percent of the U.S. population according to the 2000 census, self-identified as Jehovah's Witnesses. There were 8,547 congregations ("Largest Religious Groups in the United States of America," http://www .adherents.com/rel_USA.html, accessed January 28, 2017).

Russell copublished *The Herald of the Morning* magazine, in 1879, with its founder, N. H. Barbour. By 1884, Russell controlled the publication and renamed it *The Watchtower*. That year, he founded Zion's Watch Tower Tract Society, known today as the Watch Tower Bible and Tract Society. *The Watchtower* magazine began with a circulation of 6,000 copies a month. Today, the Church's publishing complex located in Brooklyn, New York, publishes 100,000 books and 800,000 copies of its two magazines daily.

Russell claimed the Bible could only be understood according to his interpretation, an assertion typical among cult leaders (Bowman 1992; Penton 1997). Russell died in 1916. He was succeeded in the presidency of the Watch Tower Society, which was then known as the International Bible Students Association, by Joseph Rutherford. Rutherford changed its name, in 1931, to the Jehovah's Witnesses. The Witnesses were led after Rutherford by Nathan Knorr, then by Frederick Franz, then by Milton Henschel, who was succeeded by Don Adams.

The Jehovah's Witnesses aggressively proselytize. According to Watch Tower Society statistics, members make an estimated 740 house calls to recruit each of the nearly 200,000 new members who join each year. Members attend several book studies each week. They learn chapters and verses of the Bible by rote and can easily out-argue the average Christian when it comes to defending Jehovah's Witnesses beliefs (https://carm.org/je hovahs-witnesses-history, accessed January 28, 2017; Bowman 1992; Penton 1997).

Jehovah's Witnesses have been strident defenders of the First Amendment's freedom of religion in order to protect their ability to proselytize, which is central to their faith, and in doing so have helped to define civil liberties case law in both the United States and Canada. Their legal struggles involved 72 cases, and many important judicial decisions regarding freedom of religion, press, and speech. A number of such cases are now considered landmark decisions of First Amendment law. Of the 72 cases, 47 were won by the Jehovah's Witnesses, and even in cases in which they lost, they helped the Court to more clearly define the limits of First Amendment rights.

Between 1935 and 2002, there were a number of Supreme Court decisions involving the Jehovah's Witnesses versus various state, local, and even federal governments over issues of First Amendment freedoms, in which the Court ruling clarified the practical implications of freedom of religion, freedom of assembly, and freedom of speech. These decisions will be discussed more fully in Chapters 2 and 5 but are briefly listed here as an illustration of the conflict between the majority society and a religious minority group.

The 1935 case *Lynn v. Massachusetts* concerned a local ordinance involving a mandatory reciting of the Pledge of Allegiance in public schools. In 1938, in *Lovell v. Griffin*, the Adventists contested a local law requiring them to seek government sanction to distribute religious materials. In 1940, in *Cantwell v. Connecticut*, the issue was over whether or not the Adventists could utilize streets and parks to proselytize. Also in 1940, in *Minersville School District v. Gobitis*, the conflict was over a school district policy requiring forced recital of the Pledge of Allegiance. In 1942, the Supreme Court issued the "fighting words" doctrine, in *Chaplinsky v. New Hampshire*. In 1953, the Court overturned the earlier Gobitis ruling and ruled unconstitutional a West Virginia law requiring mandatory flag salute, in *West Virginia v. Barnette*. That same year, the Court, in *Murdock v. Commonwealth of Pennsylvania*, ruled that a state law requiring religious solicitors to obtain a license was an unconstitutional tax on a religious group. In 1946, in *Estep v. United States*, the Court ruled against a draft board that had refused to classify Jehovah's Witnesses members as ministers of a faith. In 1953, in *Niemotkov v. Maryland*, the Court reversed a lower court decision convicting two Jehovah's Witnesses lecturers of conducting public speeches in a city park without a county-issued permit.

Similarly, in 1953, in *Fowler v. Rhode Island*, the Court remanded the Supreme Court of Rhode Island's upholding the conviction of an ordained minister of Jehovah's Witnesses for holding a religious meeting in a city park of Pawtucket, ruling that a religious service of the Jehovah's Witnesses was treated differently from religious services of other denominations (Catholic and mainline Protestant) and therefore amounted to the state preferring another religious group over this one. Finally, in 2002, in *Watchtower Bible and Tract Society of New York v. Village of Stratton*, the Court ruled that the state could not require by penalty of a misdemeanor that Adventists refrain from door-to-door advocacy without first registering with town officials and applying for and receiving a permit in that the law violated the First Amendment as it applies to religious proselytizing, anonymous political speech, and the distribution of handbills.

The Nation of Islam

The Nation of Islam (NOI), better known as the Black Muslims, is an example of another millennial movement. As one NOI scholar notes:

> The rehabilitative effects of the movement on many members of the sect have been remarkable. From the nation's prisons and slums, the Black Muslims have recruited drug addicts and pushers, prostitutes and pimps, alcoholics, criminals and the despairing ghetto residents, alienated from society. These men and women have been transformed by the Muslims into employees of value in honest jobs, who conscientiously marry and raise a family. They

obey the laws, save money, and tithe to their faith. They no longer drink, use drugs or tobacco, gamble, engage in sexual promiscuity, dance, take long vacations, steal, lie, nor exhibit idleness or laziness. Their women are models of domesticity: thrifty, keeping fastidiously clean homes, devoted to their mates and children. Instead of buying expensive clothes or cars, they pool their resources to help each other. Muslim families, even in the midst of the nation's worst slums, exhibit a healthy living standard. The movement has, in its own strange way, repaired some "irreparable" damages and saved some of the damned. (Litt 1970: 78–79)

The Black Muslims began in the 1930s, during the Great Depression, arising out of various mystic, black nationalist sectarian cults located in the nation's urban ghettos, such as the Moorish-American Science Temple, founded by Timothy Drew in North Carolina (1886–1929), who proclaimed himself Prophet Noble Drew Ali in Newark, New Jersey, in 1913; he had been commissioned to preach Islam to black Americans (Lincoln 1994). The movement soon established temples in Chicago, Detroit, and Pittsburgh. Another millennial group was the Peace Mission movement of Father Divine, established on Long Island in 1919 and blended social and religious Black Nationalism, which peaked between 1931 and 1936 and claimed a following of one million. Another was the Ethiopian Pacific movement begun in Chicago in 1932 (LeMay 2009: 213–214).

The Black Muslims, first known as the Lost-Found Nation of Islam, and then simply the Nation of Islam, began in Detroit's black ghetto, led by Wali D. Fard, or Mr. W. Fard Muhammad, or simply Wallace. His most trusted follower and successor was Elijah Muhammad (nee Elijiah Poole, 1897–1975). Fard led a following of about 8,000 faithful before he disappeared in June 1934. Elijah Muhammad, declaring himself Allah's Prophet, then led the movement, which at its height was America's foremost Black Nationalist Movement, with 69 temples in 27 states, and claiming a membership in excess of one million, roughly one-third of all American Muslims at the time (Brooks 1996: 143–155). They established temples in Chicago, Milwaukee, and Washington, D.C., appealing to the black underclass.

Elijah Muhammad preached that whites were devils created by a black scientist named Yakub. Whites were held to be mentally, physically, and morally inferior to blacks, who were the original humans, the first people to inhabit the earth. Yakub angered Allah, who in punishment, ordained that the white race would rule over blacks for 6,000 years. Blacks were members of Shabazz. Black Muslims desired to free blacks from white oppression by securing land for themselves within the continental United States. Preaching an assertive, militant separatism, they formed economic self-independent groups and promoted black pride. They rejected both white society and the Judeo-Christian heritage underpinning the dominant culture and its value system (LeMay 2009: 214–215).

In 1934, the Chicago Temple Number 2 served as headquarters of the Nation of Islam and the "Mecca" of the movement. Showing remarkable growth, it grew from about 10,000 members to more than 250,000 members by 1960. Their most famous speaker, Malcolm X (nee Malcolm Little), referred to American blacks as the Lost Nation of Islam in North America. Its members immersed themselves in a new Muslim culture, with temples, schools for children, and numerous daily and weekly publications filled with black Muslim ideology, the most famous of which was *Muhammad Speaks*, with a circulation of 600,000. They set up Muslim community centers, offered employment training, ran a variety of retail and service businesses, a "University of Islam" (more like a high school), and promoted a collective identity by symbols, a flag, Allah, the star and crescent, their version of the Qur'an, and Islamic names and terms. Like the Old Order Amish and Mennonites, they have elaborate prohibitions, prescribed behaviors, and clothing styles for men and women that promote self-identification functions and black pride.

They have clashed with majority society over a number of policies—refusing to accept or pay into Social Security, opposing the draft, and have been arrested and jailed for tax evasion.

In the early 1960s, Malcolm X wrote many newspaper and magazine articles, including ones in *Muhammad Speaks*, which rose in circulation to 900,000, and was a frequent speaker on college campuses. He began to rival Elijah Muhammad for leadership. He split with the Black Muslims, founding his own group, the Organization of Afro-American Unity. He was assassinated in 1965 by three NOI followers at a rally in New York City's Harlem (LeMay 2009: 220–222).

On the death of Elijah Muhammad in 1975, the NOI was led by his son, Wallace Deen Muhammad, who soon rejected much of his father's teachings and returned Black Muslim followers to conventional Sunni Islam, forming and leading the American Society of Muslims. He formally dissolved the sect, which was revived and soon led by Minister Louis Farrakhan, who attempted to return Black Muslims to their origins under Elijah Muhammad. Today, many black American Muslims attend mainstream Islam temples of Sunni and Shi'a affiliation.

Other Non-Christian Minority Religions

There are numerous other non-Christian minority religions in America, several of which experience discrimination and outright hostility and some of which have occasional issues or conflicts with the majority society over their religious beliefs and practices. And there are the religious "nones"—atheists and agnostics—who also on occasion raise issues with freedom *from* religion.

Judaism

According to the 2001 ARIS survey, there are nearly four million persons who self-identify as Jewish, 1.3 percent of the population, which is more of a cultural identification than a religious one. The American Jewish Identity Survey of 2000 concluded there were 5.5 million Jews in the United States, among whom 1.6 million were aligned with a religion other than Judaism and 1.4 million were secular or nonreligious, leaving just over 3 million whose religion was Judaism (http://www.adher ents.com/rel_USA.html, accessed January 28, 2017). Barrett's study (2001) put the Jewish population in the United States at 5.6 million.

Judaism can be divided into three groups: Orthodox, Reformed, and Conservative. There are more than 3,700 synagogues in the United States. Among them, total Orthodox synagogues number just over 1,500, or about 40 percent of all U.S. synagogues. Total Reform synagogues number just under 1,000, or 26 percent, and total Conservative synagogues number 865, or slightly more than 23 percent. Among the Orthodox are the Hasidic synagogues, the Lubavitch/Chabad (346 in number), or mixed synagogues, the Orthodox Union/ Lubavitch, and the Young Israel and Lubavitch (Singer and Grossman 2003: 128–129).

Another study puts Jewish population at six million and found that there are 180,000 Ultra-Orthodox Jews, the Hasidic (also spelled Chasidic, from the Hebrew word meaning "pious") (http://www.news.ufl.edu/2006/11/27/hasidic-jews/, accessed March 19, 2007). They do not seek converts so their growth is almost entirely due to births, but they are nonetheless a fairly rapidly growing population—doubling every 20 years or so—because they tend to have many children. The average Hasidic family has four to six children, while non–Orthodox Jewish groups have flat or falling rates. Hasidic Jews believe in living close together, within walking distance of their synagogues. Their neighborhoods are islands of traditional Judaism. Signs on stores are in Yiddish and Hebrew; the men wear long beards and black garb, and the women wear scarves or wigs and dress in modest clothing. Their distinctiveness from the majority culture is palpable, from their apparent community tightness to their ever-present consciousness of belonging to the group: the emphasis upon custom and religious law, the high degree of ritual instructions found in the Torah, and ritual observance that permeates every corner, which include giving to charity, not mixing wool and linen, following strict kosher dietary laws, refraining from work on the Sabbath, laws regulating sexual behavior, study of the Torah, and the loving and fearing of God. Hasidic Jews live in a traditional, patriarchal system. Hasidism is a mystic and enthusiastic sect, emphasizing the importance of inner intent and carrying out ritual obligations. Their community leader is the rebbe, a social and spiritual teacher. The word "rebbe" means "rabbi" in Yiddish and is distinctly Hasidic, meaning one trained as a teacher. Historically, rebbe came from the town in which their court was located in Eastern Europe: the Lubavitch from Lubavitch in Russia; the Satmar from Satu Mare in Hungary, the Bobover from the Polish town of Bobova, and so on (Jacobson 1995; LeMay 2009: 231–232).

Their comparative growth rate means that in 50 years they will constitute a majority of American Jews, marking profound cultural and political change. Ultra-Orthodox Jews tend to be politically conservative and send their children to religious schools, making them more sympathetic to faith-based initiatives promoted by the Republican Party. Although they live apart culturally, they are politically active and vote in majority society elections. They oppose contraception, abortion, divorce, and same-sex marriages. They aim not to change beliefs but the believer.

They immigrated to the United States in the 1870s and 1880s, in large numbers after World War I, and again in 1940, fleeing strong and open anti-Semitism, mostly from what is today Poland, Belorussia, and Ukraine. In Europe, they lived in shtetls (villages). In the United States the world headquarters of the Lubavitch Hasidic sect is in Crown Heights, Brooklyn. Rebbe Manachem Schneesrohn organized three Chabad (Hasidic movement) divisions: publishing, educational outreach missions, and social services. Their children attend special schools (called a yeshiva) (Schaefer 2014). Like the Amish and Mennonites, they maintain a high degree of cultural identity despite living within the heart of the majority culture (LeMay 2009: 237).

Muslim Americans

The 2001 ARIS survey put the adult Muslim population in the United States at 1,104,000, or 0.05 percent of the U.S. population. Another study, by the National Opinion Research Center at the University of Chicago, estimated the total Muslim population to be 1,886,000 (National Opinion Research Center, www.norc.org/ Accessed August 31, 2017). Barrett's study (2001) puts them at 4.1 million. Swelled by higher immigration and conversion rates, Islam has surpassed Judaism as a minority religion, and worldwide it has more than 1.2 billion adherents, making it one of the world's largest religions. It is now the second-largest religion in Europe and Russia. Despite their being stereotyped as Arabs, only about 18 percent of all Muslims come from the Middle East—the majority live in South and Southeast Asia, in countries like Pakistan, India, and Indonesia. Islam is one of three Abrahamic faiths, the other two being Judaism and Christianity. All are called "People of the Book." Muslims regard Jesus as a Messiah, a Messenger, and Prophet, born of a virgin mother, but not as the son of God or God himself. Ritual prayer and the Qur'an are recited in Arabic.

The two main branches of Islam are Sunni (at about 90 percent worldwide) and the Shi'a (about 10 percent). The Shi'a are found predominately in Iraq, Iran, Lebanon, Yemen, and Bahrain, a fact that figures prominently in the growing anti-Islamic attitude and now policy in the United States (LeMay 2009: 228; see also Hourani 1991).

Muslims came to America during the Great Migration in the late 1800s and early 1900s, the majority from Syria, speaking Arabic. Their first permanent mosque was built in 1923, in

Cedar Rapids, Iowa, and is still often referred to as the "Mother Mosque of America."

A new post-1965 immigration flow came from Palestine and Lebanon but also from other parts of the Arabic-speaking world. Many were refugees seeking to escape violence in their homelands, such as the 1975–1990 Lebanese Civil War; Palestinians from the West Bank and Gaza Strip; displaced Kurds and Shi'ia from Iraq, war-weary Afghanis, and survivors of the 1992–1995 war in Bosnia.

Since the terrorist attacks of September 11, 2001, however, immigration from "high-risk" countries—defined by the Department of Homeland Security as Muslim-majority countries—has slowed significantly, and they are subject to special registration and more stringent vetting. The current unfavorable social climate and the threat of violence against them has kept the American Muslim community in a state of flux. Muslim organizations, such as the Council on American-Islamic Relations, the Muslim Pacific Affairs Committee, the Institute of Islamic Information and Education, and the Islamic Society of North America, are using political strength and protest to counter discrimination (Guest 2008; LeMay 2009: 228–230).

Buddhism, Hinduism, and Sikhism

The ARIS study of 2001 put Buddhists at 1,082,000, or 0.5 percent of the population, and Hindus at 766,000, or 0.4 percent of the population. Sikhism in 2004 had an estimated 80,400 adherents, or 0.03 percent of the population (http://www.adherents.com/rel_USA.html, accessed January 28, 2017). Barrett's study (2001) put their numbers at 2.4 million Buddhists and 1 million Hindus. They arrived mostly in the post-1970 immigration wave. Since Buddhists and Hindus do not proselytize and are viewed as mostly passive, even quaint, cultures and religions, they have experienced little overt discrimination and evidence few conflicts with majority society and its laws. Sikhism is equally a nonthreatening (to the majority culture) minority religion, but the fact that Sikhs wear distinctive garb (chiefly the use of turbans) has resulted in their being the misinformed target of some anti-Arab attitudes, discrimination, and even violence, especially in the immediate aftermath of the September 11 attacks.

Baha'i

The Baha'i faith is a monotheistic religion with an estimated five to seven million adherents worldwide. In the ARIS 2004 study, in the United States they numbered just more than 118,000, or 0.04 percent of the U.S. population (http://www.adherents .com/rel_USA.html, accessed January 28, 2017). It was founded in 1863 in Tehran, Iran, by Mirza Hoseyn 'Ali Nuri, known to his followers as Baha'u'llah, which in Arabic means "Glory of God." The faith has no priesthood or clergy, and their governance is by local spiritual assembly. They have no initiation ceremonies, no sacraments, and no worship rituals. Their tenets stress the unity of religion and humankind. They believe in One God, who has revealed himself progressively through the major world religions. They practice daily prayer, avoidance of intoxicants, the reading of scripture, hard work, education, and a commitment to work for social justice and equality (http:// www.religionfacts.com/bahai/facts, accessed February 1, 2017).

Native American Religion

Native American religions are quite diverse, reflecting their many tribal traditions and practices. Beyond question, however, they were the most suppressed of religious beliefs and practices by the American government, which for many decades had a policy of "forced assimilation" that targeted the eradication of Native American Indian language, culture, customs, and religious practices. Many tribes used herbal hallucinogens in their ceremonies to gain greater insight, experience visions, or communicate with the gods. Most such ceremonies included feasts, music, dances, and other performances and employed symbolism, especially with animals, as part of Native American religion. Animals were used to represent certain ideas, characteristics, and spirits and to tell the story of creation—for example, the Tlingit Indian creation story centered on a raven.

Some tribes had shaman, or medicine men, used in place of preachers or clergymen as found in Christianity. The shaman was believed to be able to communicate with their god, or Great Spirit. They considered the shaman a wise and experienced man and accorded him high status among the tribal groups. A shaman played an important role in decisions, ceremonies, and traditions (http://www.indians.org/articles/native-american-religion.html, accessed February 2, 2017). In the 2001 ARIS, about 145,000 respondents self-identified as Native Americans, or 0.05 percent.

In more recent years, they have politically mobilized and have succeeded in winning some policy concessions from the national government to reform past repression. They have won, for instance, the right to use peyote (an otherwise controlled substance) in their religious ceremonies, mostly conducted on reservation lands. The various Indian residential schools, like the Carlisle Indian Industrial School in Pennsylvania, that conducted forced assimilation suppressing native American language, religious practices, and culture have all been closed (LeMay 2009: 187–188). In 1946, perhaps in recognition of the special contributions that the *code*-talkers played in World War II, Congress created the Indian Claims Commission to settle grievances. The philosophy of these schools was to "kill the Indian to save the man." They were gradually ended with passage of the Indian Education Act (1972), the Indian Financing Act (1974), and the Indian Self-Determination and Education Assistance Act (1975). In 1978, Congress passed the American Indian Religious Freedom Act (designed to protect sacred sites and allow certain religious practices such as the use of eagle feathers and peyote), the Tribally Controlled Community College Assistance Act, and the Indian Child Welfare Act. In 1979, it enacted the Indian Archaeological Resources

Protection Act. In 1988, it passed the Indian Gaming Regulatory Act, resulting in 97 tribes in 22 states operating more than 200 casinos (LeMay 2009: 190–191, 314).

Wicca

Wicca is a religion that is a modern reconstruction of an ancient, northern European system of pagan beliefs in a fertility goddess and her consort, a horned god.

Modern-day Wicca can be traced to the writings of Charles Leland (1824–1903), Margaret Murray (1863–1963), and Gerald Gardner (1884–1964). According to Gardner (1992), Wiccans began in European prehistory with rituals associated with fire, the hunt, animal fertility, plant propagation, tribal fertility, and the curing of disease with natural herbs. They developed into a religion with a belief in a Supreme Deity, Moon-based worship, and the Sun-based faith of the Druids. It was revived in the UK by Gardner and the High Priestess Doreen Valente (1922–1999), who fleshed out surviving beliefs and practices with material from other religious, spiritual, and ceremonial magic sources (http://www.religioustolerance .org/wic_hist.html, accessed February 2, 2017). The religion expanded into the United States in the 1950s and 1960s as Neo-pagan/Wiccan. As of 2000, it had more than 400,000 claimed adherents (0.1 percent of the population), according to the ARIS 2001 survey (http://www.adherents.com/ rel_USA.html, accessed January 28, 2017). A Wiccan/Pagan poll in 2000 put their number of adherents at 766,400 (http:// www.cog.org/cogpoll_final.html, accessed February 3, 2017). Still another source, religioustolerance.org, numbers their adherents at more than 750,000, ranking them as the fifth-largest organized religion in the United States (http://www.religious tolerance.org/wic_hist.htm, accessed February 2, 2017; Leland and Pazzaglini 1999).

In the 1990s, it was virtually unknown to most of the general public because Wiccans hid their religious beliefs and practices to avoid persecution. On a per-capita basis, their members are believed (by religioustolerance.org) to be one of the most frequent victims of assaults, arson, and economic attacks and have been targets of shootings, one mass public stoning, and one lynching. Misinformed child protection officers have reportedly seized children from the homes of Wiccans for fear they would be harmed in Satanic ritual. Since 2000, they have come out of the closet and revealed their faith openly, and the general public has become more aware of Wicca and other Neo-pagan religions; the frequency of violence against them has decreased markedly, although on occasion they still have reported acts of vandalism and economic attacks against them.

Atheists and Agnostics

Avowed atheists do not believe in the existence of God, and agnostics profess that the existence of God cannot be known or proved and they simply don't know whether or not to believe in any deity. In both cases, adherents reject joining any religion or religious organization. The 2004 ARIS survey found that just more than 1.5 million persons self-identified as agnostics (0.5 percent of the 2000 population), and 1.3 million as atheists (0.4 percent of the 2000 population) (http://www.adher ents.com/rel_USA.html, accessed January 28, 2017).

In 1963, the American Atheists Organization formed, largely to fight for the civil liberties of atheists and to support the "total, absolute separation of government and religion" (http://www .atheists.org/about-us, accessed February 2, 2017). In many respects, they arose out of a Supreme Court case *Murray v. Curlett* (1959), a landmark case that challenged prayer recitation in public schools. In that ruling, Murray (1992) stated the following characterization of her atheist beliefs:

Your petitioners are atheists, and they define their lifestyle as follows. An atheist loves himself and his fellow man instead of a god. An atheist accepts that heaven is something for which we should work now—here on earth—for all men together to enjoy. An atheist accepts that he can get no help through prayer, but that he must find in himself the inner conviction and strength to meet life, to grapple with, to subdue it and to enjoy it. An atheist accepts that only in a knowledge of himself and a knowledge of his fellow man can he find the understanding that will help lead to a life of fulfillment.

Since their formation in 1963, they have consistently fought to defend the separation of church and state, appeared in all forms of the media to defend atheism from criticisms of religion and religious entities, and supported atheist public gatherings like "Atheist Pride" marches in state capitals. Its members have picketed on behalf of atheist rights and church-state separation. The American Atheists Organization publishes hundreds of books about atheism, as well as newsletters, magazines, and member alerts. It has promoted a network of activists throughout America to monitor First Amendment issues. It has preserved atheist literature and history in the nation's largest archive of its kind. It provides speakers for colleges, universities, clubs, and the news media and has granted college scholarships to young atheist activists (https://www.atheist.org/about-us, accessed February 2, 2017).

Conclusion

Since its inception and the adoption of the Constitution of the United States in 1789, the nation has struggled with how to live up to its lofty principles of the First Amendment: that government shall make no law establishing religion, nor prohibiting the right of the free exercise of religion, nor abridging the freedom of speech, of the press, or of the right to peaceably assemble and to petition the government for a redress of grievances. Through the Fourteenth Amendment and various court decisions, those principles were applied to state (and to local) governments as well (Brinton 2012).

The great diversity of religious denominations that came to or developed within the American polity has led to a perennial struggle in American politics for more than 200 years to understand, protect, and extend religious tolerance. Minority religions were often persecuted or discriminated against by the general society; by state, local, and the federal governments; and by other more dominant religious denominations. Gradually, minority religious groups used public law and especially the courts to protect themselves from such discrimination and to extend First Amendment rights.

The anti-establishment clause of the First Amendment likewise took the enactment of many laws and interpretation through many landmark Supreme Court cases to define what precisely the clause means in public policy, in law, or in the practices of government that intrude on American culture and the norms and customs of society in ways that enhance or breach the "wall of separation" between church and state. These battles, and the struggles of a host of religious and avowedly nonreligious groups, are not confined to the distant or even near-past. They are constant and ongoing, infusing American politics in a fundamental way. Freedom of religion and freedom from religion are principles requiring constant vigilance to maintain and ongoing conflict, literally a perennial struggle, to refine the practical meaning thereof (Marquardt and Vazquez 2014). The next chapter will discuss the problems, controversies, issues, and proposed solutions to those struggles for freedom of and freedom from religion in America.

References

Abanes, Richard. 2002. *One Nation under God: A History of the Mormon Church*. New York: Four Walls Eight Windows.

Ahlstrom, Sydney. 1972. *A Religious History of the American People*. New Haven, CT: Yale University Press.

Ammerman, Nancy. 1997. *Congregation and Community.* New Brunswick, NJ: Rutgers University Press.

Arrington, Leonard J., and Davis Bitton. 1992. *The Mormon Experience: A History of the Latter-Day Saints*, 2nd ed. Urbana: University of Illinois Press.

Baer, Hans. 1988. *Recreating Utopia in the Desert: A Sectarian Challenge to Modern Mormonism.* Albany: State University of New York Press.

Bailey, Thomas. 1976. *Voices of America.* New York: The Free Press.

Baltzell, E. Digby. 1996. *Puritan Boston and Quaker Philadelphia.* New Brunswick, NJ: Transaction Publishers.

Barrett, David. 2001. *World Christian Encyclopedia.* New York: Oxford University Press.

Beals, Carleton. 1960. *Brass Knuckle Crusade.* New York: Hasting House.

Billington, Ray. 1974. *The Origins of Nativism in the United States, 1800–1844.* New York: Arno Press.

Bilhartz, Terry D. 1986. *Urban Religion and the Second Great Awakening.* Madison, NJ: Fairleigh Dickinson University Press.

Bowman, Robert M., Jr. 1992. *Understanding Jehovah's Witnesses.* Grand Rapids, MI: Baker Book House.

Boyton, Linda L. 1986. *The Plain People: An Ethnography of the Holdeman Mennonites.* Salem, WI: Sheffield.

Brinton, Henry G. 2012. *The Welcoming Congregation: Roots and Fruits of Christian Hospitality.* Louisville, KY: Westminster John Knox Press.

Brooks, Roy. 1996. *Integration or Separation? A Strategy for Racial Equality.* Cambridge, MA: Harvard University Press.

Bushman, Claudia L., and Richard Bushman. 2001. *Building the Kingdom: A History of Mormons in America.* New York: Oxford University Press.

Butler, Jon. 2006. *Religion in Colonial America.* New York: Oxford University Press.

Casey, Shirley. 1918. *The Millennial Hope.* Chicago: University of Chicago Press.

The Church of Jesus Christ of Latter-day Saints. 1989. *Church History in the Fullness of Times.* Salt Lake City, UT: The Church of Jesus Christ of Latter-day Saints.

Davies, Douglas T. 2000. *The Mormon Culture of Salvation.* New York: Ashgate.

Driedger, Leo, and Donald B. Kraybill. 1994. *Mennonite Peacemaking.* Scottsdale, PA: Herald Press.

Fantel, Hans. 1974. *William Penn: Apostle of Dissent.* New York: William Morrow.

Fenn, Richard K. 1997. *The End of Time: Religion, and the Forging of the Soul.* New York: Pilgrim Press.

Gardner, Gerald. 1992, 1999. *Gardner Witchcraft Series: Witchcraft Today, The Meaning of Witchcraft.* New York: Mercury Publications, and Los Gatos, CA: Restivo Enterprises.

Gaustad, Edwin S. 1999. *Liberty of Conscience: Roger Williams in America.* Valley Forge, PA: Judson Press.

Guest, Kenneth. 2008. *God in Chinatown: Religion and Survival in New York's Evolving Immigrant Community.* New York: New York University Press.

Hardy, B. Carmon. 1992. *Solemn Covenant: The Mormon Polygamous Passage.* Chicago: University of Illinois Press.

Heimert, Alan. 1966. *Religion and the American Mind: From the Great Awakening to the Revolution.* Cambridge: Cambridge University Press.

Hening, W. W., ed. 1823. *Statutes at Large of Virginia*, vol. 12. 84–86.

Hirshson, Stanley. 1969. *The Lion of the Lord.* New York: Knopf.

Hofstadter, Richard, and Michael Wallace. 1971. *American Violence.* New York: Knopf.

Holmes, David R. 2006. *The Faith of the Founding Fathers.* New York: Oxford University Press.

Hourani, Albert. 1991. *A History of the Arab Peoples.* New York: Warner Books.

Jacobson, Simon. 1995. *Towards a Meaningful Life: The Wisdom of the Rebbe.* New York: William Morrow.

Jefferson, Thomas. 1977. *The Portable Thomas Jefferson.* Edited by Merrill Peterson. New York: Penguin Books.

Kaplan, Jeffrey. 1997. *Radical Religion in America: Millenarian Movements from the Far Right to the Children of Noah.* Syracuse, NY: Syracuse University Press.

Kornelly, Sharon. 2013. "A Holy Experiment: Religion and Immigration to the New World," in Michael C. LeMay, ed. *Transforming America: Perspectives on U.S. Immigration,* vol. 1. Santa Barbara, CA: Praeger. 189–213.

Kraybill, Donald B., and Steven M. Nolt. 1995. *Amish Enterprises: From Plows to Profits.* Baltimore, MD: Johns Hopkins University Press.

Kraybill, Donald B., and Marc A. Olshan, eds. 1994. *The Amish Struggle with Modernity.* Hanover, NH: University Press of New England.

Landes, Richard, ed. 2000. *Encyclopedia of Millennialism and Millennial Movements.* New York: Routledge.

Landes, Richard. 2011. *Heaven on Earth: Varieties of the Millennial Experience.* New York: Oxford University Press.

Launius, Roger D., and Linda Thatcher, eds. 1994. *Differing Visions: Dissenters in Mormon History.* Urbana: University Press of Illinois.

Leland, Charles, and Mario Pazzaglini. 1999. *Aradia: Gospel of the Witches.* New York: Phoenix Publications.

LeMay, Michael. 1987. *From Open Door to Dutch Door: An Analysis of Immigration Policy since 1820.* New York: Praeger.

LeMay, Michael. 2009. *The Perennial Struggle*, 3rd ed. Upper Saddle River, NJ: Prentice-Hall.

LeMay, Michael C., ed. 2013. *Transforming America: Perspectives on U.S. Immigration*, Vol. 1. Santa Barbara, CA: Praeger.

Levy, Leonard W. 1994. *The Establishment Clause and the First Amendment.* Chapel Hill: University of North Carolina Press.

Lincoln, C. Eric. 1994. *The Black Muslims in America*, 3rd ed. Trenton, NJ: Africa World Press.

Litt, Edgar. 1970. *Ethnic Politics in America.* Glenview, IL: Scott, Foresman.

Mapp, Alf. 2003. *The Faith of Our Fathers: What America's Founders Really Believed.* Lanham, MD: Rowman and Littlefield.

Marquardt, Marie T. T., and Manuel A. Vasquez. 2014. "To Persevere in Our Struggle: Religion among Unauthorized Latino Immigrants in the United States," in Louis Ann Lorentzen, ed. *Hidden Lives and Human Rights in the United States*, vol. 3: *Economics, Politics, and Morality.* Santa Barbara, CA: Praeger. 303–323.

Mauss, Armand. 1994. *The Angel and the Beehive: The Mormon Struggle with Assimilation.* Urbana: University of Illinois Press.

McConkie, Bruce R. 1966. *Mormon Doctrine.* Salt Lake City, UT: Bookcraft.

Middlekauff, Robert. 2005. *The Glorious Cause: The American Revolution, 1763–1789.* New York: Oxford University Press.

Miller, William Lee. 1986. *The First Liberty: Religion and the American Republic.* Washington, DC: Georgetown University Press.

Murray, Margaret. 1992. *God of the Witches*. New York: Oxford University Press.

Nolt, Steven M. 1992. *A History of the Amish*. Intercourse, PA: Good Books.

Nuovo, Victor. 2002. *John Locke: Writings on Religion*. New York: Oxford University.

O'Hair, Madalyn Murray. 1969 (Reprinted 2004). *What on Earth Is an Atheist?* Austin, TX: American Atheist Press. www.who2.com/bio/madalyn-murray-ohair/ Accessed August 31, 2017.

Penton, M. James. 1997. *Apocalypse Delayed: The Story of the Jehovah's Witnesses*. Toronto: Toronto University Press.

Peters, Shawn Francis. 2002. *Judging Jehovah's Witnesses: Religious Persecution and the Dawn of the Rights Revolution*. Lawrence: University Press of Kansas.

Peters, Shawn Francis. 2003. *The Yoder Case: Religious Freedom, Education, and Parental Rights*. Lawrence: University Press of Kansas.

Peterson, Merrill D., and Robert C. Vaughn, eds. 1988. *The Virginia Statute for Religious Freedom: Its Evolution and Consequences in American History*. Cambridge: Cambridge University Press.

Portman, Rob, and Cheryl Bauer. 2004. *Wisdom's Paradise: The Forgotten Shakers of Union Village*. Wilmington, OH: Orange Frazer Press.

Schaefer, Richard. 2014. *Racial and Ethnic Groups*, 14th ed. New York: Pearson.

Singer, David, and Lawrence Grossman, eds. 2003. *American Jewish Yearbook, 2002*. New York: American Jewish Committee.

Tanner, Annie Clark. 1976. *A Mormon Mother: An Autobiography*. Salt Lake City, UT: Tanner Trust Fund, University of Utah Library.

Ulrich, Laurel Thatcher. 1991. *A Midwife's Tale*. New York: Vintage Books.

Urofsky, Melvin. 2002. *Religious Freedom: Rights and Liberties under the Law*. Santa Barbara, CA: ABC-CLIO.

Vile, John R. 2015a. *Encyclopedia of Constitutional Amendments, Proposed Amendments and Amending Issues, 1789–2015*, 4th ed., vol. 1. Santa Barbara, CA: ABC-CLIO.

Vile, John R. 2015b. *Founding Documents of America: Documents Decoded*. Santa Barbara, CA: ABC-CLIO.

Walters, Kerry S. 1992. *The American Deists: Voices of Reason and Dissent in the Early Republic*. Lawrence: University Press of Kansas.

Wenger, John. 1961. *The Mennonites in Indiana and Michigan*. Scottsdale, PA: Herald Press.

Wessinger, Catherine. 2000. *Millennialism, Persecution, and Violence: Historical Cases*. Syracuse, NY: Syracuse University Press.

Wessinger, Catherine, ed. 2011. *The Oxford Handbook of Millennialism*. New York: Oxford University Press.

Wojcik, Daniel. 1997. *The End of the World as We Know It: Faith, Fatalism, and Apocalypse in America*. New York: New York University Press.

Young, Ann Eliza. 1972. *Wife No. 19: The Story of a Life in Bondage*. New York: Arno Press.

SCHOOL PRAYER

OUR HEAVENLY FATHER,

GRANT US EACH DAY THE DESIRE TO DO OUR BEST. TO GROW MENTALLY AND MORALLY AS WELL AS PHYSICALLY, TO BE KIND AND HELPFUL TO OUR CLASSMATES AND TEACHERS, TO BE HONEST WITH OURSELVES AS WELL AS WITH OTHERS. HELP US TO BE GOOD SPORTS AND SMILE WHEN WE LOSE AS WELL AS WHEN WE WIN. TEACH US THE VALUE OF TRUE FRIENDSHIP. HELP US ALWAYS TO CONDUCT OURSELVES SO AS TO BRING CREDIT TO CRANSTON HIGH SCHOOL WEST.

AMEN

2 Problems, Controversies, and Solutions

Introduction

Despite the relative simplicity of the First Amendment clauses—or perhaps, better said, because of the very simplicity of that language—religious freedom in America has often been embroiled in controversy. Such controversy over the meaning of the Establishment Clause more often involves the major or mainline religious denominations. In part, this simply reflects the fact that the various mainline religious communities have sufficient political clout to get government support, be it symbolic or financial. The religious right and many evangelicals in particular are prone to call the United States "a Christian nation." The "wall of separation" between church and state, the image and phrase coined by Thomas Jefferson (Buckley 1977; Dreisbach 2002), has never been absolute and certainly has never been without controversy. Sometimes, the problem hinged on the expression of religious allegiance and the majority society's perceived threat of foreign allegiance. At other times, it related to certain religious minorities arguing for conscientious objection to fighting during times of war. More often, problems concerning the separation of church and state related to compulsory education and the public school systems

Prayer banner in the auditorium of Cranston High School West in Cranston, Rhode Island, October 14, 2011. The banner was removed after a ruling in a federal lawsuit brought by atheist student Jessica Ahlquist. Federal courts have consistently ruled against prayers written or imposed by school officials as unconstitutional. (AP Photo/Steven Senne) of state and local governments. Public education policy raised a number of establishment questions. Is it constitutionally permissible for the government to use public funds for parochial schools? May the government give tax-exempt status to religious organizations? Is it permissible, or not, to say prayers or read from the Bible in public schools? In designing school curricula, can the government command or prohibit the teaching of subjects that are inherently religious in nature—like creationism versus evolution? Can government support clergy giving invocations at the opening of legislative sessions? Can the government require recitation of an "oath" of office? Can the government justify having "In God We Trust" on our coins or inserting the phrase "one nation under God" into our national pledge of allegiance? As will be discussed in this and subsequent chapters, there have been 50 major Supreme Court cases dealing with such controversies about the Establishment Clause (see Table 5.2).

Most establishment cases were handed down after the U.S. Civil War (after the 1880s, in fact, as will be evident from subsequent discussions). This is because originally the Bill of Rights was considered to be limitations imposed on the federal government. It was not until passage of the Fourteenth Amendment that the 10 amendments of the Bill of Rights were deemed to incorporate those freedoms to state (and by extension, local) governments as well.

More often, controversy over the meaning of the Free Exercise Clause occurs with respect to minority religious groups, cults, and sects. The Free Exercise Clause has engendered a number of questions dealt with in major Supreme Court cases. Can parents, on religious grounds, limit their children's public education? Can parents, on the basis of *their* religious beliefs, refuse medical treatment for their minor children facing life-threatening illness? Do unpopular minority religious groups have the right to proselytize in public, or may they be required to register and get approval before using public spaces for their proselytization efforts? Can government regulate the free practice of religion if it considers such behavior or actions a threat to public health or safety? Can Native American religious groups be allowed exemptions from enacted drug laws? During the 200 years of American history, there have been a dozen or so laws enacted on the subject, and many dozens of court cases that have weighed in on determining the precise meaning and the limits on government implicit in the religious freedom rights guaranteed by the First Amendment. This chapter discusses 40 such cases.

No rights, even those enshrined in the First Amendment, are absolute. Sometimes, the freedom of religion rights of members of a minority religion clashes with the rights of others. Just as the right of free speech does not guarantee a person the freedom to yell "fire" in a crowded public space when there is no fire, likewise, individuals who happen to believe that their faith allows them to handle venomous snakes cannot collect timber rattlers and toss them about in public during a religious service. The Supreme Court has ruled that members of the Latter-day Saints Church (better known as the Mormons) have the right *to believe* in plural marriage, but they do not have the guaranteed freedom to *practice* polygamy (*Reynolds v. United States*, 98 U.S. 145, 1878; *Davis v. Beason*, 133 U.S. 333, 1890).

This chapter will discuss and examine those problems and controversies and various laws and court rulings that have addressed them while searching for some degree of resolution of the issues. For the convenience of the reader, the chapter discusses religious freedom in America by dividing it into two parts: (1) problems, controversies, and solutions regarding the Establishment Clause and (2) problems, controversies, and solutions regarding the Free Exercise Clause. In both cases, understanding of the meaning of the clause evolved over time, because of subsequent legislation or court decisions. Understandably, the practical political meaning of the two clauses evolved as American society and culture changed because of ever more diverse demographic shifts that occurred as more religious groups immigrated to America or arose as new religions developed domestically.

To better understand why religious freedom in America has been subject to a long and complex struggle, it is useful to remember that the First Amendment freedoms were legally applied only to the federal government. States were free to establish churches (and many did), to direct church taxes to be paid, to mandate church attendance, and so on, if those laws were within the bounds of the state's own constitution. The Establishment Clause prevented the federal government not only from establishing a national religion but also from forcing a state government to disestablish any state religion (www.uscon stitution.net/constop_reli.html, accessed January 15, 2017; see also Amar 1998; Bonomi 1986; Buckley 1977; Butler 1990; Dreisbach 2002; Green 2010; McGarvie 2004; Sehat 2011).

In the first 15 years after the adoption of the Constitution and the Bill of Rights, 10 states disbanded their official state-sponsored religion (most were Anglican or Congregational churches). Virginia did so in 1786, when the United States was still governed under the Articles of Confederation (Buckley 1977; Dreisbach 2002). New York, North Carolina, New Jersey, Pennsylvania, Delaware, Georgia, and Maryland did so in 1789 or 1800. Of the original 13 states, 4 continued their state-sponsored religions into the 1800s: Connecticut, Massachusetts, New Hampshire, and South Carolina. The movement to separate church and state, however, was spurred on by the Great Awakening (Bonomi 1986; Green 2010; McGarvie 2004; Miller 1986; Sehat 2011).

The Establishment Clause

Until well after the Revolutionary War and the War of 1812 (specifically until 1833, when Massachusetts became the last state to disestablish its state-sponsored religion), and up to the Civil War, many Americans feared that European colonial nations (England, France, and Spain particularly) would try to reassert their control over the new nation. The issue of where an immigrant's allegiance was centered spilled over to a fear that the religious allegiances of some immigrants constituted a threat of "foreign allegiance." Such xenophobia led to enactment of the Alien and Sedition Acts of 1798 (LeMay 2013, vol. 1: 151–162). Anti-Catholicism arose in a virulent form and spread particularly after the Louisiana Purchase in 1803, which added large territories that had been French or Spanish colonies and thus had higher proportions of their population who were adherents of the Roman Catholic faith (ibid: 39; see also Abrams 2009; Alley 1999; Billington 1974; Jenkins 2003; Miller 1986). Such xenophobia is evident today in anti-Muslim sentiment for the same reasons—a question of where their allegiance lies (Bagby, Perls, and Froehle 2001; Beverley 2003).

Chapter 1 discussed the anti-Catholic violence of the 1840s, led by the Know-Nothing Party—and that led to the Ku Klux Klan in the 1880s—but important establishment questions arose and were ruled on by the U.S. Supreme Court around controversies regarding parochial schools. In 1925, for example, the state of Oregon passed a law requiring all children to attend public schools. The law made it illegal for Roman Catholic parents to send their children to Catholic parochial schools. In *Pierce v. Society of Sisters* (268 U.S. 510, 1925), the Supreme Court struck down that Oregon law as unconstitutional on grounds of Section 1, the Due Process Clause of the Fourteenth Amendment, which says simply: "No State shall make or enforce any law which shall abridge the privileges or immunities of citizens of the United States; nor shall any State deprive any person of life, liberty, or property, without due process of law; nor deny any person within its jurisdiction the equal protection of the laws." The *Pierce* decision has been hailed as the "magna carta" of the parochial school system. It is important to note that the Fourteenth Amendment states "nor deny any person" not "nor deny any citizen." While noncitizens do not enjoy all the rights, liberties, and constitutional protections afforded to citizens of the United States by the Bill of Rights, the courts have on occasion ruled that some of those rights are human rights that protect all persons, without regard to their naturalization status.

Government Aid to Church-Related Schools

While the *Pierce* ruling settled the immediate controversy of the legality of parochial schools, it did not end the question nor settle all the controversies between public and religious-based private schools. Indeed, from 1925 (in *Pierce v. Society of Sister*) up until as recently as 2011 (in *Arizona Christian School Tuition Organization v. Winn*), the Supreme Court has rendered 18 decisions drawing a line against or upholding the permissibility of state or local government laws that provided aid in one fashion or another to private church-based schools, thereby coming under the scrutiny of the Supreme Court on the Establishment Clause question (see Table 5.3).

So where does the government cross a no-establishment line in providing funding to non-public schools? Several cases have dealt with that controversy. *Everson v. Board of Education* (281 U.S. 370, 1947) concerned the state of New Jersey's public transportation law providing reimbursement to parents of parochial and private school students for the costs of busing their children to school; challengers to the law argued that such aid violated the Establishment Clause. Advocates for the parochial school system argued that it did not violate the First Amendment. Justice Black delivered the opinion of the Court upholding the state's public transportation law as not violating the Establishment Clause because (1) the financial aid went to the children and only indirectly aided the school in question and (2) the state had a legitimate public safety interest (in safely transporting children to school, whether public or private). The *Everson* decision was also significant in that it applied the Establishment Clause to the actions of state governments via the Fourteenth Amendment.

In 1971, the Supreme Court, in an 8–1 decision, ruled on the Establishment Clause in *Lemon v. Kurtzman* (403 U.S. 602), providing what became known as the *Lemon* test as to when a state or local law passed the constitutional line against establishment. The case concerned a Pennsylvania law that allowed the local government—in this case, school districts—to use public money, from the Pennsylvania Nonpublic Elementary and Secondary Education Act of 1968, to fund educational programs that taught religion-based lessons, activities, and studies (https://www.casebriefs.com/blog/law/constitutional-law/constitutional-law-keyed-to-chemerisky/first-amendment-lemon-v-kurtzman/, accessed February 17, 2017). The *Lemon* decision is considered to be a landmark Supreme Court case and decision because it set the precedent for many subsequent decisions. It did so when it stipulated a three-point test that has since been applied to virtually all subsequent cases in which a law or public policy action by a state or local government is constitutionally challenged on the basis of the Establishment Clause. The *Lemon* test asks: (1) Did the law have a secular purpose? (2) Was the law neutral on religion, that is, did the law neither advance nor inhibit religion? (3) Did the law not favor an excessive government entanglement in religion? In *Lemon v. Kurtzman*, the justices ruled that the Pennsylvania law was, in fact, an unconstitutional violation of the Establishment Clause because the law had more than a secular purpose, that it was not neutral on religion but in fact favored religious schools and religious education, and the complexity of the permissible uses of state funds did constitute an excessive entanglement in religion.

The Supreme Court's jurisprudence has waxed and waned since *Lemon*. In the 1970s and 1980s, the Court was especially skeptical of financial assistance to private sectarian schools. By 2000, the Court waned when the laws or programs were more related to indirect aid (a loan, tax relief to the parents, tax benefits that are neutral with respect to all schools—religious and nonreligious, public and private). In those decisions, the Supreme Court was more likely to uphold the state or local law or program as constitutional (http://uscivilliberties.org/cases/, accessed February 11, 2017).

Following the precedent set by *Lemon* and using the test that case stipulated as criteria on which courts (and state legislatures, for that matter) should judge whether or not aid to non-public schools is permissible, state laws come under more direct scrutiny and are more likely to be considered unconstitutional establishment when the aid or funding is provided directly to the school itself and for aspects of public education that could be construed to helping the religious (parochial) school even if the funds were not directly paying for the salary of a religious order teacher (a nun, for example). The Supreme Court, by a 6–3 vote, overturned a state of New York law as unconstitutional establishment, in *Committee for Public Education Religious Liberty v. Nyquist* (413 U.S. 756, 1973). In *Nyquist*, Justice Lewis Powell, writing for the 6–3 majority, concluded that all aspects of the New York law had the primary effect of advancing religion in violation of the Establishment Clause. The New York law provided threefold aid: (1) grants for the maintenance and repair of private schools serving primarily low-income families, (2) tuition reimbursement grants for low-income parents whose children attended private schools, and (3) tax relief in the form of a tax deduction for parents whose children attended private schools but who did not qualify for a tuition reimbursement grant (i.e., did not meet a "low-income family" means test) (http://uscivilliberties.org/legislation-and-legislative-action/2963-abortion-laws-and-the-establishment-clause.html, accessed February 11, 2017).

In its defense in *Nyquist*, the state of New York argued that the maintenance grants were to ensure the health, welfare, and safety of children attending such schools. It further argued that if the private school enrollments declined and those children were thereby forced to attend public schools, it would aggravate a serious financial crisis for public education in New York, at the time already fiscally stressed—in the 1970s, about 85 percent of non-public schoolchildren attended church-affiliated, largely Roman Catholic parochial schools. In essence, New York state legislators determined that it was simply more cost effective to give some financial aid to sectarian schools than it would be to bear all the costs of having to educate all of them in public schools. The Supreme Court ruled, however, that although the maintenance and repair grants had a secular purpose, the overall primary effect of the law advanced religion. For example, the maintenance grants were not limited to upkeep of facilities used exclusively for secular purposes. Tuition reimbursement, the Court ruled, could not be given directly to sectarian schools, and the tax deductions had the same impermissible effects as the tuition reimbursement program (http://uscivilliberties.org/cases/3624-committee-for-public-education-and-religious-liberty-v-nyquist, accessed February 11, 2017.) Of note in *Nyquist's* three dissenting opinions, Chief Justice Warren Burger and Justices William Rehnquist and Byron White differed with the majority on the tuition reimbursement and tax deduction provisions of the state's plan. Their dissent cited *Walz v. Tax Commission* (1970). In *Walz*, the Court had upheld property tax exemptions for religious institutions, ruling that the granting of tax exemption is not sponsorship since the government does not transfer part of its revenues to churches but simply abstains from demanding that the church support the state through payment of taxes. It ruled there was no genuine nexus between tax exemption and the establishment of religion. In *Nyquist*, however, the majority of justices distinguished *Walz* in part by arguing that *exempting* religious property from the taxing power of the state was different from providing a tuition grant or tax deduction to private citizens who voluntarily choose to send their children to a private sectarian school. The three dissenting justices rejected that distinction.

The waning by the Court began by 1980, however, when the Court upheld a New York state law that appropriated public funds to reimburse both church-sponsored and secular non-public schools for costs regarding the administration of various services mandated by the state, for example, in grading and reporting the results of state-mandated tests that were state-prepared and teacher-prepared tests (in *Committee for Public Education and Religious Liberty v. Regan*, 413 U.S. 473, 1980). In *Regan*, the justices ruled those reimbursements were religiously neutral and therefore did not entail an excessive entanglement in religion as stipulated by the *Lemon* test.

In *Mueller v. Allen* (463 U.S. 388, 1982), the Court upheld a Minnesota state tax deduction grant program to tax-paying parents for school-related expenses, including expenses for sending their children to private secular (e.g., charter) and religious schools. In a 5–4 decision, the Court held the Minnesota law did not violate the Establishment Clause because the law contained all the elements of the three-part test promulgated in the *Lemon v. Kurtzman* decision.

Using a similar line of reasoning, in *Zobrest v. Catalina Foothills School District* (509 U.S. 1, 1993), the Court held that the Establishment Clause does not bar a school district from providing a sign language interpreter when a deaf student transferred to a Catholic school. Since the aid went to the sign interpreter and not the church school, it was religiously neutral, it had a secular purpose (educational aid to a deaf student), and it was sufficiently narrowly construed so as to not involve the state in excessive entanglement in religion.

By the 1990s and later, the Supreme Court was moving in the direction of upholding aid to religion-related schools by more expansively interpreting the *Lemon* test. For example, in *Rosenberger v. Rector and Visitors of the University of Virginia* (515 U.S. 819, 1995), the Court ruled it was unconstitutional to *withhold* funds to a religious student magazine if the university was providing such funds to other (nonreligious) student organizations or magazines devoted to purely secular interests (e.g., sports clubs, fraternities, and science clubs). Neutrality in giving aid meant that the denial of such funding to the student magazine was unconstitutionally *inhibiting* religion and thereby violated the Establishment Clause.

The "private voucher" school aid system was upheld in *Zelman v. Simmons-Harris* (536 U.S. 639, 2002). In the *Zelman* case, the Court ruled, in a 5–4 decision, that the Ohio Project Scholarship Program, which funded a school voucher system where the money was given directly to the parents who could use it for their children's educational costs whether to private secular or non-public parochial (or other religious-based) schools, did not "establish" religion. It was given to the parents and not directly to the schools. It served a secular purpose (aiding education). And the voucher nature of the program did not involve the state's excessive entanglement in religion.

In *Locke v. Davey* (540 U.S. 712, 2004), however, the Court upheld the constitutionality of a state of Washington publicly funded scholarship program that explicitly excluded using the scholarship for students pursuing a degree in devotional theology.

Religion in Public Education

In the 1830s and 1840s, and indeed up until the *Pierce* decision, the relationship between religion and education was long and contentious (McLaughlin 2013: 100–108). The primary friction prior to the Civil War was between German and Irish Catholics on the one hand and the majority Protestants on the other. The initial issue was over which version of the Bible should be used in public schools and over the very nature of what was the basic purpose of schooling. Public school reformers advocated using the schools as sites for promoting social cohesion, but that was difficult to accomplish given the different cultural and religious affiliations. In largely rural versus large city settings, the debate was often whether the schools should be Protestant or Catholic, secular or religious, monolingual or bilingual (McLaughlin: 103). In 1854, then newly elected governor Henry Gardner advocated that the national government should ordain that all schools use English and should retain the Bible in our common schools (public schools in the terminology of the time) in order to nationalize the immigrants before we naturalize them and educate them before either (Glenn 1988: 72–73). Henry Joseph Gardner (1819–1892) served as governor of Massachusetts from 1855 to 1858. He was the candidate of the Know-Nothing movement and was elected governor as part of the sweeping electoral victory of the American Party in the Massachusetts elections of 1854 (http://www.scrip poplicly.net/hejgagoandco.html, accessed February 16, 2017).

This was a significant problem and issue because by the 1860 census one-third of Germans were Roman Catholic adherents (Daniels 2002: 152) and the Irish immigrants who came in between 1848 and 1852, numbering well over one million, were overwhelmingly adherents of Roman Catholicism. Between 1850 and 1870, two-thirds of all immigrants to the United States came from Germany and Ireland. In the eyes of the American Party voters (more commonly known as the Know-Nothing Party) and indeed of many if not most Protestants, Roman Catholicism was a dangerous, alien religion. In 1835, Samuel Morse wrote "Popery is opposed in its very nature to Democratic Republicanism; and it is therefore, as a political system, as well as religious, opposed to civil and religious liberty, and consequently to our form of government" (cited in McLaughlin 2013: 106; see also Gjerde 1998: 137). Samuel Morse (1791–1872) was very influential, a famous painter, and a more famous inventor. He contributed to the invention of the single-wire telegraph and was codeveloper of the Morse code that helped developed the commercial use of the telegraph.

Throughout the 1830s, 1840s, and 1850s, Protestant school leaders insisted that religious instruction in common (i.e., public) schools be nondenominationally Christian through the reading of the King James version of the Bible. Catholic leaders, of course, objected and referred to the common schools as Protestant schools. In the 1840s and 1850s, in New York City, a virtual war between Catholic and Protestant school leaders ensued (Ravitch 1974: 33–76). Similar strife occurred in Philadelphia in 1842, over whether public school children should read from the King James or the Douay (Catholic) version of the Bible (Spring 2008: 113).

These debates and controversial battles between Catholics and Protestants over the place of religion in public schools continued into the 1960s and beyond, raising questions over the issue. Periodically, the Supreme Court grappled with the question of religion in public education and the Establishment Clause. Can public school officials compose an "official prayer" and encourage its recitation in public schools? Such prayer offended non-Protestant parents of public elementary school children: Catholics, Jews, Orthodox, Atheists, and so on. In a landmark decision, *Engel v. Vitale* (370 U.S. 421, 1962), the Supreme Court ruled that it was unconstitutional for New York state officials to do so, by its law requiring that public schools open each day with the Pledge of Allegiance and a non-denominational prayer in which the students recognized their dependence upon God on the grounds that such prayer and its recitation in public schools amounted to the state favoring religion over nonreligion and protestant Christianity over other denominational churches.

In *Abington School District v. Schempp* (374 U.S. 203, 1963), the Supreme Court similarly struck down a Pennsylvania law that required that each public school day open with Bible reading as violating the Establishment Clause. While the state and local school officials argued that the Bible was a historical document, not just a religious one, and that it taught civic morality and behavior, the Court rejected that defense. It held that Bible reading was teaching religion, that a specific version of the Bible favored one denomination over others, and religion over nonreligion, and that such mandated Bible reading inherently entangled the government in religion and was therefore unconstitutional on the basis of the Establishment Clause.

In addition to the Bible-reading question, the justices ruled on the issue of prayers in public schools in a number of cases challenging local, public school district laws or policies on the matter, again based on Establishment Clause grounds. In *Wallace v. Jaffree* (472 U.S. 38, 1985), the Court struck down an Alabama law that set aside a moment for voluntary prayer that allowed teachers to lead willing students in a prayer to "Almighty God, the Creator and Supreme Judge of the world." The justices ruled that the Alabama law had no secular purpose and that it endorsed religion, thereby violating the Establishment Clause.

Issues around problems, and subsequent controversies, over prayer in public schools were often intentionally confused by religious proponents. They typically argued that the Establishment Clause was anti-religion and was being used to ban all prayer in schools. No one is preventing school children, however, from praying in school. The issue is not prayer in school, per se, but mandated prayer written or endorsed by public school officials.

Lee v. Weisman (505 U.S. 577, 1992) involved a state of Rhode Island, officially approved, clergy-led prayer at public school graduations. In a 6–3 decision written for the majority by Justice Kennedy, the Court held that the state law may not sponsor clerics to conduct even nondenominational prayers as they led to subtle religious coercion, thus violating the Establishment Clause. Justices Rehnquist, White, and Thomas dissented (https://www.law.cornell.edu/supct/html, accessed February 17, 2017).

In a similar 6–3 decision, in *Santa Fe Independent School District v. Doe* (530 U.S. 290, 2000), the Court struck down a New Mexico law permitting the practice of student-led prayers at sports games (in this case, football games) as a violation of the Establishment Clause (http://www.oyez.org/cases/1999/99-62, accessed February 17, 2017).

In *Elk Grove Unified School District v. Newdow* (542 U.S. 1, 2004), a California daily prayer and recitation of the Pledge of Allegiance, with its phrase "one nation under God," was challenged by the atheist parent of a public school child. The Court ruled that the parent in question, as the noncustodial parent of the child, lacked the standing to sue. The Court did not rule on the merits of the case with respect to the pledge issue, although we will see later that it has ruled in other cases on a related controversy with respect to legislative chaplains and legislative sessions opening with a nondenominational invocation.

The Court dealt with the Establishment Clause issue as it influenced the teaching of secular subjects, like biology and evolutionary science, inasmuch as such subjects had significant implications for some religious beliefs. In *Epperson v. Arkansas* (393 U.S. 97, 1968), the Supreme Court invalidated a state law that prohibited the teaching of evolution in its public schools. Justice Abraham Fortas, writing for the majority, held that the Arkansas law was an unconstitutional violation of the Establishment Clause, holding that the government must be neutral in matters of religious theory, doctrine, and practice. It ruled that creationism was, in fact, religious theory.

In *Stone v. Graham* (449 U.S. 39, 1980), the Supreme Court ruled that a Kentucky law that mandated the posting of the Ten Commandments on the wall of each public school classroom in the state violated the Establishment Clause because the law lacked a nonreligious legislative purpose (one of the principles of the three-part *Lemon* test) and was not neutral on religion versus nonreligion.

The Court, however, did not allow a state law or policy to discriminate against providing aid to a student group even if the students were organized with a religious focus when the state was providing equal aid to a secular student group. In *Rosenberger v. Rector and Visitors of the University of Virginia* (515 U.S. 819, 1995), the Court held that it was unconstitutional to withhold funds from a religious student magazine when they funded student sports, fraternity, and similar magazines. The Court held the state had to treat such student groups with neutrality. The Court's rationale was evident in a 1997 decision, *Agostini, et al. v. Felton, et al.* (473 U.S. 401), when it held that a federally funded program providing supplemental, remedial instruction to disadvantaged children on a neutral basis is not invalid under the Establishment Clause when such instruction is given on the premises of sectarian schools by government employees under a program containing safeguards such as those present in New York City's Title 1 program.

Finally, in *Mitchell v. Helms* (530 U.S. 793, 2000), the Court held it was permissible for *loans* to be made to religious schools under Chapter 2 of the Education Consolidation and Improvement Act of 1981 as the loan program did not involve the state in an excessive entanglement with religion.

Government-Sponsored Religious Displays

Another problem that required a number of Supreme Court decisions to clarify just where the limits should be drawn to comply with the Establishment Clause is over the use of religious displays on public property, for example, erecting a large cross, displaying the Ten Commandments, and putting up a crèche (Christmas nativity scene) on public property during the Christmas holiday season.

In *Lynch v. Donnelly* (465 U.S. 668, 1984), the Court upheld a nativity display that was one among other symbols in a public park "to celebrate the Christmas holiday and to depict the historical origins of that holiday." Likewise, the Court, in a per curiam decision, upheld a lower federal court decision that allowed as constitutional the display of a nativity scene placed on public land but paid for and erected by a private group when it was part of a number of holiday scenes, including secular ones (Santa Claus, Christmas Trees, carolers, etc.), holding that observers of the displays would not interpret the nativity scene as the Village Board endorsement of a religion (in *Board of Trustees of the Village of Scarsdale v. McCreary*, 492 U.S. 83, 1985).

The Court reached a different decision, however, in another later case. In *Allegheny County v. Greater Pittsburgh ACLU* (492 U.S. 573, 1989), Justice Blackmun, writing for the majority decision and citing the *Lemon v. Kurtzman* tests, struck down as an unconstitutional infringement of the Establishment Clause a display of a crèche and cross in the city hall, ruling that those displays paid for by the city government and displayed in the city hall indicated a government allegiance to a particular creed or sect. In the opinion of a majority of the Court, those displays amounted to government proselytizing. Likewise, in *McCreary County v. ACLU* (545 U.S. 844, 2005), the Court ruled that two large, framed copies of the Ten Commandments in Kentucky courthouses lacked a secular purpose and were not religiously neutral and, therefore, they violated the Establishment Clause.

By contrast, in that same year, in *Van Orden v. Perry* (545 U.S. 677, 2005), a six-foot monument displaying the Ten Commandments donated by a private group and placed with other historical monuments on the public grounds next to the Texas State Capitol had a secular purpose and therefore would not lead an observer to conclude that the state endorsed the religious message. As such, it therefore did not violate the Establishment Clause.

Prayers in Public Schools

Whether or not and under what circumstances prayers could be allowed in public schools was a concern addressed in several landmark Supreme Court decisions. The fact that the prayers were led by teachers was a subtle endorsement of religion.

In *Lee v. Weisman* (505 U.S. 577, 1992), the Court, asked to address the constitutionality of an officially approved, clergy-led prayer at public school graduations, ruled that such prayers led to subtle religious coercion and thereby violated the Establishment Clause. At issue was the policy and practice that the school district had to provide a sign-language interpreter to a deaf child at a religious school. The Court ruled that the aid was constitutional because it went to the student, not the church, and even though it was at the religious school, it was not an excessive entanglement of the state in religion.

A degree of coercion was the critical element in the Court's decision in a 2000 case. In *Santa Fe Independent School District v. Doe* (530 U.S. 290, 2000), at issue was a public school district's policy of having students vote on a prayer to be read by a student at football games. The Court ruled the policy violated the Establishment Clause because the voting policy resulted in religious coercion of the minority by the majority.

In *Elk Grove Unified School District v. Newdow* (542 U.S. 1, 2004), a student's father challenged the constitutionality of requiring public school teachers to lead the Pledge of Allegiance, which included the phrase "under God" since 1954. The Court determined that since Newdow was the noncustodial parent, he did not have standing to bring the case to court and therefore the Supreme Court did not answer the constitutional question. The case illustrates the fact that often the Court will reach a decision on narrow or technical grounds and avoid deciding or ruling on the constitutional question or issue in the case, thereby avoiding setting a precedent.

Sabbatarian Laws (Blue Laws)

Occasionally, state laws and more often local laws (usually city ordinances) have frequently set aside Sunday as a day of rest, prohibiting certain stores to be open to sell their wares, thereby requiring their employees to work on the Sabbath or discriminating against those members of a religious faith who celebrate Saturday as their Sabbath day. Cases challenging such blue laws have typically been brought by members of the Jewish faith, by Seventh-day Adventists, and by Jehovah's Witnesses. One of the first and landmark decisions by the Supreme Court on this issue was in the case *McGowan v. Maryland* (366 U.S. 420, 1961). It was the first of several blue law cases. Chief Justice Earl Warren wrote the majority opinion in the 8–1 decision that held that laws with a religious origin are not by that mere fact unconstitutional on Establishment Clause grounds. They may be permissible if they have a secular purpose, in this case to provide a uniform day of rest, set aside for rest and recreation.

In *Braunfeld v. Brown* (366 U.S. 599, 1961), the Court upheld a Pennsylvania law requiring stores to be closed on Sundays, even though Orthodox Jews had argued that such a law unduly burdened them since their religion required them to close their stores on Saturdays as well. The Court ruled that the Pennsylvania law did not target Jews specifically as a group and that therefore the state law did not violate the Establishment Clause (http://billofrightsinstitute.org/cases, accessed September 29, 2016).

That same year, the Court issued another and similar decision in *Gallagher v. Crown Kosher Market of Massachusetts, Inc.* (366 U.S. 627, 1961). The appellees were a group of Orthodox Jews whose religion forbids them to shop on their Sabbath, which is from sundown on Friday until sundown on Saturday, and requires them to eat kosher food. They were a group of rabbis and a corporation that sold kosher food to such customers. They sued in a federal district court seeking to have declared unconstitutional a Massachusetts Sunday closing law that forbids them to sell kosher food, except kosher meat, until 10:00 a.m. on Sunday. The law forbade keeping open shops and the doing of any labor, business, or work on Sundays, with some stipulated exceptions (e.g., dairy and other perishable food items, prescriptions, and other medicines). The appellees were joined in by amici curiae (friend of the court) briefs filed by the Synagogue Council of America, the American Jewish Committee, the American Civil Liberties Union, and the General Conference of Seventh-day Adventists. The appellees and the amici curiae briefs argued that the Sunday closing law was an unconstitutional violation of the Equal Protection Clause of the Fourteenth Amendment, the Establishment Clause, and the Free Exercise Clause of the First Amendment. A majority of the justices held that the statute does not prohibit Sunday business and labor by Sabbatarian observers so long as it disturbs no other persons and that the law provides for special licenses for emergency Sunday work, which may be obtained from local officials. In a 6–3 decision, the Court upheld the Massachusetts law, citing the precedent set in *Braunfeld v. Brown.*

Finally, the Court considered a case wherein the state law required employers to grant employees unqualified right not to work on their Sabbath. It was held unconstitutional because it lacked a secular purpose and therefore fostered excessive entanglement with religion. Justice Burger wrote the majority opinion in *Thorton v. Caldor* (472 U.S. 703, 1985), which the Court rendered in an 8–1 decision. It held that private companies are free to fire people who refuse to work on any day they claim to be their Sabbath, because the First Amendment applies only to government, not to private employers (https://billofrightsinstitute.org/cases, accessed September 29, 2016).

Religious Institutions Functioning as Government Agencies

Another problem area arises when religious institutions seem, in whole or in part, to function as a public body or government agency in providing a service or in regulating access to the use of space or the location of certain types of business deemed offensive or threatening to the religious institution. The Supreme Court rendered three decisions that addressed such concerns raised by that problem.

In the case of *Larkin v. Grendel's Den* (459 U.S. 116, 1982), the Court considered a Massachusetts statute that vests in the governing bodies of schools and churches the power to prevent the issuance of liquor licenses for business premises located within a 500-foot radius of the church or school by objecting to the license application. In this case, the appellee was a restaurant operator whose application for a liquor license was denied when a church located 10 feet from the business objected to the application. They then sued the licensing authority in federal district court arguing that the statute on its face and as applied in this case violated the Establishment Clause (http://caselaw.com/us-supreme-court/459/116.html, accessed February 18, 2017). The Court held that the statute did violate the Establishment Clause. It held the Massachusetts law is not simply a legislative exercise in zoning power, but rather that it delegates to private, nongovernmental entities the power to reject certain liquor license applications. Such power is normally invested in governmental agencies. Under the circumstances of the *Larkin* case, the Court did not give the deference normally due to a legislative zoning judgment. It further held that the valid secular objective of the law in protecting schools and churches from the commotion associated with liquor outlets could readily be accomplished by other means than giving the schools or churches essentially a veto power over the licensing board. The power of the churches was held to no specified standards by the statute, which called for no reasons, findings, or reasoned conclusions, and therefore can be seen as having a "primary" and "principal" effect of advancing religion. The Court ruled that the statute substitutes the unilateral and absolute power of a church for the reasoned decision making of a public legislative body acting upon specified evidence and guided by standards as to issues with significant economic and political implications; therefore it enmeshes (entangles) the processes of government and creates the danger of political fragmentation and divisiveness on religious lines, citing *Lemon v. Kurtzman*, which argued that few entanglements could be more offensive to the spirit of the Constitution and as protected by the Establishment Clause (http://caselaw.find law.com/us-supreme-court/459/116.html).

In a 1988 decision, *Bowen v. Kendrick* (487 U.S. 589, 1988), a group of federal taxpayers, clergy, and the American Jewish Congress filed a suit in federal district court seeking declaratory and injunctive relief by challenging the constitutionality, under the First Amendment's Establishment Clause, of the Adolescent Family Life Act (AFLA). That act authorizes federal grants to public or nonprofit private organizations or agencies for service and research in the area of premarital adolescent sexual relations and pregnancy. The AFLA requires: (1) that the grantee (recipient of the grant authorized by the law) furnish certain types of services, including counseling and education relating to family life and problems associated with adolescent premarital sexual relations; (2) that the complexity of the problems requires the involvement of religious and charitable organizations, voluntary associations, and other groups in the private sector, as well as government agencies; and (3) that grantees not use funds for certain purposes, including family planning services and the promotion of abortion. AFLA funding has been granted to a wide variety of recipients, including organizations with institutional ties to denominations. Granting summary judgment for the appellees, the federal appellate court declared that the act, both on its face and as applied, violated the Establishment Clause insofar as it provided for the involvement of religious organizations in federally funded programs. The Supreme Court held that the AFLA Act, on its face, does not violate the Establishment Clause as it satisfies the Lemon test conditions (https://supreme.ustia.com/cases/federal/us/487/589, accessed February 18, 2017).

Finally, in *Board of Education of Kiryas Joel Village School v. Grumet* (512 U.S. 587, 1994), the Supreme Court struck down a New York law creating a special school district to benefit disabled Orthodox Jewish children because it benefited a single religious group and was therefore not neutral to religion.

Tax Exemptions for Religious Institutions

Three major Supreme Court cases rendered decisions as to whether or not religious institutions could be granted tax exemption without violating the First Amendment's Establishment Clause.

In *Walz v. Tax Commission of the City of New York* (397 U.S. 664, 1970), the Supreme Court held that grants of tax exemption to religious organizations do not violate the Establishment Clause. The case was brought by a property owner who unsuccessfully sought an injunction to prevent the City of New York Tax Commission from granting property tax exemption to religious organizations for properties used solely for religious purposes. The appellant argued that the exemptions violated the provision prohibiting establishment of religion under both the First and the Fourteenth Amendments. The Supreme Court held (1) that the First Amendment tolerates neither governmentally established religion nor governmental interference with religion; (2) that tax exemption is not aimed at establishing, sponsoring, or supporting religion; (3) that tax exemption creates only minimal and remote involvement between church and state, far less entanglement than would taxation of churches, and restricts the fiscal relationship between them, thereby tending to complement and reinforce the desired separation insulating each from the other; and (4) that tax exemption has been used for two centuries and has not led to an established church or religion, and, on the contrary, has helped to guarantee the free exercise of all forms of religious beliefs (https://supreme.justia.com/cases/federal/us/397/664/case.html, accessed February 20, 2017).

The Supreme Court reached a different decision in a 1983 case. In *Bob Jones University v. United States* (461 U.S. 574), the Court held that the religion clauses of the First Amendment did not prevent the Internal Revenue Service (IRS) from revoking the tax-exempt status of a religious university or school whose practices are contrary to compelling public policy, such as the eradication of racial discrimination (IRS ruling 71–447, 1971). Bob Jones University denied admission to applicants in interracial marriage, who advocated such marriage, or who were engaged in interracial dating. The Supreme Court held that Bob Jones University (and the Goldsboro Christian School, which accepts only Caucasian students) maintained a racially discriminatory policy and that therefore the IRS could revoke their tax exempt status (https://www.law.cornell.edu/supremecourt/text/461/574, accessed February 20, 2017).

The case of *Texas Monthly, Inc. v. Bullock* (489 U.S. 1, 1989) tested the legality of a Texas law that exempted religious publications from having to pay a state sales tax.

The Texas Monthly, a nonreligious publisher, claimed that the tax exemption granted to religious publications violated the Establishment Clause and sought recovery of the sales taxes it had paid in 1985. In a 6–3 decision, the Supreme Court ruled that the exemption violated the Establishment Clause by advancing religion and the Free Press Clause by discrimination based on the content of the publications. The majority opinion of Justices Brennan, White, Marshall, Blackmun, Stevens, and O'Connor cited *Lemon v. Kurtzman*. The Court could not rewrite tax statutes, but it invalidated the taxes levied on nonreligious publishers and ordered the state of Texas to refund the *Texas Monthly's* sales taxes paid for 1985. In dissent were Justices Rehnquist, Scalia, and Kennedy. The majority held that by taxing nonreligious publications but not taxing religious publications, the state of Texas advantaged religious publications over nonreligious publishers.

Legislative Chaplains and Prayers

The Supreme Court used the *Lemon* test in the case of *Marsh v. Chambers* (462 U.S. 783, 1983). The case concerned the Nebraska legislature's chaplaincy practice (paying a small stipend to clergy to deliver an invocation at the start of a legislative session). In a 6–3 decision, with Justice Burger writing the opinion for the majority, the Court held that the Nebraska practice did not violate the Establishment Clause, finding that the chaplaincy was constitutional because of the unique history of the United States having Congress opened by chaplains giving an invocation.

Standing to Sue

There were two Supreme Court decisions that dealt with the question about having the standing to sue challenging a law over the Establishment Clause. The first case was a 1968 decision of the Court: *Flast v. Cohen* (392 U.S. 83, 1968). In the *Flast* case, the Supreme Court dealt with an earlier (1923) decision, *Frothingham v. Mellon*, in which the Court had decided that the taxpayer did not have standing to sue the federal government in order to prevent expenditures if her only injury was an anticipated increase in her taxes. The case had no issue of a constitutional barrier against federal taxpayer lawsuits. In the *Flast* case, the plaintiffs, Florance Flast and others, joined in filing the lawsuit against Wilbur Cohen, then secretary of Health, Education, and Welfare (HEW), now the Department of Health and Human Services, contesting the constitutionality of spending federal funds on religious schools on Establishment Clause grounds. A district court had denied standing, and the Supreme Court heard the case on appeal. Chief Justice Earl Warren wrote the 7–2 opinion, holding that the taxpayers did have standing to sue to prevent the spending of federal funds in contravention of the Establishment Clause's prohibition against government support of religion. In *Flast,* the Court established a "double nexus" test that a taxpayer must satisfy in order to have standing to sue: (1) establish a logical link between the taxpayer status and the type of legislative enactment contested and (2) show that the challenged law exceeds a specific constitutional limitation upon the exercise of the taxing and spending power, not simply that the enactment in general is beyond powers delegated to Congress. Only when both nexuses have been satisfied may the petitioner have standing to sue. The Court ruled that the petitioners had satisfied both nexuses and therefore had standing to sue. As to the law at issue allocating funds to parochial schools and therefore potentially violating the Establishment Clause, the Court expressed no views as to the merits of the appellants' claims in this case (https://supreme.justia.com/cases/federal/us/392/83/case.html, accessed February 20, 2017).

Another standing to sue case was the 1982 decision in *Valley Forge Christian College v. Americans United for Separation of Church and State, Inc.* (454 U.S. 464). The *Valley Forge* case contested the Federal Property and Administrative Services Act of 1949, which provided an economical and efficient system to dispose of surplus federal government property that had outlived its usefulness and been declared surplus and that then may be transferred to private or other public entities. The act authorized the HEW secretary to assume responsibility to dispose of surplus real property for educational use, and the secretary could sell such property to nonprofit, tax-exempt educational institutions. In the *Valley Forge* case, the property in question was a surplus military hospital under the act and was conveyed by HEW to a church-related college, the petitioner. The appraised value of the property was more than $577,000 and was discounted 100 percent by the HEW secretary as a public benefit allowance. The respondent (the Americans United for Separation of Church and State, Inc.) challenged the conveyance as a violation of the Establishment Clause. The Court ruled that the respondents lacked standing to sue as taxpayers under the *Flast v. Cohen* decision and as citizens to challenge the conveyance. The justices ruled 7–1 that Americans United lacked standing as taxpayers because the action was by a decision by HEW, not the Congress, and thus was not an exercise of Congress's authority conferred by the Taxing and Spending Clause but rather by the Property Clause. The respondents alleged no other basis for standing to sue, claiming that the Constitution had been violated, but nothing else. They failed to identify any personal injury suffered. Claimed injury sufficient to confer standing is not measured by the intensity of the litigant's interest or the fervor of his advocacy, observed Justice Rehnquist while delivering the opinion of the Court (http://www.law.cornell.edu/supremecourt/text/454/464, accessed February 20, 2017).

Teaching Creationism and Evolution in Public Schools

The Court dealt with the controversy of teaching creationism in public schools, as to whether or not that violated the Establishment Clause, in *Edwards v. Aguillard* (482 U.S. 578, 1987). The *Edwards* case challenged a Louisiana state law that required that if public schools teach evolution, they also had to teach creationism as "creation science." A teacher could choose not to teach evolution or creationism, but if one was taught, then the other also had to be taught. The Court held that the law was on its face a violation of the Establishment Clause because it lacked a clear secular purpose. Furthermore, the act did not further its stated secular purpose of "protecting academic freedom." The Court held the act did not enhance the freedom of teachers to teach what they choose and failed to further the goal of "teaching all the evidence." Forbidding the teaching of evolution when creationism is not also taught undermines the provision of comprehensive scientific education, nor does making them teach creationism if they teach evolutionary theory give teachers flexibility that they did not already possess to supplement the present science curriculum with the presentation of theories, besides evolution, about the origin of life. Finally, the Court ruled that teaching creation science impermissibly endorses religion by advancing the religious belief that a supernatural being created humankind. The act is designed either to promote the theory of creation science that embodies a particular religious tenet or to prohibit the teaching of a scientific theory disfavored by certain religious sects. In either case, it violates the First Amendment (https://www.law.cornell.edu/supremecourt/text/482/578, accessed February 20, 2017).

Unequal Government Treatment of Religious Groups

The Supreme Court considered the issue of equality of treatment of religious groups in a state of Minnesota law that was challenged on Establishment Clause grounds in *Larson v. Valente* (456 U.S. 228, 1982). The Court heard the case on appeal from the Eighth Circuit. At issue was a section of Minnesota's Charitable Solicitations Act that provides that only those religious organizations that receive more than half of their total contributions from members or affiliated organizations are exempt from the registration and reporting requirements of the act. The appellees, members of the Unification Church, sued in the federal district court, seeking a declaration that the statute, on its face and as applied to them, violated the Establishment Clause of the First Amendment and also seeking injunctive relief. After obtaining a preliminary injunction, appellees moved for summary judgment. Upon finding that the "overbreadth" doctrine gave appellees standing to challenge the statute, the lower court held that the application of the statute to religious organizations violated the Establishment Clause and therefore recommended declaratory and permanent injunctive relief. The district court, accepting this recommendation, entered summary judgment for appellees. The Court of Appeals affirmed both on the standing issue and on the merits. But the court, disagreeing with the district court's conclusion that appellees and others should enjoy the religious organization exemption from the act merely by claiming to be such organizations, held that proof of religious organization status was required in order to gain the exemption and left the question of the appellees' status "open . . . for further development." Accordingly, the Court of Appeals vacated the district court's judgment and remanded for entry of modified injunction and further proceedings.

The Supreme Court held:

1. Appellees have standing to raise their Establishment Clause claims.

2. The state of Minnesota attempted to use a fifty percent rule to compel the Unification Church to register and report under the act. The fact that the fifty percent rule only applies to religious organizations compels the conclusion that, at least for purposes of this suit challenging that application, appellee Unification Church is a religious organization within the meaning of the act. The controversy between the parties is not rendered any less concrete by the fact that appellants, in the course of this litigation, have changed their position to contend that the Unification Church is not a religious organization within the meaning of the act, and that therefore it would not be entitled to an exemption even if the fifty percent rule were declared unconstitutional. This is so because the threatened application of its fifty percent rule to appellees amounts to a distinct and palpable injury to them, in that it disables them from soliciting contributions in Minnesota unless they comply with the registration

and reporting requirements of the act. Moreover, there is a causal connection between the claimed injury and the challenged conduct. The fact that appellees have not yet shown an entitlement to a permanent injunction barring the state from subjecting them to the act's registration and reporting requirements does not detract from the palpability of the particular and discrete injury caused to appellees.

3. In setting up precisely the sort of official denominational preference forbidden by the First Amendment, it violates the Establishment Clause. Since the challenged statute grants denominational preferences, it must be treated as suspect, and strict scrutiny must be applied in adjudging its constitutionality. And even assuming, *arguendo*, that appellants' asserted interest in preventing fraudulent solicitations is a "compelling" interest, appellants have nevertheless failed to demonstrate that the fifty percent rule is "closely fitted" to that interest. Appellants' argument to the contrary is based on three premises: (1) that members of a religious organization can and will exercise supervision and control over the solicitation activities of the organization when membership contributions exceed fifty percent; (2) that membership control, assuming its existence, is an adequate safeguard against abusive solicitations of the public; and (3) that the need for public disclosure rises in proportion with the percentage of nonmember contributions. There is no substantial support in the record for any of these premises. Where the principal effect of the fifty percent rule is to impose the act's registration and reporting requirements on some religious organizations but not on others, the "risk of politicizing religion" inhering in the statute is obvious.

The majority opinion of the Supreme Court was written by Justice Brennan, and by its 6–3 decision, the Court affirmed that the Minnesota statute was in violation of the Establishment Clause.

The Free Exercise Clause

Problems and controversies over the precise meaning of the Free Exercise Clause and on the limits it imposes on governments have most often involved minority religions, sects, or cults. Laws and Supreme Court decisions sometimes discerned a difference between members of a minority religion being free to exercise a belief versus their freedom to put that belief into practice when the resulting behavior was viewed by the majority society as threatening to the health and safety or similar "public interest."

This section discusses 38 Supreme Court decisions involving a Free Exercise Clause challenge to a governmental law or policy. Minority religions involved include, for example, the Amish and Mennonites, the Jehovah's Witnesses, the Church of Jesus Christ of Latter-day Saints, and the Unification Church.

Solicitation by Religious Groups

Ten U.S. Supreme Court decisions that involved problems with the rights of members of a religious group to solicit the public for donations were decided between 1940 and 1980. The first such case, *Cantwell v. Connecticut* (310 U.S. 296, 1940), ruled on a Connecticut state law requiring permits for religious solicitation. The Supreme Court specifically incorporated the First Amendment protection of the free exercise of religion to states via the Fourteenth Amendment. The Court ruled that state governments could not require special permits for religious solicitation when such permits were not required for nonreligious solicitation. Jesse Cantwell, a Jehovah's Witnesses adherent, was convicted on a charge of breach of peace for playing a record while soliciting on the streets of New Haven, Connecticut, that was sharply critical of the Catholic religion. His intent was to proselytize his listeners. Although the message on the record was offensive, it was only played to persons who voluntarily agreed to listen. The *Cantwell* decision was a unanimous decision and a landmark free exercise case. In it, the Court held that

1) the peaceful expression of beliefs—including religious views that might offend some listeners—is protected from infringement by the federal as well as state governments, and 2) that the government has no role in determining religious truth. (http://www.billofrightsinstitute.org/educa tor-resources/lesson-plans/landmark-supreme-court-cases/ Cantwell-v-Connecticut, accessed February 21, 2017)

In *Minersville School District v. Gobitis* (310 U.S. 586, 1940), the Court ruled in an 8–1 decision that public schools could compel students—in this case, Jehovah's Witnesses—to salute the American flag at the start of a school day. The two students, a girl aged 12, and her brother, aged 10, were expelled from the public school of Minersville, Pennsylvania, for refusing to salute the national flag. School board policy required both teachers and students to participate in the Pledge of Allegiance ceremony. The children were brought up to believe that such a gesture of respect was forbidden by command of scriptures. Given their ages of 10 and 12, they were subject to compulsory school attendance law. The Pennsylvania law made no exemptions for children who had sincere conscientious objection. Justice Frankfurter delivered the opinion of the Court, which upheld the state law. Their ruling, however, was overturned just three years later, in the decision in *West Virginia State Board of Education v. Barnette* (319 U.S. 624, 1943).

The Court similarly upheld a state law in a case also involving the Jehovah's Witnesses in *Cox v. New Hampshire* (312 U.S. 569, 1941). In *Cox*, a New Hampshire town required that a license be obtained before a sidewalk parade could be held within the town. A group of Jehovah's Witnesses held a parade without first obtaining a license and were fined for violating the law. They challenged the law's provisions as violating their First Amendment rights. The Court ruled 9–0, in an opinion written by Justice Charles Evans Hughes, that although it cannot regulate the content of speech, the town government can place reasonable time, place, and manner restrictions on speech for the public safety when such speech took the form of a parade or other large gathering and it could impose a reasonable fee for the permit that was proportional to the amount of police presence required to ensure the peaceable conduct of the event (www.uscourts.gov/educational-resources/education-activities/ facts-and-case-summary-cox-v-new-hampshire, accessed February 21, 2017).

The Jehovah's Witnesses were similarly involved in a 1942 case, *Jones v. City of Opelika-1* (316 U.S. 584). The Supreme Court heard the case *certiorari* from the Supreme Court of Alabama. It concerned a challenge to a city ordinance that required that licenses be procured and that taxes in reasonable amount be paid for the conduct of various businesses within the municipality, including the selling of books and pamphlets on the streets or from house to house, which is general and nondiscriminatory in its incidences and which does not infringe the liberties of free speech, free press, or free exercise of religion when applied to a member of a religious organization engaged in selling the printed propaganda of his sect. The Supreme Court, in a 6–3 decision, upheld the ordinance as the regulation was for an individual, not the religion or religious group per se. Justice Reed wrote the majority opinion (www.supreme .justia.com/316/jones-v-opelika, accessed February 21, 2017).

The Jehovah's Witnesses were also party to a suit on freedom of religion in the case *Marsh v. State of Alabama* (326 U.S. 501, 1943). Chickasaw, Alabama, was a company-owned town (the Gulf Shipbuilding Corporation), a suburb of Mobile, with a business block. The appellant, a Jehovah's Witnesses adherent, stood near the post office to distribute religious literature without written permission to do so from the company management. The deputy sheriff, employed by the company, arrested her, and she was charged with violating a 1940 Alabama code that makes it a crime to enter or remain on the premises of another after having been warned not to do so. She sued charging that the state law violated her freedom of religion and press, contrary to the First and Fourteenth Amendments.

The Alabama Court of Appeals affirmed the conviction. The Alabama Supreme Court denied certiorari. The U.S. Supreme Court granted certiorari to hear the case. It found that the conviction must be reversed, finding that ownership of the town by a single company is not enough to give that company the power, enforceable by a state law, to abridge those freedoms. Chickasaw does not function differently from any other town, and the shopping area is freely accessible and open to the public. The manager appointed by the corporation cannot curtail the liberty of press and religion. Their use of the power of state law enforcing such action by criminally punishing those who attempt to distribute religious liberty clearly violates the First and Fourteenth Amendments to the Constitution. The Court reversed and remanded the case to the lower court (http://www.caselaw.findlaw.com/us-supreme-court-326/501.html, accessed February 21, 2017).

In *Murdock v. Pennsylvania* and *Jones v. City of Opelika-II* (319 U.S. 103, 1943), the Supreme Court once again considered a case brought by the Jehovah's Witnesses. In these cases, the Supreme Court held that a municipal ordinance requiring solicitors to purchase a license was an unconstitutional tax on the Jehovah's Witnesses' right to freely exercise their religion. Justice Douglas delivered the opinion of the Court. The city of Jeannette, Pennsylvania (and of the City of Opelika), had an ordinance requiring all persons soliciting within the Borough to procure a license to conduct said business and pay a tax to the Borough Treasurer. The petitioners, members of the Jehovah's Witnesses, went door to door distributing literature and soliciting people to purchase certain religious books and pamphlets published by the Watch Tower Bible and Tract Society. The book and pamphlets cost 5 cents each. None of the members obtained a license to solicit. Petitioners were arrested, convicted, and fined for violation of the ordinance. Their convictions were sustained by the Superior Court of Pennsylvania. The case(s) were brought to the Supreme Court on a writ of certiorari, along with petition to rehear *Jones v. Opelika*. The

Supreme Court reversed the lower court's decision and held that the municipal ordinance violated the free expression of religion clause of the First Amendment (http://www.constitu tion.org/ussc/319-105a.html, accessed February 21, 2017).

Likewise, the Jehovah's Witnesses scored a significant court victory in a decision overturning Gobitis (*Minersville School District v. Gobitis*, 310 U.S. 586, 1940). This 6–3 decision was in the case *West Virginia Board of Education v. Barnette* (321 U.S. 158, 1943). Justice Jackson delivered the opinion of the Court. The Court held (1) that state actions against which the Fourteenth Amendment protects includes state boards of education; (2) actions by the state making it compulsory for children in public schools to salute the flag and recite the pledge of allegiance violates the First and Fourteenth Amendments; (3) held the decision as applicable to children who were expelled, for those who refused to comply and for whose absence thereby became unlawful, subjecting them and their parents or guardians to punishment; (4) those who refused compliance did so on religious grounds; and (5) under the federal Constitution, compulsion as here employed is not a permissible means of achieving "national unity." (https://www .law.cornell.edu/supremecourt/text/319/624, accessed February 21, 2017).

Another Jehovah's Witnesses case concerned the use of minor children to sell religious literature on the streets in contradiction of state child labor laws. In *Prince v. Massachusetts*, 321 U.S. 158, 1944), the Court held that the government had broad authority to regulate actions and treatment of children. It specified that parental authority is not absolute and can be permissibly restricted if doing so is in the interest of a child's welfare. The Supreme Court heard the case on appeal from the Superior Court of Massachusetts, Plymouth County. Justice Rutledge delivered the opinion of the Court. The case involved an appeal from a Jehovah's Witnesses adherent, Sarah Prince, who was the aunt and custodian of a girl 9 years of age. The justices rule the following: (1) that the state law at issue provides that no minor (defined in the law as a boy under 12 or a girl under 18) shall sell or offer to sell on the streets or other public places any newspaper, magazine, periodicals, or other articles of merchandise; (2) that it is unlawful for any person to furnish a minor any article that he or she knows the minor intends to sell, in violation of the law; (3) that whether a sale or offer to sell and whether the minor is doing work within the meaning of the state law were questions of local law for which the decision of the state court is binding; (4) as to the proclaiming of religion in streets or other public places, the power of the state to control the conduct of children is broader than the state's power over adults; and (5) there is no denial of equal protection of the law in excluding children of a particular sect from such use of the streets as by state law such action is barred to all other children (https://suprem.justia.com/cases/federal/us/321/158/case.html, accessed February 21, 2017).

The Hare Krishna cult was involved in a 1980 Supreme Court case *Heffron v. International Society for Krishna Consciousness* (452 U.S. 640, 1981). The *Heffron* decision involved a state of Minnesota law that allowed the Minnesota Agricultural Society to devise rules to regulate the state fair in St. Paul, Minnesota. One rule required organizations wishing to sell or distribute goods and written material to do so from an assigned location on the fair grounds. Walking vendors or solicitors were not allowed. The International Society for Krishna Consciousness challenged the rule, arguing that the rule restricted the ability of its followers to freely exercise their religious beliefs at the state fair. The question before the Court was could a state, consistent with the First and the Fourteenth Amendments, confine religious organizations wishing to sell or distribute religious literature at a state fair to an assigned location on the fairgrounds? In a 5–4 decision, the Court upheld the rule. Using the valid time, manner, and place criteria the Court employs to assess government restrictions of First Amendment Freedoms (the *Cox* test), the Court held the rule did not violate the Constitution as it was applied equally to all groups wanting to solicit on the fairgrounds. The majority held that allowing all religious, nonreligious, and commercial groups to move about the grounds distributing literature and soliciting funds would be potentially dangerous to the fair's visitors. Justices Burger, Stewart, White, Powell, and Rehnquist were in the majority. Justices Brennan, Marshall, Blackmun, and Stevens were in the minority (*Heffron v. International Society for Krishna Consciousness, Inc.*, *Oyez*, https://www.oyez.org/cases/1980/80-795, accessed February 21, 2017).

Using Religious Tests for Public Benefits or Services

In *Chaplinsky v. New Hampshire* (315 U.S. 568, 1942), the Court dealt with a case that involved a Jehovah's Witnesses member who challenged the constitutionality of a New Hampshire state law that forbids under penalty that any person shall address "any offensive, derisive or annoying words to any other person who is lawfully in any street or public place" (referred to as the fighting words doctrine). The Jehovah's Witnesses member was convicted in the municipal court of Rochester, New Hampshire, in violation of the law for calling, on the public street outside the city hall, government officials and workers "God damned fascists" and the whole government of Rochester as being fascists or agents of fascists, thereby using offensive, derisive, and annoying words and names. (In 1942, the United States was at war with fascist Germany and Italy.) Chaplinsky was found guilty and fined. Upon appeal, the Supreme Court of the state affirmed his conviction. He then appealed to the U.S. Supreme Court arguing that the state law was a violation of free speech, free press, and the free exercise of religion, as he was distributing Jehovah's Witnesses literature at the time and denouncing all religion as a "racket." The Supreme Court upheld the state law as constitutional on its face and as applied not to violate the Fourteenth Amendment.

Can an atheist be required to swear an oath in order to be appointed to a public office? That was the issue in the case of

Torcaso v. Watkins (376 U.S. 488, 1961). In *Torcaso*, the Supreme Court reaffirmed that the U.S. Constitution prohibits state and federal governments from requiring any kind of a religious test for public office, in this case, as a notary public. Torcaso, an atheist, was denied a commission as a notary because he would not swear an oath declaring his belief in God, as required by the state of Maryland's Constitution. He sued first to the Court of Appeals of Maryland, which affirmed the state constitution. He then appealed to the U.S. Supreme Court, which reversed the Maryland Court of Appeals decision. Justice Black delivered the unanimous opinion of the Court (https://supreme.justia.com/cases/federal/us/367/488/case.html, accessed February 21, 2017).

Conflict between the meaning of the Establishment Clause and the Free Exercise Clause and between religious belief versus religious action and the right to religious belief versus the right to run for public office was at issue in a 1978 Supreme Court case, *McDaniel v. Paty* (435 U.S. 618). Appellee Paty, a candidate for a Tennessee constitutional convention, sued in the State Chancery Court, for a declaratory judgment that appellant McDaniel, an opponent who was a Baptist minister, was disqualified from serving as a delegate by a Tennessee law establishing the qualifications for constitutional convention delegates to be the same as for membership in the State House of Representatives, which barred ministers of the Gospel or priests of any denomination whatsoever. The Tennessee Supreme Court upheld the statutory provision, ruling that the clergy disqualification provision imposed no burden on "religious belief" and restricted religious action only in the lawmaking process where religious action is absolutely prohibited by the Establishment Clause. The U.S. Supreme Court, in a unanimous decision written by Chief Justice Warren Burger, reversed the judgment of the Tennessee Supreme Court, holding that the challenged provision violates the appellant's right to the free exercise of his religion, applied to the states by the Fourteenth Amendment, because it conditions his right to the free exercise of his religion on the surrender of his right to seek office, thus violating the First and the Fourteenth Amendments (https://www.law.cornell.edu/supremecourt/text/435/618, accessed February 21, 2017).

Conflict between free exercise and establishment was again at issue, in *Thomas v. Review Board of the Indiana Employment Division* (450 U.S. 707, 1981). In *Thomas*, the Supreme Court ruled, 7–2, that the Indiana's denial of employment compensation benefits to petitioner Thomas violated his right to free exercise of religion (https://www.law.cornell.edu/supremecourt/text/450/707, accessed February 21, 2017).

The petitioner, Thomas, a Jehovah's Witnesses adherent, was hired to work at his employer's roll foundry fabricating sheet steel for industrial uses. When that foundry was closed, he was transferred to a department of the company that fabricated turrets for military tanks. All the other departments also fabricated weapons. He asked to be laid off, asserting his religious beliefs prevented him from participating in the production of weapons. He applied for unemployment compensation benefits and was denied benefits.

The Indiana Court of Appeals reversed the review board's decision, holding the statute improperly burdened his right to free exercise of his religion. The Indiana State Supreme Court vacated the Court of Appeals' decision and denied benefits, holding that he quit voluntarily for personal reasons, his belief being more a "personal philosophical choice" than religious belief. The U.S. Supreme Court reversed the Indiana State Supreme Court decision. Chief Justice Burger, writing the majority opinion, held that a person may not be compelled to choose between First Amendment right and participation in an otherwise available public program and that the payment of benefits would not involve the state in fostering a religious faith in violation of the Establishment Clause.

Free exercise of religion and the need for military uniformity were the conflicts at issue in *Goldman v. Weinberger* (475 U.S. 503, 1986). Petitioner Goldman was a Jewish Air Force officer and a practicing Jew. He was denied the right to wear a yarmulke when in uniform on the grounds that the Free Exercise Clause applies less strictly to the military than to ordinary (i.e., civilian) citizens. Goldman, an Orthodox Jew and ordained rabbi, was ordered not to wear a yarmulke while on duty and in uniform indoors as a commissioned officer at the March Air Force Base pursuant to air force regulations that while authorized headgear may be worn outdoors, such headgear may not be worn indoors except by armed security police in the performance of their duties. The Supreme Court upheld the air force regulations, drawing the line essentially between religious apparel that is visible and that which is not and observing that the challenged regulation reasonably and evenhandedly regulated dress in the interest of the military's perceived need for uniformity (https://supreme.justia.com/475/Goldman-v-Weinberger, accessed February 21, 2017).

That same year the Supreme Court heard the case *Bowen v. Roy* (476 U.S. 693, 1986). This Supreme Court case established limits on freedom of religion in the United States in an 8–1 decision, with Chief Justice Warren Burger writing for the majority. The plaintiffs were Native American parents who applied for financial aid under a U.S. government welfare program (Aid to Families with Dependent Children, [AFDC]).

The appellee, Stephen Roy, and Karen Miller, and their daughter, Little Bird of Snow, sued the appellant, Otis Bowen, secretary of Health and Human Services, John Block, secretary of Agriculture, and Walter Cohen, secretary of the Pennsylvania Department of Public Welfare. Roy and family were receiving AFDC and food stamps. When they refused to provide a Social Security number for Little Bird, arguing it would violate their Native American religious beliefs, the Pennsylvania Department of Welfare terminated their AFDC benefits. The parents sued, arguing the Free Exercise Clause provided an exemption to the Social Security number requirement. In testimony in lower court, Roy disclosed that Little Bird had a Social Security number but that the widespread use of the number would "rob the spirit" of Little Bird, violating their religious beliefs.

The Court restrained the government from denying benefits for Little Bird until she was 16 but denied Roy's request for damages.

Public Education

This section reviews five Supreme Court cases that drew lines and distinctions on limits on the free exercise law and public policy and law regarding public education. The first such case is the landmark decision in *Wisconsin v. Yoder* (406 U.S. 205, 1972). In this case, the Supreme Court ruled that Amish adolescents could be exempt from a state law requiring school attendance for all 14- to 15-year-olds, since their religion required living apart from the world and worldly influence. The state's interest in students attending two more years of school was not enough to outweigh the individual right to free exercise. The *Yoder* case involved Old Order Amish and Conservative Amish Mennonite Church members who objected to the compulsory education law requiring their children be placed in public education school past the eighth grade. The Supreme Court noted ample evidence that showed that the Amish provided continuing informal vocational education to their children designed to prepare them for life in the rural Amish community and that the respondents sincerely believed that high school attendance was contrary to the Amish beliefs and way of life and that they would endanger their own salvation and that of their children by complying with the law. The Court recognized that the Old Order Amish and the Conservative Amish Mennonites demonstrated three centuries of an identifiable religious sect and that they had a long history of being a successful and self-sufficient segment of American society. The Court held that the state's interest in universal education is not totally free from a balancing process when it infringes on other fundamental rights, such as those protected by the Free Exercise Clause (https://www.law.cornell.edu/supremecourt/text/406/205, accessed February 21, 2017).

In *Widmar v. Vincent* (454 U.S. 263, 1981), the Supreme Court ruled against the University of Missouri at Kansas City, a state university, which makes its facilities available for activities of registered student groups. One such registered religious group of students was denied access to university buildings for the purpose of holding religious worship or religious teaching. The student group sought relief in federal district court, alleging the university regulation violated their free exercise of religion and free exercise of speech under the First Amendment. The district court upheld the regulations as being justified and, indeed, required by the Establishment Clause. The Court of Appeals reversed the decision of the district court, holding that the regulations were content-based discrimination against religious speech and found no compelling justification to bar equal access to facilities that were open to groups and speakers of all kinds. The Supreme Court held that the university's exclusionary policy violated the fundamental principle that a state regulation of speech should be content neutral and affirmed the Court of Appeals decision in a 7–2 decision, the majority opinion being written by Justice Powell (https://www .law.cornell.edu/supremecourt/text/454/263, accessed February 21, 2017).

Equal access for religious groups in public schools was also at issue in the *Board of Education of Westside Community Schools v. Mergens* (496 U.S. 226, 1990). In 1990, Congress passed the Equal Access Act, which required that public schools give religious groups the same access to facilities as given to other extracurricular groups. *Mergens* ruled that allowing religious clubs to meet is not a violation of the Establishment Clause. Westside High School, in District 66 of Omaha, Nebraska, refused to let a student group wishing to form a Christian Bible Study Club have the same terms and privileges as other student clubs. When the school board and administration denied access, the students sued, alleging that Westside's refusal violated the Equal Access Act. On appeal from an adverse district court ruling, the Court of Appeals found in favor of the students. The Supreme Court granted Westside certiorari. In an 8–1 decision, the justices held that the Equal Access

Act did not violate the Establishment Clause, distinguishing between "curriculum" and "noncurriculum student groups." Since Westside permitted other noncurricular clubs, it was prohibited under the Equal Access Act from denying equal access to any other after-school club based on the content of its speech. (https://www.oyez.org/cases/1989/88-1597, accessed February 21, 2017).

Could a public school prohibit the use of its property for any religious group? That was the question at issue in *Lamb's Chapel v. Center Moriches Union Free School District* (508 U.S. 384, 1993). The state of New York enacted a law authorizing schools to regulate the after-hours use of school property and facilities. The Center Moriches School District prohibited the use of its property for any religious group, refusing repeated requests by Lamb's Chapel to use the school's facilities for an after-hours religious-oriented film series on family values and child rearing. The Supreme Court, by unanimous vote, held that the district violated the First Amendment's freedom of speech on two grounds: (1) denying their request solely on the basis that such movies were religious oriented and (2) the district's granting of permission would not have amounted to an establishment of religion since the showing of the films would be neither school sponsored during school hours nor closed to the public (https://www.oyez.org/cases/1992/91-2024, accessed February 22, 2017).

The problem of religion in education was also an issue in another case, as noted earlier with respect to the Establishment Clause, *Rosenberger v. Rector and Visitors of the University of Virginia* (515 U.S. 819, 1995), which also had freedom of religious expression considerations. Ronald Rosenberger, a University of Virginia student, requested $5,800 from a student activities fund to subsidize the cost to publish "Wide Awake: A Christian Perspective at the University of Virginia." The university refused funding solely because the publication "primarily promotes or manifests a particular belief in or about a deity or an ultimate reality," thereby prohibited by university guidelines. In a 5–4 opinion, the Court held that the university's denial of funding due to the content of the message imposed a financial burden on his speech and amounted to viewpoint discrimination. The Court ruled that if the university chooses to promote free speech at all, it must do so equally and be content neutral. It held the university must provide financial subsidy to a student religious publication on the same basis as other student publications (https://www.oyez.org/cases/1990-1999/1994/1994_94_329, accessed February 21, 2017).

Religion and Right to Work Laws

The beliefs of some religions affect when and on what their adherents can work. Five Supreme Court decisions have addressed problems arising from religious beliefs and work to clarify the limits and the rights accorded to persons with such religious beliefs by the First Amendment's Free Exercise Clause and devised tests or guidelines to determine those limits.

In *Sherbert v. Verner* (374 U.S. 398, 1963), the Supreme Court specified what became known as the *Sherbert* test, in its 7–2 decision in the case. The appellant, Sherbert, was a member of the Seventh-day Adventist Church. She was fired by her South Carolina employer, a textile mill, because she would not work on Saturday, her Sabbath day. She filed a claim for unemployment compensation benefits and was denied under the South Carolina Unemployment Compensation Act. The State Commission denied her benefits, which action was sustained by the State Supreme Court. The U.S. Supreme Court held that the South Carolina law abridged Sherbert's right to the free exercise of her religion, violating the First Amendment as applicable to the states by the Fourteenth Amendment. The majority of the justices held the state showed no compelling state interest enforced under the eligibility provisions of the state law. The *Sherbert* test stipulated that there must be a compelling state interest shown, and provisions justifying denial of benefits must be narrowly tailored (https://www.law.cornell.edu/supremecourt/text/374/398, accessed February 23, 2017).

Work shift scheduling can involve highly complex issues of agreements with the employer, employee, unions, and state laws. Such complexities are exemplified in *Transworld Airlines, Inc. v. Hardison* (432 U.S. 63, 1977). Respondent Hardison worked for TWA at an airplane maintenance and overhaul base in which work scheduling was based strictly on a seniority system, the most senior employee having first choice in job and shift assignment as per a collective bargaining agreement between TWA and the Machinists and Aerospace Workers union. When he was transferred to a job at which he had less seniority, he was assigned to work on Saturdays, his Sabbath day. The union and TWA refused to violate the seniority system and respondent sued. A Court of Appeals affirmed judgment for the union but held that TWA had not satisfied its duty to accommodate respondent's religious needs under the Equal Employment Opportunity Commission (EEOC) guidelines. The Supreme Court reversed the decision of the Court of Appeals. In its decision, the Supreme Court held: (1) the seniority system itself was a significant accommodation to the needs, both religious and secular, of all of TWA's employees; (2) TWA could not be faulted for failing to work out a shift or job swap for respondent; (3) absent a discriminatory purpose, the seniority system cannot be an unlawful employment practice; and (4) to require TWA to bear additional cost in order to give respondent Saturdays off would be an undue hardship. Justice White delivered the 7–2 decision of the Court.

Work cases can sometimes raise complex issues involving state and federal jurisdiction as well as Free Exercise, Establishment, and Equal Protection clauses. One such case is *Ohio Civil Rights Commission v. Dayton Christian Schools* (477 U.S. 619, 1986). The appellee was the Dayton Christian School, a nonprofit elementary and secondary private Christian school that requires its teachers to subscribe to a particular set of religious beliefs including internal resolution of disputes through the "biblical chain of command." After a pregnant teacher was told her contract would not be renewed because their doctrine said mothers should stay at home with pre–school age children, she contacted an attorney. The school then fired her for violation of the internal dispute resolution. She filed suit with the Ohio Civil Rights Commission alleging sex discrimination. The Civil Rights Commission started proceedings versus the school, which answered the complaint by asserting that the First Amendment prevented the Commission from exercising jurisdiction over the complaint. A district court then refused to issue an injunction, ruling that the Commission's actions would not violate the First and Fourteenth Amendments. The Court of Appeals then heard the case and ruled that the Commission's actions would not violate the First and Fourteenth Amendments. The Supreme Court held: (1) the district court should have abstained from adjudicating the case and (2) reversed and remanded the case, that it is sufficient under Ohio law that constitutional claims may be raised in state court judicial review of administrative proceedings (the Civil Rights Commission). Chief Justice Rehnquist delivered the 5–4 majority opinion. The Court of Appeals erred in ruling that the Commission's jurisdiction violated both Free Exercise and Establishment Clauses and the Equal Protection Clause of the Fourteenth Amendment. Instead, they should have invoked federal abstention doctrine (www.caselaw.findlaw.com/us-supreme-court-477/619. html, accessed February 23, 2017).

The Mormon Church was involved in a similarly complex issue in 1987: *Corporation of the Presiding Bishop of the Church of Jesus Christ of Latter-day Saints v. Amos* (483 U.S. 327). In this case, Arthur Mayson had worked for the Deseret Gymnasium, a nonprofit facility in Salt Lake City, Utah, for 16 years as an engineer. The Corporation of the Presiding Bishop (CPB) fired him when he failed to obtain a certificate authorizing him to attend the Church's religious temple. He filed a class action suit in district court alleging the CPB and the Corporation of the President (COP) violated the Civil Rights Act of 1964 by dismissing him because he failed to satisfy certain religious conditions. The CPB and COP claimed that Section 702 of the act exempted them from claims of religious discrimination. Mayson claimed that Section 702 violated the Establishment Clause by allowing religious organizations to practice discriminatory hiring for nonreligious jobs. The district court agreed that his job was nonreligious. It further held that Section 702 violated the Establishment Clause because it allowed religious adherents exclusive participation in nonreligious activities. The Supreme Court in a unanimous decision held that Section 702 did not violate the Establishment Clause. Section 702 passed the three-part test that the Supreme Court had established in *Lemon v. Kurtzman*. In this case, the government allowed for a church to advance its religion but did not directly intervene. Thirdly, by allowing the religious organization to employ whom they pleased, the state became less entangled in religion (https://www.oyez.org/cases/1986/86-179, accessed February 23, 2017).

Finally, the Native American Church was involved in a case involving freedom of religion versus the government's right to enact drug laws. *Employment Division v. Smith* (494 U.S. 872, 1990) involved two Native American workers who served as counselors in an Oregon-located private drug rehabilitation organization. They used peyote—a powerful hallucinogen—as part of their religious ceremonies as members of the Native American Church. Their rehabilitation organization fired them. They filed for unemployment compensation benefits, which the government denied because their dismissal was considered for work-related misconduct. They lost their case in state courts. The U.S. Supreme Court vacated the Oregon Supreme Court's judgment against the employees and remanded the case for determination whether or not sacramental use of illegal drugs violated Oregon's drug law. On remand, the Oregon Supreme Court ruled that while Oregon drug laws prohibited use of illegal drugs for sacramental religious uses, this prohibition violated the Free Exercise Clause. The case then returned to the U.S. Supreme Court, where the Court was asked to determine if a state can deny unemployment benefits to a worker fired for using illegal drugs for religious purposes. In a 6–3 decision, the Court ruled that it could so deny benefits. Writing for the majority, Justice Antonin Scalia held that an individual's religious beliefs did not excuse him from compliance with an otherwise valid law prohibiting conduct that the government is free to regulate. "Allowing exceptions to every state law or regulation affecting religion would open the prospect of constitutionally required exemptions from civic obligations of almost every conceivable kind." Scalia cited compulsory military service, payment of taxes, vaccination requirements, and child-neglect laws (http://www.oyez.org/cases/1989/88-1213, accessed February 23, 2017).

Government Intrusion into Church Controversies

Can the government intervene into a church or religious belief by asking a jury to judge whether or not the defendants truly believe their claimed belief? The case of *United States v. Ballard* (322 U.S. 78, 1944) was an appeal of a fraud conviction of two leaders of a new religious I Am Activity movement for fraudulently seeking and collecting donations (amounting to $3 million) on the basis of religious claims that they themselves did not believe. The Supreme Court held that the question of whether or not their claims about their religious beliefs and experiences were actually true should not have been submitted to a jury. The Court held "freedom of religious belief embraces the right to maintain theories of life and death and of the hereafter which are rank heresy to followers of orthodox faiths." Justice Douglas, writing for the majority in the 5–4 decision, wrote: "The First Amendment does not select any one group or any one type of religion for preferred treatment. It puts them all in that position." The Court overturned the conviction (https://supremejustia.com/cases/federal/us/322/78/case .html, accessed February 23, 2017).

Can the fear of potential subversive activity by a church leader justify the intrusion of the government into internal church disputes? That was the controversy at the heart of a 1952 case (during the Korean war) involving a dispute within the Russian Orthodox Church in New York City. *Kedroff v. St. Nicholas Cathedral* (344 U.S. 94, 1952) was a case brought to state court by a New York corporation holding title to a property in a suit to determine which prelate was entitled to the use and occupancy of a cathedral of the Russian Orthodox Church in New York City. The Court of Appeals held for the plaintiff on the grounds that the Religious Corporations Law of New York had the purpose of affecting the transfer of administrative control of the Russian Orthodox Church in North America from the Supreme Church Authority in Russia to authorities selected by a convention of the North American churches. The Supreme Court held that the New York State statute interferes with the free exercise of religion, contrary to the First Amendment as applied to states by the Fourteenth Amendment. The Court held that the New York law had acted inappropriately when it determined for the Russian Orthodox Church, a hierarchical church, its ecclesiastical administration, appointment of clergy, or the transfer of property of a church from one group to another within the broader church. Doing so interferes with the free exercise of religion and is contrary to the Constitution (https://supreme.justia.com/federal/us/344/94/case.html, accessed February 23, 2017).

Can the state, or courts, settle internal property disputes? That question was at the heart of the issue in *Presbyterian Church v. Hull Church* (393 U.S. 440, 1969). By writ of certiorari to the Supreme Court of Georgia, the U.S. Supreme Court heard a case in which respondents, two local churches, voted to withdraw from the petitioner, the general church, with which they had a doctrinal dispute, and wanted to reconstitute themselves as autonomous religious organizations. A tribunal of the general church took over the respondent's property on behalf of the general church. The respondents sued in the Georgia state Supreme Court to enjoin the general church from trespassing on the disputed property. The general church moved to dismiss the case and cross-claimed for injunctive relief on the grounds that civil courts had no power to determine whether the general church had departed from its tenets of faith and practices. The motion to dismiss was denied, and the case went to jury on the theory that Georgia law implied a trust of local church property for the benefit of the general church on condition that the latter adheres to doctrinal tenets existing at the time of the affiliation by the local churches. The jury, having been instructed to determine whether the general church had substantially abandoned its original doctrines, found for the respondents, and the trial judge issued an injunction against the general church, which the Supreme Court of Georgia affirmed. The U.S. Supreme Court reversed, holding that civil courts cannot, consistent with the First Amendment, determine ecclesiastical questions in resolving property disputes. Georgia's "implied trust" theory requires civil courts to weigh the significance and meaning of religious doctrine. It can play no role in judicial proceedings (https://supreme.justia.com/cases/federal/us/393/440/case.html, accessed February 23, 2017).

Another dispute within the Georgia Presbyterian Church was the concern in the Supreme Court decision in *Jones v. Wolf* (443 U.S. 595, 1979). This case involved a dispute over the ownership of church property, following a schism in a local church affiliated with a hierarchical church organization. The property of the Vineville Presbyterian Church of Macon, Georgia (the local church), is held in the names of the local church or trust for the local church. The church was established affiliated with the Presbyterian Church in the United States (PCUS), a hierarchical form of government. At a congregational meeting of the local church, 164 voted to separate from PCUS, and 94 opposed the resolution. The minority faction brought class action in state court seeking declaratory and injunctive orders giving them exclusive right to the property as members of the PCUS. The trial court purporting to apply Georgia's "neutral principles of law" granted judgment to the majority, and Georgia's Supreme Court affirmed, rejecting the minority's challenge based on the First and Fourteenth Amendments. The U.S. Supreme Court held that the process of identifying the factions is to be determined by the laws and regulations of the PCUS. Therefore, the First Amendment requires that Georgia courts give deference to the Presbyterian commission's determination that the minority faction represents the "true congregation." The Georgia Supreme Court's decision was vacated and remanded (https://supreme.justia.com/cases/federal/us/443/595/case.html, accessed February 23, 2017).

Finally, the Court grappled with internal church disputes in the case of *Hosanna-Tabor Evangelical Lutheran Church and School v. EEOC* (565 U.S. ___, 2012). The case reached the Supreme Court by certiorari from the U.S. Court of Appeals, Sixth Circuit. Chief Justice Roberts delivered the unanimous decision of the Court.

The petitioner, Hosanna-Tabor Evangelical Church and School, is an affiliated church and a congregational member of the Lutheran Church—Missouri Synod. They have two types of teachers: "called" and "lay." Lay are not required to be trained by the Synod. Respondent Perich completed her synod training and Hosanna-Tabor asked her to become a called teacher. She accepted and was designated a commissioned minister. She later developed narcolepsy and began the 2004–2005 school year on disability leave. When she reported that she would be able to return to work in February, the school principal responded that the school had contracted a lay teacher to fill her position for the year. The congregation offered to pay a portion of her health insurance premiums in exchange for her resignation as a called teacher. She refused to resign and reported for work in February but was not allowed to teach. The school board and congregation voted to rescind her call and Hosanna-Tabor sent her a letter of termination. She filed a charge with the EEOC claiming termination was in violation of the Americans with Disabilities

Act. Hosanna-Tabor invoked the "ministerial exception" to the act. The district court agreed and granted summary judgment to Hosanna-Tabor. The Sixth Circuit Court of Appeals vacated and remanded, concluding Perich did not qualify as a "minister" under the exception rule.

The Supreme Court held: (1) the Establishment and Free Exercises Clauses bar suits on behalf of ministers against their churches; (2) because Perich was a minister within the meaning of the exception, the First Amendment requires dismissal of the employment discrimination suit against her employer; (3) held that the ministerial exception only bars an unemployment suit brought on behalf of a minister challenging her church's decision to fire her. The Court expresses no views on whether the exception bars other types of suits (https://www.supreme.court/gov/opinions/11pdf/10-533.pdf, accessed February 23, 2017).

Eminent Domain

In *Lyng v. Northwest Indian Cemetery Protective Association* (485 U.S. 439, 1988), the Supreme Court ruled on a case involving the U.S. Forest Service's eminent domain authority and the claims by Native American Indians on their Free Exercise Clause rights. The U.S. Forest Service approved a road-building and timber-harvesting plan, rejecting the recommendations of its own earlier study, through the Chimney Rock area of the National Forest (in California). Opposed to the plan's effect on nearby sacred sites used for religious ceremonies, an Indian organization, individual Indians, nature organizations, and the state of California sued in federal district court challenging both the road building and the timber harvesting plans, contending that such actions violated the respondent Indians' rights under the Free Exercise Clause and would violate certain federal statutes (the American Indian Religious Freedom Act). The Supreme Court affirmed that the Free Exercise Clause does not prohibit the government from permitting timber harvesting in the Chimney Rock area, nor the construction of the proposed road. Justice O'Connor delivered the 5–3 majority opinion of the Court, Justice Kennedy not participating in the case (https://www.law.cornell.edu/supremecourt/text/485/439, accessed February 24, 2017).

In the case of *City of Boerne v. Flores* (521 U.S. 507, 1997), the Court had to rule on a conflict between a local zoning ordinance board and a church. The archbishop of San Antonio filed suit claiming that the local zoning authority violated his rights under the 1993 Religious Freedom Restoration Act (RFRA) by denying him a permit to expand his church in Boerne, Texas; the zoning authority argued that it had to refuse the permit because the church was located in an historic preservation district governed by an ordinance that forbids new construction and that the RFRA was unconstitutional as it sought to override this local preservation ordinance. On a writ of certiorari appeal from the Fifth Circuit's reversal of a district court's finding against the archbishop, the Supreme Court agreed to hear the case. The Court, in a 6–3 decision, ruled for the city of Boerne holding that the U.S. Congress had exceeded its Fourteenth Amendment enforcement powers by enacting the RFRA, which, in part, subjected local ordinances to federal regulation. The majority opinion held that there was no evidence to suggest that Boerne's historic preservation ordinance favored one religion over another or that it was based on animus or hostility for free religious exercise (https://www.oyez.org/cases/1990-1999/1996/1996_95_2074, accessed February 24, 2017).

Freedom of Speech

The Supreme Court heard and had to decide two cases in which the conflict was between two sacred First Amendment rights: free exercise of religion versus free speech. In *R.A.V. v. City of St. Paul* (505 U.S. 377, 1992), the issue was whether or not a hate crime or speech was protected free speech. In *R.A.V.* (a teenage boy), the Supreme Court unanimously struck down a St. Paul, Minnesota, ordinance that proscribed cross burning and other actions that "one knows or has reasonable grounds to know" will cause "anger, alarm or resentment in others on the basis of race, color, creed, religion, or gender." In essence, the local ordinance joined a "hate crime" to the "fighting words" exemption of free speech. The Court found the St. Paul ordinance unconstitutional but based on different grounds. Justices White, Blackmun, Stevens, and O'Connor did so solely on the grounds that the ordinance was overly broad, thereby sweeping within its proscription expression that should be protected. The other five members, concurring in the majority opinion written by Justice Scalia, found the ordinance "an unconstitutional content-based regulation of speech" (https://uscivillib erties.org/cases/4344-rav-v-city-of-st-paul-505-us-377-1992 .html, accessed February 24, 2017).

Conflict between the RFRA of 1993 and the Controlled Substance Act was at issue in the 2006 Supreme Court decision in *Gonzales v. O Centro Espirita Beneficente Uniao do Vegetal* (546 U.S. 418). UDV is a small religious sect from the Amazon region of Brazil. It sued the federal government (specifically, Attorney General Gonzales, in this case) to prevent the government from interfering with its use of *hoasca*, a hallucinogenic herbal tea, used during religious ceremonies on the grounds that the RFRA of 1993, which prohibits substantial imposition on religious practices in absence of a compelling government interest, established their right to use hoasca. The district court ruled in favor of the UDV, which the Tenth Circuit Court of Appeals affirmed. The appellate court found that the federal government failed to sufficiently prove the alleged health risks of hoasca and could not show it would be used recreationally. Attorney General Gonzales argued prohibiting the drug was required by international treaty. The Court of Appeals held that the government had not "narrowly tailored" its prohibition of the drug. The Supreme Court had to decide if the RFRA required the government to permit the importation, distribution, possession, and use of an otherwise illegal drug by a religious organization when Congress found that the drug had high potential for abuse, is unsafe, and violates an international treaty when so imported and distributed. In a unanimous 8–0 decision, with Justice Alito not participating, the Court answered yes. Chief Justice Roberts wrote the majority opinion, holding that the government had failed to prove a compelling interest in regulating UDV's use of the drug for religious purposes. The Court rejected the attorney general's argument that the Controlled Substances Act could accommodate no exceptions. The Court held it was required by the RFRA to examine individual religious freedom claims and grant exceptions to generally applicable laws absence showing a compelling government interest (http://www.oyez.org/cases/2005/04-1084, accessed February 24, 2017).

The problem or issue over the practice of polygamy by the Mormon Church and the freedom of religious exercise was decided in two Supreme Court cases. In *Reynolds v. United States* (98 U.S. 145, 1878), the U.S. Supreme Court upheld a federal law banning polygamy. The Court ruled that while the Free Exercise Clause of the First Amendment forbids the government from regulating belief, it does allow the government to regulate actions, such as marriage. George Reynolds was convicted and sentenced to two years' hard labor and a fine in the third judicial district court of the Territory of Utah with bigamy in violation of Section 5352 of the revised statutes (the Morrill Anti-Bigamy Act, 1862). *Reynolds* was the first Supreme Court opinion to address the impartial jury and the Confrontation Clause of the Sixth Amendment. George Reynolds was a member of the Church of Jesus Christ of Latter-day Saints charged with bigamy under the Morrill Anti-Bigamy Act. Chief Justice Morrison Waite wrote the unanimous opinion of the Court holding that religious duty was not a sustainable defense to a criminal indictment (https://supreme.justia.com/cases/us/98/148/case.html, accessed February 24, 2017).

In a follow-up 1890 decision, the Supreme Court was even more blunt and direct in deciding on the question of freedom of exercise of religion in the First Amendment. In *Davis v. Beason* (133 U.S. 333), the Supreme Court affirmed by a 9–0 vote that the federal laws against polygamy did not conflict with the

Free Exercise Clause of the First Amendment. In its opinion, the Court stated: "Bigamy and polygamy are crimes by the laws of the United States, by the laws of Idaho, and by the laws of all civilized and Christian countries, and to call their advocacy a tenet of religion is to offend the common sense of mankind. A crime is nonetheless so, nor less odious, because sanctioned by what any particular sect may designate as religious" (https://supreme.justia.com/cases/federal/us/133/333/case.html, accessed February 24, 2017).

Finally, there is the problem of a conflict between religious belief and practice that involves the ritual sacrifice of animals (in this case, chickens) and the applicability of the Free Exercise Clause of the First Amendment. That problem was squarely at issue in the case of *Church of Lukumi Babalu Aye v. City of Hialeah* (508 U.S. 520, 1993). Justice Kennedy delivered the unanimous opinion of the Court (with differences on the precise grounds). The Yoruba people were brought as slaves by the hundreds of thousands to Cuba, and they brought with them the practices of Santeria religion, of which the Church of Lukumi Babalu Aye was a small sect that located to the city of Hialeah, Florida. Kennedy's opinion wrote that the principle that the government may not enact laws that suppress religious belief or practices is so well understood that few violations are recorded in the Court's opinions (citing *McDaniel v. Paty* and *Fowler v. Rhode Island*).

The Court's review confirmed that the laws in question (municipal ordinances of the City of Hialeah, Florida) were enacted by city officials who did not understand, failed to perceive, or chose to ignore the fact that their official actions violated the nation's essential commitment to religious freedom. Justice Kennedy stated bluntly: "The challenged laws had an impermissible object; and in all events the principle of general applicability was violated because the secular ends asserted in the laws were pursued only with respect to conduct motivated by religious beliefs. We invalidate the challenged enactments and reverse the judgment of the Court of Appeals." The ordinance passed by Hialeah, Florida, specifically forbade the "unnecessarily" killing of "an animal in a public or private ritual or ceremony not for the primary purpose of food consumption." The Court ruled that that ordinance was unconstitutional (https:// .www.law.cornell.edu/supct/html/91-948.html, accessed February 24, 2017).

Solutions

One thing the chapter's review of these cases makes clear is that a "solution" is often quite difficult to achieve; sometimes "resolution" of a conflict is more often the result of the Supreme Court's decisions. When the Court decides unanimously or nearly so (e.g., 7–2 or 8–1), the decision more decisively settles the matter. When the Court is closely split in its decision (5–4), the controversy is resolved but not solved, and on occasion, the dissenters in one decision prevail in a subsequent decision.

The Supreme Court is the final arbiter between federal district courts and federal appellate courts when those courts have disagreed in their interpretation of the Establishment and the Free Exercise Clauses. The Court has even disagreed with itself over time, on occasion overturning a prior Supreme Court ruling in freedom of religion matters.

By far, however, the Supreme Court has been the final arbiter as to the meaning of the two clauses with respect to state government actions, such as state compulsory education laws, limits of government aid to church institutions, state public transportation laws and policies, state "blue" (or Sunday closing/Sabbatarian) laws, rulings by state civil rights commissions, and state laws enforcing seniority systems in employment. The Supreme Court, as this chapter has shown, is the final arbiter and reviewer of decisions by state lower courts, state appellate courts, and state Supreme Courts over interpretation of the meaning of the Establishment and Free Exercise Clauses. At times, courts at all levels may disagree based upon the judicial philosophy being applied, that is, whether a judge or judges (in appellate and higher courts) adhere to a strict constructionist (or textualist) versus a living/evolving interpretation of the Constitution.

Conclusion

This chapter's review of several dozens of Supreme Court cases makes clear the great complexity of problems, controversies, and solutions inherent in the Establishment Clause and the Free Exercise Clause. Only complex matters of jurisprudence (the interpretation of law) rise to the level of Supreme Court decision making. The First Amendment's Establishment and Free Exercise Clauses sometimes seem to conflict with one another. National congressional actions can raise First Amendment issues, some of which require decisions by the U.S. Supreme Court to "resolve" if not fully solve. The First Amendment and the Fourteenth Amendments usually coincide in cases, although not always in agreement.

The Supreme Court has been called upon to review the constitutionality of acts of Congress with respect to the First Amendment's Establishment and Free Exercise Clauses. The Alien and Sedition Acts of 1798 had implicit anti-Catholicism issues. The Louisiana Purchase in 1803 added not only huge amounts of land to U.S. territory but a greater percentage of Catholics in the population, which raised fears among many in the Protestant majority.

The Supreme Court distinguished several "tests" to serve as guidelines to lower courts and to state and local governments about how to assess the constitutionality of state and local laws on the First Amendment's religious freedom clauses: the *Everson*, *Lemon*, *Flast*, *Cox*, *Sherbert*, and *Chaplinski* tests or doctrines ("fighting words," "secular purpose," "neutrality" doctrine, and so on).

Sometimes, national legislation enacted for one purpose has implications for freedom of religion in America that must be resolved by the Supreme Court: for example, the Elementary and Secondary Education Act, the Equal Opportunity Employment Act, federal treaties, the Civil Rights Act versus the Religious Liberty Act, the Educational Consolidation and Improvement Act, the AFLA, AFDC, the Equal Access Act, the Civil Rights Act of 1964, the Americans with Disabilities Act, the Controlled Substance Act, and the RFRA. At other times, First Amendment challenges had to be considered by the Supreme Court with regards to rules and regulations of federal agencies, such as the IRS and the U.S. Forest Service.

On numerous occasions and in a number of landmark cases, the Supreme Court has reviewed constitutional challenges on First and Fourteenth Amendment grounds of local government actions: local school regulations, religious symbols erected on local public property, local blue laws, local tax boards, and local zoning boards.

In recent years, presidents have used executive actions and orders in an attempt to resolve highly contentious issues, typically when after many years requesting legislative action Congress refuses to act. In 2014, for example, President Obama issued an Executive Order concluding the Congress was not going to act on a broader measure prohibiting discrimination on sexual discrimination or gender identity by companies and later relating to schools and the provisions or school policy regarding the use of gender-assigned bathrooms. A number of faith leaders urged him to include an exemption for government contractors with a religious affiliation, such as some social service agencies. President Obama refused to include those exemptions. His use of executive actions and orders led his Republican opponents to accuse him of abusing the powers of his office, although in point of fact he had issued fewer such actions and orders per year than any modern president. An issue with use of such executive action, of course, is that the policy may be quite temporary—binding only while that president is in office. President Obama's DACA and DAPA orders were halted by a federal district judge. Even more impactful, President Trump, on succeeding President Obama, quickly took executive actions to undo all or most of President Obama's actions and orders, especially relevant here for immigration enforcement and the RFRA, building a border wall, and announcing a temporary immigration ban on seven mostly-Muslim countries that a federal district court placed a stay order upon, pending judicial review as to its constitutionality on allegations that it was it fact an unconstitutional "Muslim ban."

Perhaps in a nation as demographically complex as the United States, with so many diverse religious affiliations, it should not be surprising that the wall of separation is at times breached or rendered porous and requires continuous vigilance and action by the Supreme Court to uphold the lofty but often contentious principles of freedom of and freedom from religion.

References

Abrams, Paula. 2009. *Cross Purposes: Pierce v. Society of Sisters and the Struggle over Compulsory Education.* Ann Arbor: University of Michigan Press.

Alley, Robert S. 1999. *The Constitution and Religion: Leading Supreme Court Cases on Church and State.* Amherst, NY: Prometheus Books.

Amar, Akhil Reed. 1998. *The Bill of Rights.* New Haven, CT: Yale University Press.

Bagby, Ihsan, Paul M. Perls, and Bryan T. Froehle. 2001. *The Mosque in America: A National Portrait.* Washington, DC: Council of American-Islamic Relations.

Beverley, James A. 2003. *Islamic Faith in America.* New York: Facts of File.

Billington, Ray A. 1974. *The Origins of Nativism in the United States, 1800–1844.* New York: Arno Press.

Bonomi, Patricia U. 1986. *Under the Cope of Heaven: Religion, Society, and Politics in Colonial America.* New York: Oxford University Press.

Buckley, Thomas. 1977. *Church and State in Revolutionary Virginia, 1776–1787.* Charlottesville: University of Virginia Press.

Butler, Jon. 1990. *Awash in a Sea of Faith: Christianizing the American People.* Cambridge, MA: Harvard University Press.

Daniels, Roger. 2002. *Coming to America: A History of Immigration and Ethnicity in American Life*, 2nd ed. New York: Perennial.

Dreisbach, Daniel. 2002. *Thomas Jefferson and the Wall of Separation of Church and State.* New York: New York University Press.

Gjerde, Jon, ed. 1998. *Major Problems in American Immigration and Ethnic History.* Boston: Houghton Mifflin.

Glenn, Charles L., Jr. 1988. *The Myth of the Common School.* Amherst: University of Massachusetts Press.

Green, Steven K. 2010. *The Second Disestablishment: Church and State in Nineteenth Century America.* New York: Oxford University Press.

Jenkins, Philip. 2003. *The New Anti-Catholicism: The Last Acceptable Prejudice.* New York: Oxford University Press.

LeMay, Michael C., ed. 2013. *Transforming America: Perspectives on Immigration: The Making of a Nation of Nations: The Founding to 1865*, vol. 1. Santa Barbara, CA: Praeger.

McGarvie, Mark Douglas. 2004. *One Nation under Law: America's Early National Struggle to Separate Church and State.* DeKalb: Northern Illinois University Press.

McLaughlin, H. James. 2013. "The Common and Uncommon Schooling of Immigrants to the United States, 1787–1865," in Michael C. LeMay, ed. *Transforming America: Perspectives on Immigration*, vol. 1. Santa Barbara, CA: Praeger. 97–120.

Miller, William Lee. 1986. *The First Liberty: Religion and the American Republic.* Washington, DC: Georgetown University Press.

Ravitch, Diane. 1974. *The Great School Wars: New York City, 1805–1973.* New York: Basic Books.

Sehat, David. 2011. *The Myth of American Religious Freedom.* New York: Oxford University Press.

Spring, Joel. 2008. *The American School: From the Puritans to No Child Left Behind.* New York: McGraw-Hill.

NO HATE
IN MY STATE

HUMAN
RIGHTS

This chapter presents nine original essays about religious freedom in America that have been contributed by their authors to expand upon the perspective and expertise of this author. They write from a variety of professional backgrounds, which give them a perspective different from the author's: artist/administrator, constitutional law professor, lawyer, nurse, priest, writer. They give voice to activism on religious freedom and articulate the need for additional legislation or court action addressing problems and controversies with religious freedom matters, both freedom of and freedom from religion in American politics and society.

Why Mixing Religion and Political Activity Leads to a Poisoned Chalice: Ending Compelled Taxpayer Support for Religious Political Activity
Christina Ann-Marie DiEdoardo

Few areas of public policy better illustrate the maxim of Samuel Johnson that "Hell is paved with good intentions" (Boswell 1824) than government regulation of political activity by tax-exempt religious organizations. A system designed to

Rob Hill, state director of the Human Rights Campaign Mississippi, speaks on the steps of the Mississippi Capitol in Jackson, Mississippi, on July 1, 2016. Hill and other citizens celebrated a recent federal ruling that blocked a Mississippi law on religious objections to same-sex marriage moments before it was set to take effect. The court ruled that the law was unconstitutional. (AP Photo/Rogelio V. Solis) keep religion out of politics has mutated into a *de facto* government subsidy for religious political speech in violation of the spirit of the Establishment Clause of the First Amendment.

On its face, federal law restricting political activities by tax-exempt religious organizations seems clear enough. A nonprofit corporation like a church, mosque, temple, or synagogue that "operate[s] exclusively for religious . . . purposes" can qualify for a tax exemption so long as "no substantial part of the activities of which [it] is carrying on [is] propaganda or otherwise attempting, to influence legislation . . . and which does not participate in, or intervene in (including the publishing or distribution of statements) any political campaign on behalf of (or in opposition to) any candidate for public office" (26 U.S.C. 501(c)(3)).

However, the devil is in the details, as we'll see in subsequent text.

Hands Off and Eyes Closed

As the Internal Revenue Service (IRS 2015) points out in "The Restriction of Political Campaign Intervention by Section 501(c)(3) Tax-Exempt Organizations" published on its website on December 15, 2015, "*Contributions to political campaign funds or public statements of position (verbal or written) made on behalf of the organization in favor of or in opposition to any candidate for public office* clearly violate the prohibition against political campaign activity" (emphasis added).

If that's the case, then how can Senator Ted Cruz issue a press release on his campaign website (TedCruz.org 2015), on November 20, 2015, proclaiming the endorsement of "more than 200 faith leaders" for his presidential campaign without those ministers endangering their church's tax exemption?

As it turns out, quite easily. Under the IRS's *own* rules, set forth in its article "Other Eligible Donees," which was published February 12, 2016, on IRS.gov, unless a church or nonprofit organization usually has more than $5,000 in reportable gross receipts each year, it "may be treated as tax-exempt without having to file an application." However, while non-church charitable organizations have to file at least a postcard informational return (and a more detailed return if their gross receipts exceed certain levels), *churches are exempt from this requirement.*

Accordingly, if a church stays completely off the IRS's radar by keeping its gross receipts under $5,000, it need not *ever* report any of its expenditures (political or otherwise) to the IRS.

Why Render Unto Caesar?

The IRS's decisions in this area aren't completely irrational. There's a strong public policy argument that the government—whether through its taxation arm or through another entity—shouldn't be in the business of determining the legitimacy of religious organizations, as in France (Hadden 2014).

Indeed, since the Establishment Clause prohibits the government from establishing or preventing the establishment of a religion, there are constitutional reasons for the IRS to tread carefully in this area. Unlike France, churches in the United States don't typically receive direct support from the state, so the only way they can exist and operate is through donations.

Moreover, as Senator Cruz has shown during the 2016 Republican caucuses in Iowa, members of religious organizations can form powerful political blocs. That power often gives them access to members of Congress, who can then cause trouble for any IRS official who dares to challenge those religious groups who wish to have their tax-deductible cake and eat it too through open endorsement of a candidate.

One Person's Tax Exemption Is Another Person's Compelled Subsidy

Given that Americans make approximately *$100 billion* in tax-deductible donations a year to religious groups (Bekiempis 2013), it's reasonable for both those who adhere to a particular religious practice and those who do not to ask if the groups receiving that largess are meeting their corresponding obligations with regard to staying out of politics. Sadly, under current IRS practices it's virtually impossible for the IRS to meaningfully verify the compliance of these groups with federal law, particularly when most religious groups don't even need to file an informational return (IRS 2015).

The rationale behind a government recognizing any organization as a public charity is that the organization is providing services (e.g., food for the hungry, shelter for the homeless) to the public, thereby saving the government the cost or aggravation of doing so—which therefore justifies the grant of a tax exemption.

That business case falls apart in the area of political speech. If I donate $1,000 to the Democratic or Republican Party tomorrow, it has no effect on my tax situation when I pay my taxes the following year. However, if I donate $1,000 to a religious organization which then aggressively advocates for my favored candidate in violation of the law, I gain *both* the tax exemption and the ability to effectively hide my financial support of a particular candidate, which otherwise might have to be publicly disclosed.

This is an outcome that is both inequitable and unsustainable. If churches wish to retain the tax exemptions that apply to their overall operations, they must accept the imposition of real and enforceable safeguards to keep them out of the political system. If they are unwilling to accept that, they must pay taxes as every other political actor does.

References

Bekiempis, Victoria. 2013, October 24. "Are Churches Making America Poor?" Retrieved from http://www.news week.com/2013/10/25/are-churches-making-america-poor-243734.html

Boswell, James. 1993. *The Life of Samuel Johnson (Everyman's Library)*, 1st ed., 1824, this edition, 1993. New York: Alfred A. Knopf/Random House, Inc.

Hadden, Gerry. 2014, July 12. "The French Want to Make Society Safe for Religion by Banning So-Called Cults."

Retrieved from http://www.pri.org/stories/2014–07–12/
french-want-make-society-safereligion-banning-so-called-cults

Internal Revenue Service. 2015, March 20. "Annual
Exempt Organization Return: Who Must File."
Retrieved from https://www.irs.gov/charities-non-profits/
annual-exempt-organization-return-who-must-file

Internal Revenue Service. 2015, December 15. "The
Restriction of Political Campaign Intervention by Section
501(c)(3) Tax-Exempt Organizations." Retrieved from
https://www.irs.gov/charities-non-profits/charitable-organi
zations/the-restriction-of-political-campaign-intervention-
by-section-501-c-3-tax-exempt-organizations

Internal Revenue Service. 2016, February 12. "Other
Eligible Donees." Retrieved from https://www.irs.gov/
charities-non-profits/contributors/other-eligible-donees

TedCruz.com. 2015, November 20. "More Than 200 Faith
Leaders Endorse Ted Cruz for President." Retrieved from
https://www.tedcruz.org/news/more-than-200-faithleaders-
endorse-ted-cruz-for-president/

*Christina Ann-Marie DiEdoardo is an attorney who practices
criminal defense and nonprofit law at the Law Offices of Christina DiEdoardo P.C. in San Francisco, California. She earned
her juris doctorate* cum laude *from the William S. Boyd School
of Law at the University of Nevada Las Vegas in 2005 and is li-
censed to practice law in California and Nevada as well as before
the U.S. Supreme Court. Nothing in this article should be construed as legal advice or establishing an attorney-client relationship
and all opinions expressed are her own.*

Say a Prayer for Me
Stacy Mintzer Herlihy

When I was 8 years old, I was bused to Hebrew school because
my mom was afraid of all the black children in the local public

school. Why my mom should fear 8-year-old black children and not 8-year-old religious fanatics would remain a mystery to me during my five-year stay in the precincts of Orthodox Judaism.

My yeshiva was built of orange and red ceramic brick and it was surrounded by old maple trees and three playgrounds. I would have been very happy at the Hebrew Academy of the Five Towns and Rockaway had it not been for the fact that everyone at the school, from the bus driver to the students, teachers, and principal, was an Orthodox Jew—except me. I was not an Orthodox Jew. If you asked my classmates, they would have said I was not a Jew at all and I would have agreed with them.

Mom made us ham and cheese sandwiches, fed us shrimp salad, and drove us to the movies on Saturdays. She loved Christmas because dad the mailman made a lot of money in tips. Our holidays were winter recess, spring break, the 4th of July, and Thanksgiving.

At 8, I thought of myself as an American.

Everyone here was a Jew every month, every day, except at Thanksgiving. Our lives were governed not by the Constitution but by the 613 things the Mishnah said we were supposed to do and the 612 that it forbid. The year began not, as I had thought, in January but in September. It was followed not by Columbus Day but by Rosh Ha'shanah, Yom Kippur, and Succos.

After two months, I felt like I was being pulled underwater. I wore pants to school (underneath the dresses mandated by HAFTR), defiantly ignored all attempts to increase my fluency in Hebrew, and put a comic book on top of my Siddur (prayer book).

Contempt felt good until the day Miriam invited me to her house for Shabbos. Miriam was my only friend, a fellow bookworm with long brown hair, glasses thicker than mine, and acceptance of the rules of Orthodox Judaism I secretly envied. Miriam's house was clean, white, and big: the perfect house for a doctor's family.

On Friday, an hour after I had arrived, Miriam's mom Rifka lit Shabbos candles and said the brochot (blessings) to welcome in the holiday. We walked to temple for prayers that were unfamiliar to me and returned to a house filled with the aroma of foods Miriam's mom had baked so she wouldn't have to cook for her family on Shabbos. The next day was again spent in morning prayer, afternoon reading, and quiet talking and then evening candles and prayers. Miriam's mom lit havdalah candles—thick, braided candles whose melting would mark the end of the rest day. Her family began to read aloud in Hebrew in the quiet living room. I did not follow their voices because I did not know the words.

At the end of the first prayer, Miriam's father paused and pulled his children toward him. He put his hands on their heads and began to recite in Hebrew. At the end of the prayer, perhaps for my benefit, he repeated his word in English. The prayer thanked God for his children, prayed for their good fortune, and reminded them of his love. When he was done, Miriam looked at me and asked her father if he could say a prayer for me. As I had suspected, her father gently reminded her that only my father could say that prayer. For the first time in my life, my father's lack of Hebrew and my mother's determined ecumenicism hurt.

The rest of the service continued as Miriam's family chanted in unison in Hebrew until the havdalah candles became unbraided and the voices stopped.

On the week that followed, I could not remove the voices of Miriam and her family from my ears or my mind. I began to realize a few things about my religion I had not understood before. I knew, as I always would, that the Orthodox Judaism practiced at my school did not fit me and never would. But it did fit perfectly, effortlessly, at Miriam's house. The rules that continually chafed at me were used by Miriam and her family as a framework in which to fit their lives. Prayers I had previously mocked as hollow were different in meaning when said voluntarily. A day spent without television, cooking, or money became a day filled with inner calm. It wasn't how I wished to spend the rest of my Saturdays but I understood in the smallest of ways why Miriam and so many of my classmates did.

I knew my father would never recite the Shabbos blessing over my head, and a very small part of me grieved for it. It wasn't the prayer I wished for. It was the expression of love behind it and the serenity of the daughter who received it. Much of my time at Hebrew school was spent asking why things were as they were. Jewish tradition places value on questions but the answers supplied to me were rigorously demanding and I could not accept them. Miriam accepted these answers and in her scrubbed white house I finally understand why.

My visit to Miriam's house did not make everything magically fine at school. But I was never quite able to think of my classmates and their chosen version of Judaism with the same rancor. So many years later, I still think of myself as an American: a Jewish American. This is what religious freedom means to me in my America. Like the Orthodox Jews in my school, I was free to leave school, leave Orthodoxy, and find my own path here. Just as they sought a fiercely traditional Judaism, I sought and finally found my own Judaism, a Judaism that remains as determinedly secularist as my parents and yet still full of lit candles, kindness, and love. This is what America is to me—a place where we find our own truly American religious freedom.

Stacy Mintzer Herlihy is a freelance writer based in New Jersey. She is the coauthor with Allison Hagood of Your Baby's Best Shot: Why Vaccines Are Safe and Save Lives *(2012, paperback 2015). Herlihy is presently at work on another book.*

Religious Choice in Medicine: When Cancer Patients Have Religious Objections to Life-Saving Blood Transfusions
Angela Quinn

Nurses and health care professionals care for people at times when they are most vulnerable. We are there when people take their first breaths and when they take their last. We are there to hold someone's hand when they must contemplate a difficult health care decision that completely contradicts their religious beliefs. We provide compassion and caring to people of all backgrounds, genders, ages, and religions without judgment or prejudice. While some days are challenging, working as a nurse offers some of the most rewarding, beautiful moments. There are patients whom we never, ever forget; Susan* is a patient who will stay with me forever.

I'll never forget the dreadful feeling I got as I received the report from Susan's night nurse. Susan had leukemia, a rare type of blood cancer that severely reduces a patient's ability to fight infection and causes symptoms such as systemic pain and shortness of breath. As we reviewed Susan's blood chemistry together, my heart sank. Susan's white blood cells were almost nonexistent. Without those, she would be extremely vulnerable to infection. Her red blood cells were so low in number that I wondered how her body was carrying around any oxygen at all. "Wow, I'm going to be hanging blood all day," I said to the night nurse. "Susan won't be receiving any blood transfusions today. She's a Jehovah's Witness," the nurse replied.

This was not the first time I had encountered this very situation. Patients who are practicing Jehovah's Witnesses do not accept blood transfusions due to the belief that blood signifies "life" and thus taking the blood transfusion would go against God's plan (https://www.jw.org/en/jehovahs-witnesses/faq/jehovahs-witnesses-why-no-blood-transfusions/). As Susan's nurse and advocate, I instantly accepted her decision to forgo her recommended treatment. There is no room for our personal beliefs and customs in nursing; we treat our patients according to the health care plans that they decide for themselves regardless of how we feel about them.

As I entered Susan's room with her night nurse to do our introductions, I took a deep breath and prepared to encounter a very sick patient. I anticipated that with such a serious disease and poor prognosis, especially without those blood transfusions, I would be encountering a sad and depressed patient. I had cared for patients with a very poor prognosis many times before and I knew from these experiences that it can be extremely challenging to hold it together emotionally in front of the patient and their family. I prepared mentally for the mindset one needs to care for a patient in this condition and I entered the room to meet my patient. The bright, amazing smile that greeted me instead of a worried, sad face I expected is one that will stay with me for the rest of my life.

Over the next three months or so, I visited Susan every shift that I worked. Visiting her became the highlight of my day as her bright smile was uplifting and contagious. "When are you working again?" she would ask. I made a promise to her each and every time that I would be back in a few days. I was feeling a little run down one day; so I didn't want to take the chance of visiting Susan and getting her sick so I just called her to say hello instead. "You made my day," she told me, but the truth is that hearing her voice made mine! "Don't worry, today will get better for you" she told me during one visit when my face still showed the stress of my shift despite trying to hide it from her. It's always a touching moment when your patient becomes your nurse instead!

As I walked into Susan's room one afternoon for a quick visit, I paused before entering when I heard a few voices. Susan had visitors and they were praying. I listened from outside of the room, expecting to hear prayers for Susan and her recovery. Instead, I heard the most beautiful words of awareness and encouragement for Susan's roommate Yolanda,* who was also suffering from leukemia. Yolanda didn't have any religious objections to her much-needed blood transfusions and thus had a much better prognosis than Susan. However, Yolanda wasn't handling her diagnosis well at all and a deep depression had set in. Tears ran down my face as I listened to Susan praying for less suffering for Yolanda even though she herself was in tremendous pain. To say that Susan was one of the most genuinely beautiful people I've ever met is an understatement.

Susan adopted Yolanda and became her unofficial nurse, speaking to her from across the room and offering her the most encouraging words. When Susan lost the strength to do her daily walk through the halls, she fought with every bit of strength she had to keep her spirits up. I'd pop by and find Susan in bed with her religious readings close by. I watched as Susan's body weight diminished, yet her internal strength just continued to grow. Her wall of cards and letters from loved ones and friends grew as long as the space between her breaths.

The world lost a beautiful soul when Susan left it. One might feel that Susan's religious objections to her blood transfusions could have lessened her life, but her religious beliefs are what gave her the strength to hold on until the very end. Sometimes, it isn't the nurse who touches the life of the patient; it is the patient who forever touches the life of the nurse.

*Names changed for anonymity.

Angela Quinn is a registered nurse on Long Island, New York. Angela is passionate about nursing and public health. She is a volunteer with Executive Board Member of Nurses Who Vaccinate, a non-profit organization that positions nurses and the public as advocates for public health wellness through vaccinations. Angela is also the founder of Correcting the Misconceptions of Anti-Vaccine Resources, a professional blog that refutes anti-vaccine articles and blogs that promote misinformation and misconceptions about vaccines.

When Children Pay the Price of Freedom of Religion
Dorit R. Reiss

Over five days in February 1991, two sisters in a religious group in Philadelphia called the Faith Tabernacle died of measles. Monica died first. In a 2015 book, Dr. Paul Offit describes Monica's death:

> Monica's illness began with a rash and progressed to labored breathing and unconsciousness. By the time the police arrived, her heart had stopped beating. (Offit 2015)

Monica's father explained that "his religion forbade him from calling a doctor when Monica had a rash, or when she had a high fever, or when she was gasping for air, or when she slipped into unconsciousness. It was only after she had stopped breathing that he called the police." Monica was 9.

Five days later, on the day of Monica's funeral, her sister, Tina Louise, died of measles. She was 13.

Since the 1960s, the United States had a very effective measles vaccine. But Wayne Johnson, Tina and Monica's father, decided not to give it to his children because his religion forbade it, and he had no remorse, seeing this as a test of faith. If Monica and Tina had been vaccinated, they would almost certainly not have died.

Freedom of religion is important. But sometimes, a parent's freedom of religion conflicts with a child's health and welfare. In several important cases, our legal institutions—courts and legislatures—had to weigh parents' religious freedom against a child's welfare. Courts have consistently preferred the child's welfare; legislatures, less so.

One of the oldest cases addressing the tension between parental religious freedom and the child's interests is *Prince v. Massachusetts* (321 U.S. 158, 166–167 [1944]). In *Prince*, a Jehovah's Witnesses adherent took her niece with her in the evening to hand out religious materials. She was prosecuted for violating child labor laws and found guilty. She appealed, claiming that her freedom of religion was violated. The case went all the way to the U.S. Supreme Court, which said:

> But the family itself is not beyond regulation in the public interest, as against a claim of religious liberty. . . . And neither rights of religion nor rights of parenthood are beyond limitation. Acting to guard the general interest in youth's wellbeing, the state, as parens patriae, may restrict the parent's control. . . . [A parent] cannot claim freedom from compulsory vaccination for the child more than for himself on religious grounds. The right to practice religion

freely does not include liberty to expose the community or the child to communicable disease or the latter to ill health or death.

And the Court went on to explain:

Parents may be free to become martyrs themselves. But it does not follow they are free, in identical circumstances, to make martyrs of their children before they have reached the age of full and legal discretion when they can make that choice for themselves.

Freedom of religion, *Prince* powerfully says, does not allow parents to sacrifice the child. In other cases, too, courts have stepped in to protect children from parental decisions that may be against their welfare—even if the issue was not one of life and death. In *In re Sampson* (317 N.Y.S.2d 641 [Fam. Ct. 1970], *affirmed*, 323 N.Y.S.2d 253 [App. Div. 1971], *affirmed*, 278 N.E.2d 918 [N.Y. 1972]), for example, young Kevin had a disease that made his face deformed. It could be fixed by surgery; but while his Jehovah's Witnesses mother did not oppose the surgery, she opposed a blood transfusion during it. The deciding court, convinced by the doctors that surgery without transfusion was too dangerous, ordered the transfusion.

The logic, again, was that young children are too young to choose their religious faith independently, and the parents' religious freedom does not justify sacrificing the child's life.

If only legislatures were as careful with children's well-being. But they were not. Let us examine, again, the case of vaccination. In the 1960s and 1970s, requirements that children be vaccinated before attending schools spread across the states. The logic was to protect children from dangerous, preventable diseases. But in several states, religious exemptions were added to the bills, allowing those with religious opposition to send children to school unvaccinated. New York was the first to do so. Most of the time, it was lobbying by Christian Scientists who led to these exemptions (Colgrove 2006). In 1972, the price of such exemptions became clear when, after years of no polio cases, a polio outbreak occurred in a Christian Scientists high school in Connecticut, where many children were unvaccinated for religious reasons. Eleven of the children were paralyzed, the youngest 7, the oldest 18, paying the price for their parents' beliefs.

In Philadelphia in 1991, again, an outbreak of measles centered on two religious communities whose members did not vaccinate their children against measles. Nine children died, including Monica and Tina, discussed in the beginning of this article, paying with their lives for their parents' beliefs. Again, the state offered a religious exemption allowing that.

Sometimes, people lie and use a religious exemption to not vaccinate a child for reasons that are not religious (Reiss 2014). In fact, there is an entire church created to allow people to obtain religious exemptions from vaccines even if they don't have real religious objections. But even if people are sincere, they are still making a choice to risk their child's life and health because of religious faith the child is too young to join voluntarily. Religious freedom is important; but children's lives should not be sacrificed to it.

References

Colgrove, James. 2006. *State of Immunity: The Politics of Vaccination in Twentieth-Century America*. Berkeley: University of California Press.

Offit, Paul A. 2015. *Bad Faith: When Religious Belief Undermines Modern Medicine*. New York: Basic Books. 96.

Reiss, Dorit R. 2014. "Thou Shalt Not Take the Name of the Lord Thy God in Vain: Use and Abuse of Religious Exemptions from School Immunization Requirements." *Hastings Law Journal* 65: 1551.

Dorit R. Reiss is a professor of law at UC Hastings College of the Law and a member of the Parent Advisory Board of Voices for Vaccines.

Transgender Rights: A Religious Freedom Wedge Strategy
Rani Baker

In February 2016, Charlotte, North Carolina, added protections for sexual orientation and gender identity to its antidiscrimination ordinance (Ring 2016). A month later, over the course of less than 12 hours, state-level lawmakers in North Carolina quickly pushed through during an overnight emergency session what would later be known as House Bill 2 (Domonoske 2016). House Bill 2, also known as the Public Facilities Privacy and Security Act, is a sweeping measure that blocked employment protections for LGBT folks and also included distinctly specific and detailed regulations about bathroom and changing room use (General Assembly of North Carolina 2016). It also sought to supersede both local and federal attempts to address antidiscrimination through exercise of states' rights, seemingly as an attempt to present a blueprint for similar bills.

House Bill 2 was clearly a response to protections being awarded in the city of Charlotte. The state's General Assembly called its first emergency session in 35 years to address this (Lee, Stasio, and Tiberii 2016). Ironically, the governor at the time, Pat McRory, said that one of the issues with the Charlotte protections was "government over-reach," even as he ratified a statewide bill to shut down a city policy.

Between 2013 and 2016, 24 states have considered similar "bathroom" bills. In 2017 alone, 19 states have attempted to pass similar legislation (Kralik 2017). While it remains true so far that North Carolina is the only state to pass (and later retract) this sort of legislation, these attempts are clearly escalating. This is also clearly planned, the second-stage strategy for the religious right culture war due to waning support on same-sex marriage: a wedge issue they can use to divide centrists from progressives and a front they expect to conquer with less resistance for their constituency in the 2016 election cycle.

Even in seemingly progressive stronghold cities like Seattle, which has had transgender protections on the books for a decade, there has been a battle taking place over transgender rights. Right-wing activists proposed one of the most extreme anti-trans initiatives of 2016, setting back decades of progress (Ford 2016). Despite the fact that there are similar ordinances in Austin, Dallas, Fort Worth, Plano, San Antonio, and El Paso, in 2015, Houston lost a battle for transgender employment and housing protection due to activist campaigns against it spearheaded by the religious right (Fernandez and Smith 2015).

The planning for this strategy goes back to at least the summer of 2014. During the Southern Baptist Convention (Ford 2014) in June 2014, the Southern Baptists released a statement (Southern Baptist Convention 2014) on transgender individuals among their congregation and outlined their public political position on gender-identity-related antidiscrimination. During the conference, transgender rights were presented as the "next phase" of the gay rights fight after same-sex marriage.

The Family Research Council, still reacting from its inability to defeat *Obergefell v. Hodges*, the Supreme Court gay marriage ruling in June 2015, soon afterward released their own statement and platform on transgender rights (O'Leary and Sprigg 2015). It lays out broad-stroke quotables and strategies about pathology and politics, a veritable cliff notes of the tactics and rhetoric they employ in promoting legislation to undermine LGBT rights.

In January 2016, the Republican National Committee approved a resolution focusing specifically on pushback against recently passed gender-identity-based employment and housing protections, couching its reversal in terms of privacy and religious expression (Ennis 2016). While the language of the resolution is populated with references specifically to sex-segregated facilities, the resolution also makes references to other "Obama administration gender identity policies," such as the 2014 Executive Order protecting transgender folks from employment and housing discrimination (Hudson 2014). Besides limiting employment, housing, and public accommodations access, these platforms also bring the suggestion that doctors and other medical professionals can withhold treatment or medical care from transgender individuals based on a religion-based objection to the transgender person's lifestyle or very existence (Stern 2017). These concerns add to the growing uneasiness of 2017's already turbulent dialogue about who will have access to medical care in the future.

Make no mistake, this isn't just about bathrooms.

References

Domonoske, Camila. 2016, March 24. "North Carolina Passes a Law Blocking Measures to Protect LGBT People." National Public Radio. Retrieved from http://www.npr .org/sections/thetwo-way/2016/03/24/471700323/north-carolina-passes-law-blocking-measures-to-protect-lgbt-people

Ennis, Dawn. 2016, February 25. "Republican National Committee Endorses Anti-Trans 'Bathroom Bills.'" *The Advocate*. Retrieved from http://www.advocate.com/ transgender/2016/2/25/republican-national-committee-endorses-anti-trans-bathroom-bills

Fernandez, Manny, and Mitch Smith. 2015, November 3. "Houston Voters Reject Broad Anti-Discrimination Ordinance." *The New York Times*. Retrieved from https:// www.nytimes.com/2015/11/04/us/houston-voters-repeal-anti-bias-measure.html?_r=0

Ford, Zack. 2014, October 31. "How the Southern Baptists Are Still Completely Failing Transgender People." *ThinkProgress*. Retrieved from https://thinkprogress.org/ how-the-southern-baptists-are-still-completely-failing-transgender-people-173dac9fcf11

Ford, Zack. 2016, March 3. "The Most Radical Anti-Trans Initiative Ever Submitted in Washington State." *ThinkProgress*. Retrieved from https://thinkprogress.org/the-most-radical-anti-trans-ballot-initiative-ever-submitted-in-washington-state-7eb36c3f8ea5

General Assembly of North Carolina. 2016, March 23. Public Facilities Privacy & Security Act, House Bill 2, Session Law 2016–3. General Assembly of North Carolina.

Hudson, David. 2014, July 21. "President Obama Signs a New Executive Order to Protect LGBT Workers." Obama White House Archives. Retrieved from https://obamawhitehouse.archives.gov/blog/2014/07/21/president-obama-signs-new-executive-order-protect-lgbt-workers. Accessed May 13, 2017.

Kralik, Joellen. 2017, April 12. "'Bathroom Bill' Legislative Tracking." National Conference of State Legislatures. Retrieved from http://www.ncsl.org/research/education/-bathroom-bill-legislative-tracking635951130.aspx

Lee, Laura, Frank Stasio, and Jeff Tiberii. 2016, March 23. "NAGA Special Session: Non-Discrimination Measures Voided." WUNC Public Radio. Retrieved from http://wunc.org/post/ncga-special-session-non-discrimination-measures-voided#stream/0

O'Leary, Dale, and Peter Sprigg. 2015, June. "Understanding and Responding to the Transgender Movement." Family Research Council. Retrieved from http://downloads.frc.org/EF/EF15F45.pdf

Ring, Trudy. 2016, February 22. "Charlotte OK's LGBT-Inclusive Ordinance." *The Advocate*. Retrieved from http://www.advocate.com/politics/2016/2/22/charlotte-oks-lgbt-inclusive-accommodations-ordinance

Southern Baptist Convention. 2014. "On Transgender Identity." Southern Baptist Convention. Retrieved from http://www.sbc.net/resolutions/2250/on-transgender-identity

Stern, Mark Joseph. 2017, January 3. "Judge: Doctors Have 'Religious Freedom' to Refuse to Treat Trans Patients, Women Who've Had Abortions." *Slate*. Retrieved from http://www.slate.com/blogs/outward/2017/01/03/doctors_ may_refuse_to_treat_transgender_patients_and_women_ who_ve_had_abortions.html

Rani Baker is a freelance writer and illustrator as well as a performing musical artist and programmer. She has written about LGBT rights and history for nearly two decades. She lives in Portland, Oregon.

The First Amendment and Immigration
John R. Vile

Of all the amendments to the U.S. Constitution, none has a more hallowed place than the First Amendment, which was proposed by the first Congress in 1789, ratified by the necessary number of states in 1791, and is the first of 10 amendments known today as the Bill of Rights. The amendment guarantees the free exercise of religion and prohibits its governmental establishment, as well as providing for freedom of speech, press, peaceable assembly, and petition. Court decisions have also tied it to the right of association.

The amendment was one of the first that federal courts also applied to limit actions by state governments. Although a majority of the U.S. Supreme Court has never interpreted the amendment to provide an absolute right to anything (unless it might be freedom of thought), the Court has interpreted most provisions of the amendment quite liberally. To qualify as subversive, for example, speech must present a clear and present danger of imminent danger of unlawful action, typically by advocating violent actions in dangerous situations.

Whereas the Constitution largely limits government when it comes to restricting First Amendment freedoms, it specifically empowers Congress with the power "[t]o establish a uniform

Rule of Naturalization." It further limited state taxes or duties on the personal imports to no more than $10 per person (a provision intended to apply to the importation of slaves).

Congress has not always exercised its right of naturalization in an unbiased fashion. The first naturalization law, which Congress adopted in 1790, limited naturalization to "free white" persons, which recognized the dubious status that blacks had at the time. In the latter part of the 19th and early part of the 20th centuries, Congress excluded groups and imposed quotas (especially Japanese and Chinese) on the basis of race. Not until the adoption of the Nineteenth Amendment in 1920 did the Constitution prohibit discrimination against women voters, and not until 1924 did Congress extend citizenship to Native American Indians.

During World War II, President Franklin D. Roosevelt issued an Executive Order rounding up and detaining individuals of Japanese ancestry, including those who had been born in the United States and were thus citizens according to the first paragraph of the Fourteenth Amendment (1868). It overturned the notorious Dred Scott decision of 1857 by recognizing the citizenship of "all persons born or naturalized in the United States." After the Supreme Court decision in *Brown v. Board of Education* (1954) overturning segregation, it is doubtful that such orders would pass constitutional muster today; indeed, Congress eventually adopted a law compensating victims of these exclusion orders.

What about laws related to First Amendment freedoms? Notably, under an international convention adopted in 1951, the United States accepts refugees who are fleeing persecution "for reasons of race, religion, nationality, membership of a particular social group or political opinion." Indeed, such individuals have priority over those who are seeking citizenship because of their inability to find work, famine, or other economic hardships.

Pointing in part to recent terrorist incidents, many of which have been provoked by Islamic radicals, 2016 Republican presidential candidate and now president Donald Trump proposed not only building a wall that would deter immigrants from Mexico and the rest of Latin America but also suspending temporarily the immigration of all immigrants who are Muslim or who are from nations that are known terrorist hotbeds. Such a proposal would be unlikely to survive judicial scrutiny.

Even before Congress ratified the First Amendment, Article VI of the U.S. Constitution contained a provision prohibiting a "religious test," which would require candidates for office to affirm their belief in God or in a particular set of religious beliefs. The nation currently includes many citizens who are Muslims, and, like Roman Catholics and Jews in the 19th century who were often the subject of similar suspicions, many Muslim immigrants have come to the United States seeking religious freedom and have assimilated into the nation. The 2016 Democratic National Convention featured a Muslim father who waived a copy of the U.S. Constitution as he told how his son gave his life fighting for the U.S. military in Iraq.

In times of declared war, the United States has the right to incarcerate or deport citizens who are citizens of enemy nations, and during World War II, the U.S. Supreme Court upheld the conviction of Nazi saboteurs who had entered the nation with the purpose of engaging in terrorist activities. Before becoming citizens, immigrants (especially those from troubled areas of the world) undergo extensive background checks and take a test on the nation's Constitution and political system. The United States has the right to exclude individuals who have been convicted of major crimes. When individuals take an oath of citizenship, they pledge to abjure allegiance to any foreign nation.

Especially in the early 20th century, it was common to exclude individuals who advocated the forceful overthrow of governments (communists) or no government at all (anarchists). At the time, members of both groups were often associated with terrorist acts. The elected branches of government have special obligations to protect citizens against both foreign and domestic attacks, and the government is free to ask questions designed to ferret out those who might seek citizenship for nefarious purposes or whose violent actions, anti-democratic values, or known association (membership in ISIS, for example) are so antithetical to the U.S. Constitution that they would pose a threat if they were allowed to stay in the country. The United States is not required to extend citizenship to those who would seek to deny religious or political freedoms to others.

Given the knowledge that there are many peaceful and law-abiding U.S. citizens who already share the Muslim faith, and given the First Amendment's commitment to religious freedom, it is highly doubtful that the United States can legally exclude individuals on the basis of their religious faith any more than it can exclude them simply on the basis of their race or ethnicity. Moreover, a law that excluded all individuals from nations dominated by terrorists would deny asylum to individuals, including children, who are fleeing such religious and political persecution sometimes because they have aided U.S. military forces in such areas. Albert Einstein was one who fled a dictatorial government in order to migrate to the United States.

There is a difference between being cautious and prudent and being intolerant and bigoted. Americans need to be wary not only of allowing terrorists to gain a domestic foothold but also of adopting a mind-set that excludes individuals not by their illegal actions and known associations with terrorist groups but by stereotypes based on their race, religion, or nation of origin. Such a policy is antithetical to the First Amendment.

John R. Vile, PhD, is a professor of political science and dean of the University Honors College at Middle Tennessee State University.

Many Are Called—By the Supreme Court of the United States
Courtney Wilder

In January 2012, the Supreme Court ruled on *Hosanna-Tabor Evangelical Lutheran Church and School v. EEOC* (U.S. 10–553

[2012]), a case that "may be its most significant religious liberty decision in two decades" (Liptak 2012). The Court upheld the ministerial exception, long recognized by lower courts, which is a legal position "grounded in the First Amendment, that precludes application of [civil rights] legislation to claims concerning the employment relationship between a religious institution and its ministers" (*Hosanna-Tabor*). Employment law that protects most employees in the United States no longer covers some people who work at religious organizations. The ruling was unanimous. Numerous religious organizations, including mainline and evangelical Protestant denominations, the Roman Catholic Council of Bishops, and several Jewish, Sikh, and Hindu organizations, publicly supported Hosanna-Tabor in this matter (Taylor 2012). The Becket Fund for Religious Liberty, a law firm that served as cocounsel for Hosanna-Tabor, lauds the decision as the Court's "most important religious liberty case in years" ("Supreme Court Sides with Church 9–0" 2012). It would seem as though this ruling is a clear victory for religious freedom.

However, while the ruling was warmly welcomed by some, others voiced concern that religious organizations were no longer bound by employment law and thus the civil rights of people deemed "ministers" could be set aside by religious organizations, including churches, synagogues, temples, and mosques and affiliated schools, hospitals, and social service agencies (Taylor 2012). Even legal scholars who agreed with the ruling warned that the affirmation of religious freedom for churches has its dangers (Horowitz 2012).

What are the facts of the case in *Hosanna-Tabor*? The situation began when Cheryl Perich got sick. A teacher at the Hosanna-Tabor elementary school in Redford, Michigan, a school affiliated with the Lutheran Church—Missouri Synod (LCMS), Perich began to experience a serious illness in June 2004. Perich was a "called" teacher, who had completed required theological study, passed an oral exam, been endorsed by the local synod, and called by a congregation. Her teaching duties, including participation in chapel and providing religious instruction to her students, were identical to those of non-called or lay teachers (*Hosanna-Tabor*). When Perich became ill, she took disability leave and was assured that when she was able to return to work, she would have a job (Pew Research Center 2011). She was eventually treated for narcolepsy, a neurological disorder that causes a person to fall asleep unexpectedly (*Hosanna-Tabor*).

In December 2004, when Perich anticipated being cleared by her physician to return to work within a few months, the school hired another teacher to replace her. Faced with the prospect of fulfilling two separate contracts for the same position, the school asked Perich to voluntarily resign, expressing concern about her capabilities. She refused and, in the conversations that followed, told the school she had consulted a lawyer. Perich was fired for insubordination. She then pursued legal action through the Equal Employment Opportunity Commission, arguing that she should be protected by the Americans with Disabilities Act, which prohibits retaliatory terminations of employees with disabilities who have sought legal protection (*Hosanna-Tabor*).

The Supreme Court ruled instead that Perich was a minister, and thus not protected by the act. Her status as a called teacher and her religious role at work meant that she qualified for the ministerial exception, despite the fact that the LCMS does not ordain women (Barry, https://www.lcms.org/document .fdoc?src=lcm&id=1099). For its part, Hosanna-Tabor argued that Perich lost her job not because of her disability but for insubordination; the LCMS maintains an internal dispute resolution process and by seeking legal counsel and indicating she might pursue legal action to protect herself, Perich had violated the terms of her employment. The denomination grounds this process in I Corinthians 6:1–11, which instructs believers to take their dispute to "the saints" rather than "to court before the unrighteous" (Taylor 2012). This doctrine did not prevent the LCMS from pursuing legal action in response to Perich.

The Supreme Court, however, ruled that a religious organization does not need to provide a religious reason for terminating the employment of a minister apart from the organization's right as a religious entity to choose its own leaders. Herein lies the problem. There is significant evidence that people with disabilities are subject to unjust practices in the workplace, which is one reason for the existence of the Americans with Disabilities Act and the provisions within that act protecting people from retaliatory firing. Unfortunately, religious organizations have in many cases participated in the characterization of people with disabilities as particularly prone to sin, as needing religious healing to reverse their disabilities, and as less valuable and less deserving of equal treatment in society, public and private, than able-bodied people. This happens even when the stated positions of individual denominations and congregations strongly condemn this behavior. That is, when left to their own devices, churches are just as likely to discriminate against people with disabilities as anyone else (Eiesland 1994).

What has happened in the wake of *Hosanna-Tabor*? Later in 2012, a lower court ruled that the ministerial exception applied in the firing of a tenured professor of history of religions, who was a scholar of Jewish studies and a practicing Jew, from a Christian seminary on the grounds that he was a "minister" (Laurence H. Kant. *Appellant v. Lexington Theological Seminary*. S.W.3d. [2014 WL 1511387; the case was decided July on 27, 2012]). That is, in its efforts to uphold religious freedom and to apply both the Establishment Clause and the Free Exercise Clause, the Supreme Court ruled that an individual person can, against his or her will, be assigned the status of "minister" in a religious tradition of which he or she is not a part, thus allowing employers to avoid compliance with civil rights law. There are also other implications. Caroline Corbin argues: "A church may [now] . . . be able to terminate without interference a minister who helps a colleague file a sexual harassment claim. Likewise, a church, religious school, or religious hospital may be able to fire as insubordinate and spiritually unfit a minister who reports any wrongdoing, whether it be discrimination, embezzlement, or the sexual abuse of children" (Corbin 2012, 951).

Although religious freedom for institutions is affirmed by *Hosanna-Tabor*, there is no guarantee that religious institutions will exercise that freedom in accordance with their stated religious ideals, nor that those ideals are morally sound. In addition, the religious and other freedoms of individuals may well be at odds with the actions of the institutions with which they are affiliated as members or employees.

References

Barry, A. L. "What about . . . the Ordination of Women to the Pastoral Office." https://www.lcms.org/document.fdoc?src=lcm&id=1099.

Corbin, Caroline Mala. 2012. "The Irony of Hosanna-Tabor Evangelical Lutheran Church and School v. EEOC." *Northwestern University Law Review*. 106, no. 2: 951.

Eiesland, Nancy. 1994. *The Disabled God*. Nashville, TN: Abingdon Press.

Horowitz, Paul. 2012. "Act III of the Ministerial Exception." *Northwestern University Law Review*. 106. http://scholarly commons.law.northwestern.edu/cgi/viewcontent.cgi?article=1133&context=nulr.

Liptak, Adam. 2012, January 11. "Religious Groups Given 'Exception' to Work Bias Law." *The New York Times*. Retrieved from www.nytimes.com/2012/...court-recogni zes-religious-exceptions-to-job.

Pew Research Center. 2011, September 21. "In Brief: *Hosanna-Tabor vs. EEOC*." Retrieved from www.pewforum .org/in-brief-hosanna-tabor-v-EEOC.

"Supreme Court Sides with Church 9–0 in Landmark First Amendment Ruling." 2012, January 11. Retrieved from www.becketlaw.org/media/supreme-court-sides-church-9-0-landmark-first-amendment-ruling

Taylor, Robin M. 2012. "Special Rules for the Church: The 'Ministerial' Exception under the Americans with Disabilities Act." *Dialog.* 51: 1459–1485.

Courtney Wilder earned her Ph.D. at the University of Chicago and teaches at Midland University in Fremont, Nebraska. Her book Disability, Faith, and the Church: Inclusion and Accommodation in Contemporary Congregations *was published in 2016. She is active in Lutheran theological circles.*

The HHS Contraception Mandate and Religious Freedom Conflicts
Christina Villegas

One of the most politically contentious disputes over the nature and scope of religious freedom in the United States arose following issuance of the Health and Human Services (HHS) mandate that all health insurance plans under the Affordable Care Act (ACA) cover contraception, sterilization, and abortion-inducing drugs at no cost to the patient. Supporters celebrated the mandate as a triumph for equal rights, arguing that endowing women with the right to employer-financed contraception would make women less susceptible to unplanned pregnancy—thereby placing them on a more equal footing with men.

Opponents, on the other hand, criticized the mandate as an assault on religious freedom because it would force employers—under penalty of heavy federal fines—to fund contraception or abort a fetus, regardless of their religious or moral objections to the use of such products. Based on such opposition, hundreds of businesses, universities, nonprofit organizations, and individuals filed over 60 lawsuits seeking exemption from the mandate under the Religious Freedom Restoration Act (RFRA).

RFRA, a bipartisan act signed into law by President Bill Clinton in 1993, provides enhanced protection for freedom of conscience against federal law. Under this act, if a generally applicable law—such as the HHS mandate—imposes a "substantial burden" on a plaintiff's exercise of religion, then judges must determine whether that law furthers "a compelling government interest" and uses the "least restrictive means" to achieve that goal (Religious Freedom Restoration Act 1993). If the law fails to meet both of these standards, then petitioners are entitled to belief-based exemptions.

Due to the nature of legal challenges against the HHS mandate, the debate has largely centered on whether or not religious exemptions from the law are required under RFRA and what types of entities are entitled to such exemptions. Opponents maintain that the mandate does in fact impose a substantial burden—given the enormous fines for noncompliance—and that it does not use the least restrictive means of achieving the government goal of expanding contraception coverage (Smith 2013). Opponents further argue that RFRA's protection against such a burden extends to for-profit businesses, as well as churches, nonprofit organizations, and individuals (Meese, Eastman, and Caso 2014). In contrast, defenders of the mandate argue that the ordinance is "justified as the least restrictive means of protecting compelling government interests" and that it does not impose "a substantial burden" on the exercise of religion (Gedicks 2012: 4).

In spite of the preoccupation with whether RFRA exemptions should be granted in particular cases, support for and opposition to the HHS mandate is ultimately rooted in a more fundamental disagreement over what freedom consists in and how it is protected by the state. On the one hand, petitioners largely interpret the right to free exercise of religion according to the original understanding of liberty, generally the ability to live, work, and use one's own faculties and resources in accordance with one's personal beliefs free from arbitrary injury or restraint. James Madison (1792), the father of the Bill of Rights and author of the First Amendment, for instance, identified the right to freedom of conscience as part of the broader right to property—that is, the rightful claim to one's own beliefs, faculties, and possessions. According to this understanding, individuals should be free to live out the dictates of their faith in both private and public life, so long as the actions mandated by their faith do not cause tangible harm or threaten the well-being and preservation of the social order. The role of government, accordingly, is to create conditions where individuals can cultivate their talents, worship God following the dictates of their conscience, and pursue goals free from arbitrary control or injury by other people or from the government itself. In this sense, the HHS mandate violates individual liberty because it dictates how employers and individuals must spend and invest their own money, regardless of personal beliefs and opinions, and it restricts the ability of individuals as consumers to enter into contracts based on personal needs and preferences.

In contrast, advocates of the mandate clearly adhere to a different understanding of liberty. Many even assert that the liberty to spend one's own resources or enter into contracts in accordance with personal preferences and beliefs is actually a violation of liberty. For instance, in reference to petitioners' request for exemption, Frederick Gedicks (2012: 1) writes, "Must government excuse religious persons from complying with a law they find burdensome, when doing so would violate the liberty of others by imposing on them the consequences of religious beliefs and practices that they do not share and which interfere with their own religious and other fundamental liberties? To pose this question is to answer it: One's religious liberty does not include the right to interfere with the liberty of others." Likewise, Caroline Corbin (2012: 1481) argues that employers requesting exemption from the contraception mandate not only "discriminat[e] against female employees" but also seek to "impose [their] religious values onto them."

It is important to clarify that in spite of widely publicized accusations that petitioners want to use the "police power of the state to prevent women from taking birth control" (Star 2012), the conflict over the HHS mandate is not based on an attempt to outlaw or restrict access to certain products. In the absence of the mandate, employers would still have the option to purchase insurance policies that cover contraception, sterilization, and abortion, and women could also choose to purchase such plans on their own. Those seeking exemptions from the mandate are concerned with the issue of whether individuals should be forced to directly finance or facilitate their use. Testifying before Congress, Archbishop-Designate William Lori of Baltimore explained: "This is not a matter of whether contraception may be *prohibited* by the government. This is not even a matter of whether contraception may be *supported* by the government. Instead, it is a matter of whether religious people and institutions may be *forced* by the government to provide coverage for contraception or sterilization, even if that violates their religious beliefs" (Ad Hoc Committee for Religious Liberty of the United States Conference of Catholic Bishops 2012).

By obscuring the distinction between the legal ability to purchase products and forcing others to directly pay for and facilitate their use, mandate supporters clearly reject the traditional understanding of liberty in favor of a competing definition. Freedom, according to the new view, generally espoused by the progressive left, is not the ability to make decisions about one's own life or the employment of one's faculties free from arbitrary injury or restraint. Instead, it is an evolving concept requiring whatever conditions or resources are necessary to achieve autonomy—freedom from constraints imposed by poverty, traditional morality, religion, culture, race, gender, and even biology. On these grounds, rights must not be limited to individual freedom, choice, and opportunity but should be extended to whatever financial and legal privileges are necessary to "free" individuals from nature and necessity based on their membership in a specific race, class, or gender.

The HHS mandate is motivated by this modern understanding of freedom. If women are to be free from the limitation to their autonomy caused by unplanned pregnancy, it is not enough that they have unrestricted legal access to contraception or abortion. Rather, they must have unfettered access without the burden of having to pay for it themselves. As Caroline Corbin (2013: 1480) argues, "[D]enying women free access to contraception results in serious and direct harms to women's autonomy, equality." In so far as religious free exercise prevents individuals from contributing financially to or actively promoting such redistributive policies, it directly threatens women's autonomy and equality and must be restricted accordingly.

In summary, although the debate surrounding the HHS contraception mandate seemingly centers on the issue of whether narrow exemptions to the law are justified to protect religious freedom, the dispute in reality is based on a more fundamental disagreement over what freedom consists of and the types of laws necessary to secure it. As long as the traditional view that individuals have a right to freely exercise the dictates of their faith outside the walls of their church, mosque, or synagogue uneasily coexists with the belief that liberty requires the rightful claim to the resources of others, such conflicts are bound to persist.

References

Ad Hoc Committee for Religious Liberty of the United States Conference of Catholic Bishops. 2012. *Our First, Most Cherished Liberty: A Statement on Religious Liberty.* Washington, DC: United States Conference of Catholic Bishops. Retrieved from http://www.usccb.org/issues-and-action/religious-liberty/upload/Our_First_Most_Cherished_Liberty.pdf

Corbin, Caroline Mala. 2012. "The Contraception Mandate." *Northwestern University Law Review Colloquy* 107: 1459.

Gedicks, Frederick Mark. 2012. *With Religious Liberty for All: A Defense of the Affordable Care Act's Contraception Coverage Mandate.* Washington, DC: American Constitution Society for Law and Public Policy. Retrieved from https://www.acslaw.org/sites/default/files/Gedicks_-_With_Religious_Liberty_for_All_1.pdf

Madison, James. 1792, March 29. "On Property." Retrieved from http://press-pubs.uchicago.edu/founders/documents/v1ch16s23.html

Meese, Edwin, III, John Eastman, and Anthony Caso. 2014. "Amici Curiae Brief of Center for Constitutional Jurisprudence and St. Thomas More Society of Orange County in Support of Hobby Lobby and Conesto-GA, et al." Nos. 13–354 and 13–356. Counsel for Amici Curiae Center for Constitutional Jurisprudence and St. Thomas More Society of Orange County. Retrieved from http://www.adfmedia.org/files/HobbyLobbyConestogaAmicusCCJ.pdf

Religious Freedom Restoration Act. 1993. Public Law 103–141, U.S. Statutes at Large 107 (1993): 1488.

Smith, Steven D. 2013. "Debate: The Contraception Mandate and Religious Freedom." *University of Pennsylvania Law Review Online* 161: 261. Retrieved from https://papers.ssrn.com/sol3/papers.cfm?abstract_id=2279463

Star, Penny. 2012, March 1. "NOW President: Bishops Want 'Police Power of the State' to Prevent Women from Taking Birth Control." *CNS News.* Retrieved from http://www.cnsnews.com/news/article/now-president-bishops-want-police-power-state-prevent-women-taking-birth-control

Dr. Christina Villegas is assistant professor of political science at California State University-San Bernardino. Her research and teaching interests include American government, American

political thought, modern political thought, Congress and the legislative process, and the formulation of public policy.

The Episcopal Church—Foundations of Religious Freedom
Christopher Johnson

The Episcopal Church (also known as the Protestant Episcopal Church in America, or PECUSA) is one of the early examples of a religious community in the United States that distinguished its ecclesial freedom from the authority of the civil government under whose laws it existed. The Revolutionary War birthed our country's independence from England in 1776. That same liberation extended its reach to the continuing churches founded in its former colonies. Many of the framers of the Constitution of the United States of America were also churchmen of these same continuing churches. They applied the same reasoning that would assure their church's balance of power as they did assuring that balance of civil power.

The Episcopal Church is governed by a presiding bishop, who presides over meetings of the Church and functions as chief pastor and as representative of the Church and the episcopate, among other roles. Houses of Bishops and Deputies exist much as the Senate and House of Representatives. Together, these Houses legislate the laws and policies that guide the Church. Every three years since 1785, the General Convention of the Episcopal Church has convened. Between those triennial conventions, governance is assured by the oversight of an Executive Council that is representative of the various regions of the Church. A judicial body exists to preside over cases where Church laws are alleged to have been broken. This judicial body functions independently of any civil action that may likewise occur.

The Episcopal Church appealed to the Scottish Episcopal Church for the consecration of its first bishop, Samuel Seabury. This was necessary because English canon law required clergy to make an oath of allegiance to the English Crown, which citizens of the newly formed United States of America could not in clear conscience do. Scotland was in the midst of redefining its own relationship to the Realm of England and was receptive to Seabury's consecration as bishop. In 1784, provision for the new bishop's consecration was made by the Scottish Episcopal Church without requiring such an oath of allegiance.

Two Expressions of Religious Freedom Exercised within the Episcopal Church

Over its first 200-plus years, the governing bodies of the Episcopal Church have exercised their understanding of religious freedom in numerous ways. In 1970, women were first authorized to serve as members of the General Convention, though one woman, Elizabeth "Betsey" Dyer, did serve irregularly as a "layman" delegate in 1946. In 1974, 11 women were ordained to the priesthood in an "irregular" service. By 1976, those ordinations were approved by the General Convention. By 1989, the first woman was ordained as a bishop in the Episcopal Church. These major revisions of the roles women fulfill in the Episcopal Church occurred over a period of 19 years! While many would argue that the changes were long overdue, it is important to acknowledge that it was the bicameral structure of the Church's governance that facilitated that revised understanding and practice of religious freedom.

Likewise, The Episcopal Church has exercised the use of its bicameral structure to facilitate its care for members of the LGBT community in support of equal protection under the law, inclusion as members in its common life as parishioners, marriage equality, as deputies to the General Convention, and eventually as ordained clergy, including bishops. These changes took twice as long to effect, but nevertheless became generally accepted within the Episcopal Church more readily than by most other mainline churches as well as by state and federal governments.

Expressions of Religious Freedom Expressed through Episcopal Commitment to Interreligious Dialogue with Abrahamic Traditions

We also speak of interreligious relationships, that is, relationships with religious traditions that are not based on the teachings of one's particular faith, such as Christian and Jewish relations, Christian and Muslim relations, or Jewish and Muslim relations. In the case of these three religious traditions, we all claim a stake in the Hebrew scriptures that date to the person of Abraham. We call these Abrahamic traditions. At their foundation, each recognizes a single entity as God and each is nurtured by a desire to love and serve that God. For these Abrahamic traditions, loving the neighbor is an expression of what God asks us to do for the sake of reciprocating God's love for us.

Religious freedom as extended by the Episcopal Church to Jewish and Muslim traditions has been generously directed at relationships with each tradition in particular and with both Jewish and Muslim traditions together. The expression of our commitment to religious freedom has often come as demonstration of our shared desires to better understand the nature of Jewish and Palestinian relations and proposals for a two-state solution to resolve current tensions. We also lean on our respect for religious freedom when there is public aggression toward Muslims because of the anger and fear generated by terrorist attacks. When the times are reasonably calm, we are intent to invest in these relationships so that they can be durable when they are under external threat. The Executive Council writing in response to the September 11, 2001, terrorist attacks made resolves that seem ever prescient in today's U.S. political culture. These are timely and important to note because of our current climate of fear and polarization. Executive Council minutes from it October 15–19, 2001, meeting in Jacksonville, Florida, resolved

> That the Council calls upon the whole Church to engage
> in local interfaith dialogues among peoples of the three

Abrahamic faiths with resources developed by the office of Ecumenical and Interfaith Relations, condemning in the strongest terms all actions by any groups that pervert the values of Islam, Judaism, and Christianity, especially the core belief of non-violence as expressed in salaam, shalom and peace, noting that such interfaith dialogue can help reduce incidents seen in recent weeks of backlash violence against Muslims, Sikhs, Hindus and others, . . .

That the Council, while recognizing legitimate security concerns in wake of September 11, urges the protection of constitutional rights and civil liberties which are founding principles of our democracy, so that the rights of certain persons will not be wrongfully jeopardized because of their ethnicity or race, . . .

That the Council urges that the tradition of offering safe haven to refugees and asylum seekers be respected, not permitting security-based procedural safeguards to impinge upon the rights of asylum seekers based on their country of origin, race, ethnicity or religion, but ensuring that their claims for protection are adjudicated fairly, and further urges congregations and dioceses to continue their ministries of hospitality to refugees and immigrants of all traditions.

Conclusion

The Episcopal Church has been actively exercising its practice of religious freedom both within and outside of its institutional boundaries. The Church's bicameral structure has most likely served to facilitate this practice because it has allowed for a process that gives voice to many and not only to those who occupy direct leadership roles on an institutional level. In some sense, we might even argue that we use our freedom to aid and support our civil authorities as well, as they look for language and precedence to undergird their own legislative reasoning. From my perspective, what began as a religious transition out from under the authority of civil government (the English Crown) successfully adopted a structure of governance capable of assuring both an elasticity of reasoning as well as the preservation of the essential elements of its tradition and theology. I suspect that the Episcopal Church has evolved well precisely because it has been free from the burden of autocratic, or, at least directive, oversight for its means of governance. The wisdom of our bicameral approach to governance is probably our best assurance for continuing to negotiate a culture of peace because it is born out of a shared respect for the preservation of true justice for all.

The Reverend Christopher Johnson is rector of St. Raphael Episcopal Church in Colorado Springs, Colorado. He has a Doctor of Ministry degree from Drew University. Previously, he served as the church-wide program officer for Jubilee Ministry and Poverty Alleviation, the Episcopal Church. He has served General Conventions of the Episcopal Church as a site volunteer, as a staff officer, and as an elected delegate.

4   Profiles

Introduction

Many organizations and people have been and continue to be involved in the political conflict over religious freedom in America, an enduring issue in American politics. This chapter provides a list and brief descriptions of some of the leading players in the arena of that perennial political struggle. For the convenience of the reader, the chapter is structured as follows: governmental organizations, nongovernmental organizations, governmental people, then nongovernmental people.

Governmental Organizations

This section lists and briefly discusses some major federal government offices and agencies.

Attorney General of the United States and Solicitor General of the United States

The office of the attorney general of the United States was established by the Judiciary Act of 1789. The attorney general's office gradually evolved over time to become the Department

---

David Silverman, president of American Atheists, addresses the American Atheists National Convention in Salt Lake City on April 18, 2014. In an effort to raise awareness and attract new members, the organization held their national conference over Easter weekend in the city headquarters of the Church of Jesus Christ of Latter-day Saints. American Atheists are the largest such group lobbying for freedom from religion. (AP Photo/Rick Bowmer)

of Justice (DOJ), when that department was created in 1870, making the attorney general the chief law enforcement officer of the federal government. The attorney general represents the United States in legal matters, giving legal advice to the president of the United States and to heads of the executive branch departments when asked to do so. In matters of exceptional gravity, the attorney general appears before the U.S. Supreme Court to argue the government's case, although that task is usually performed by the solicitor general of the United States. The attorney general is appointed by the president and confirmed by the U.S. Senate, and the office, like other cabinet-level secretaries, is subject to impeachment by the House of Representatives and trial in the Senate for "treason, bribery, and other high crimes and misdemeanors" (Article II, Section 4, U.S. Constitution; and Judiciary Act of 1798, 28 U.S.C. 503). As head of the DOJ, the attorney general is arguably second only to the U.S. Supreme Court in impact on legal matters pertaining to the First Amendment's Establishment and Free Exercise clauses. The attorney general has fairly wide latitude in deciding whether or not to bring cases to federal court on the basis of constitutionality questions or issues. When a case is brought to the federal court level by other litigants challenging a law or government action on the matter of establishment or Free Exercise clause grounds, the attorney general must represent the government's side, although the solicitor general is normally the person who actually presents the federal government's case.

The solicitor general is likewise appointed by the president and confirmed by the Senate (28 U.S.C. 505). The position was created by the 1870 act. The solicitor general determines the legal position that the federal government will take to the Supreme Court and supervises and conducts cases in which the government is a party. The office also files amici curiae briefs in which the federal government has a significant interest and in federal courts of appeal argues in most of the cases in which an amicus curiae brief has been filed. The Office reviews cases decided against the United States in federal district courts and approves every case in which the federal government files an appeal. The solicitor general has an office in the DOJ as well as in the Supreme Court building and is the most frequent advocate before the Supreme Court; when the office endorses a petition for certiorari, review is most often granted by the Court. Five solicitors general have gone on to serve on the Supreme Court and numerous others on the U.S. Courts of Appeals.

In addition to deciding whether or not to bring a case on such grounds, the attorney general may opt to submit an amicus curiae brief in cases involving First Amendment rights, even if the case does not involve a federal government act, when the attorney general deems challenges to state or local government actions on religious freedom grounds are of likely import to the national level as well.

Office of the President of the United States

The president of the United States is both the head of state and head of the federal government (the executive branch of the United States). By constitutional powers (Article II), the president directs all the departments and executive agencies and is the commander in chief of the armed forces. The office's constitutional powers include execution of all federal law; appointment of federal executive, diplomatic, regulatory, and judicial offices; and concluding treaties with foreign powers (with the advice and consent of the Senate). The president can grant pardons, reprieves, and clemency and convenes and adjourns either or both houses of the Congress under extraordinary circumstances. The president increasingly has set the legislative agenda of the party to which the president is titular head and directs both foreign and domestic policy.

The president impacts religious freedom in America in several ways. The president appoints some 8,000 to 14,000 offices, from ambassadors, to cabinet members, to other federal officers, who by their actions and departmental rules and regulations may affect religious freedom. The president can also affect religious freedom issues by executive orders, reviewable by federal courts and which can be superseded by legislation enacted by the Congress. Historically, the greatest impact has been through the president's power to nominate federal judges, including the U.S. Courts of Appeals and the Supreme Court of the United States. Arguably, the greatest impact historically has been through the president's appointment of the chief justice.

The Supreme Court of the United States

The Supreme Court is the government organizational entity that has had the most profound impact on religious freedom in America. The Supreme Court oversees the federal court system comprised of 94 district-level trial courts in 12 regional circuits and 13 Courts of Appeals. The federal district courts are the workhorses of the federal judicial system in that almost every civil or criminal case heard in the federal courts starts at the district-court level. These courts review petitions, hear motions, hold trials, and issue injunctions, all of which can have an impact on freedom of religion matters. Chief justices have particularly important impact in that they assign the justice among the majority who will write the Court's opinion.

U.S. Federal Departments

Virtually any of the cabinet-level departments of the U.S. government can, by their rules and regulations and implementation of federal laws, play a role in defining freedom of religion issues. Space does not allow here a discussion of each of those departments. This section discusses three such departments as exemplary of how federal departments and agencies can impact our understanding of and the politics of freedom of religion in America: the Department of Homeland Security, the DOJ, and the Department of the Interior.

The Department of Homeland Security

The Department of Homeland Security (DHS) was established in November 2002, under President George W. Bush and in response to the terrorist attacks of September 11, 2001.

It is the third largest cabinet-level department of the U.S. government, with a workforce of 240,000 in 22 component units, among which are included the Transportation Safety Administration, Customs and Border Protection, Immigration and Customs Enforcement, and U.S. Citizenship and Immigration Services, with each of which is often involved rules, regulations, and enforcement actions that give rise to challenges on religious grounds (e.g., a travel-related "Muslim ban," anti-terrorism actions constituting racial profiling of religious minorities, conflict with cities and religious groups providing sanctuary to illegal immigrants).

The Department of Justice
The U.S. DOJ was established in 1870 by President Ulysses S. Grant. It is home to several divisions and bureaus that potentially involve the department in religious freedom matters and controversies.

- It assumed control of federal prisons in 1884. Racial and religious minorities in the federal prison system have at times involved the DOJ in religious freedom controversies.
- It established its Civil Rights Division in 1957. Civil rights on occasion have led to conflict with free exercise of religion.
- Likewise, in 1909, its Environment and Natural Resources Division was established. Matters before that division have on occasion conflicted with religious freedom issues, for example, with claimed sacred sites of Native American Indian religions versus the DOJ policy and rulings over oil pipelines.
- The DOJ established a National Security Division in 2007, which occasionally gets embroiled in controversy with Muslim Americans.

The DOJ houses several law enforcement agencies: the U.S. Marshals Service; the Federal Bureau of Investigation; the Federal Bureau of Prisons; the Bureau of Alcohol, Tobacco,

Firearms and Explosives; the Drug Enforcement Agency; the Office of Inspector General; the Executive Office of Immigration Review; the Office of Immigration Litigation; and the Office of Tribal Justice.

The department is headed by the attorney general of the United States.

The Department of the Interior

The Department of the Interior is a cabinet-level agency charged with managing the nation's natural and cultural resources. It protects those natural resources and provides scientific and other information about those resources. It employs expert scientists as well as resource-management professionals. It has nine technical bureaus in addition to various offices and helps develop future energy supplies. It holds in trust a special commitment to American Indians, Alaska Natives, and affiliated island communities (e.g., American Samoa and native Hawaiians).

It is the energy supply and special trust to Native Americans responsibilities of the Department of the Interior that have most often given rise to issues concerning freedom of religion. Cases challenging the constitutionality of the department's policies, regulations, and enforcement have been heard by the Supreme Court regarding Native American religious use of peyote and other controlled substances and the department's leasing of lands for timber harvesting and road building in public lands and parks that impinge on Native Indian claimed sacred sites. The department raises billions annually from energy, mining, grazing, and timber leases, as well as recreational permits and land sales. Critics contend that it is those revenue-raising aspects of the Department of the Interior operations that engender mixed motivations when claims of Native American sacred sites clash with the streams of revenue from energy supply and federal land use management.

The Census Bureau, housed in the department, collects and publishes census data on the U.S. population. Those data supply some of the most important information on religious affiliations claimed by the American population, as well as a host of socioeconomic data relevant to various religious groups. Those data are especially important when it comes to minority religious groups in America. Census data confirm that the United States is the most religiously diverse nation in the world.

Nongovernmental Organizations

There is a plethora of nongovernmental organizations that have been involved in controversies and conflicts over the Establishment and Free Exercise clauses or otherwise advocate and lobby on freedom of religion in American politics. Space constraints limit the discussion here to a dozen such organizations to exemplify the category. Some are lobby groups advocating for religious groups and free exercise; others seek to defend the "absolute wall of separation" between church and state and are involved in Establishment Clause cases; still others exemplify the "think tank" type of organization doing research on the religious freedom topic.

American-Arab Anti-Discrimination Committee

The American-Arab Anti-Discrimination Committee (ADC) is a civil rights organization whose mission is to defend the rights of people of Arab descent and to promote the cultural heritage of Arab Americans. The ADC was co-founded in 1980 by then U.S. senator James Abourezk (D-SD). Today, it claims to be the largest Arab American grassroots organization in the country. It supports the human and civil rights of all people and opposes racism, bigotry, and discrimination in any form and is open to participation and support of people of all ethnic, racial, and religious backgrounds. It is headquartered in Washington, D.C. Its objectives are to do the following: (1) defend and promote human rights, civil rights, and liberties of Arab Americans and other persons of Arab heritage; (2) combat stereotyping and discrimination against the Arab American community; (3) serve as the public voice of the Arab American community on domestic and foreign policy matters and issues; (4) educate the American public in order to promote greater understanding of Arab history and culture; and (5) organize and mobilize the Arab American community to further its objectives. It claims members in all 50 states, about three million Americans who trace their roots to an Arab country. It sponsors a number of programs to combat discrimination and bias against Arab Americans, including stereotypes of Arabs and Muslims, and is a member of the Leadership Council on Civil Rights. It was founded in 1980 by James Abourezk, the first Arab American U.S. senator, and Samer Khalaf, an attorney from New Jersey, who became the ADC national president in 2013. Its advisory board included Muhammad Ali; Queen Noor of Jordan; the late actor and voice actor Casey Kasem; U.S. representatives John Conyers (D-MI), Darrell Issa (R-CA), Nick Joe Rahall (D-WVA), and former representative Paul Findley (R-IL); and Archbishop Philip Saliba, the archbishop of New York and All North America of the Antiochian Orthodox Christian Church.

The legal department of the ADC offers counsel in cases of discrimination, defamation, and hate crimes and participates in selected litigation in hundreds of cases against airlines and employers for discrimination on the basis of ethnicity and national origin and against the U.S. government for discriminatory detentions without probable cause of Arabs and Muslims post–September 11. Its communications department challenges defamation, stereotyping, and bias in films, television, and news reporting and its spokespersons are considered an authoritative voice on Arab American affairs. Its government affairs department works with the Congress, the White House, and the Departments of State and Justice to promote the interests of the Arab American community (i.e., by lobbying). It contributes to the National Association of Arab Americans–Anti-discrimination Committee (NAAA–ADC) Political Action Committee to support political candidates for federal office. Its research institute, begun in 1981, sponsors research studies, seminars, conferences, and publications about discrimination faced by Arab Americans, promotes better understanding of Arab cultural heritage, and provides lesson plans, background articles, fact sheets, bibliographies, and other resources to educators.

Its offices suffered a series of violent attacks in 1985, as well as attacks on mosques in southern California. In 1991, during the Gulf War, it was targeted by violent anti-Arab telephone messages and the ADC documented more than 100 hate crimes against Arab Americans. The 1996 Antiterrorism and Effective Death Penalty Act and the Illegal Immigration Reform and Immigrant Responsibility Act allowed for the deportation of immigrants for minor offenses and allowed secret classified evidence and the denial of bond for those under threat of deportation. One 1999 case involving the targeting of Arab Americans reached the Supreme Court, in *Reno v. American-Arab Anti-Discrimination Committee* (525 U.S. 471). In its decision, delivered by Justice Antonin Scalia, joined by Chief Justice Rehnquist and Associate Justices O'Connor, Kennedy, and Thomas, with concurring opinions by Justices Breyer and Stevens, with a dissenting opinion by Justice David Souter, the Supreme Court denied the case on the basis of the federal courts being deprived of jurisdiction over the respondent's suit upholding the general rule that revised procedures for removing aliens do not apply to non-citizen aliens.

American Atheists

American Atheists (AA) is a nonprofit, activist civil rights and civil liberties organization defending atheists and advocating for complete separation of church and state. It was formed in 1963 by Madalyn Murray O'Hair, following her role in removing mandatory prayer in public schools (*Abington School District v. Schempp* and *Murray v. Curlett* [1963]). Its mission is to promote atheism and secular humanism and to oppose religion in the public sphere. It is headquartered in Cranford, New Jersey, claiming 2,200 members, and led by David Silverman (president) and Amanda Knief (managing director). In 2005, it formed the Godless Americans Political Action Committee to endorse candidates who support the separation of church and state. The PAC opposes Christmas being a federal holiday or any mention of God on currency or in the Pledge of Allegiance, to date to no avail.

The organization is known for its antireligious billboards. In 2014, it launched an Internet television channel on the Roku streaming media platform, offering 24 hours programming alongside an on-demand service to "provide a breadth of content, from science to politics to comedy, all centered on *freedom from* religion."

The AA won several cases among the 23 in which it was a party, from 1963 to 2012, all involving the separation of church and state.: *Murray v. Curlett* (1963), challenging Bible reading and prayer recitation in Maryland public schools; *Murray v. U.S.* (1964), forcing the FEC to extend the fairness doctrine to atheists; *O'Hair v. Paine* (1971), challenging NASA's religious use of the space program requiring astronauts to read the Bible during a space flight; *O'Hair v. Blumenthal* (1978), challenging the use of the phrase "In God We Trust" on U.S. currency; *O'Hair v. Hill* (1978), to remove from the Texas constitution a provision requiring a belief in God of persons holding offices of public trust; *American Atheists Inc., Daniel Cooney, v. Bradford County, Florida* (2012), over a display of the Ten Commandments on public property; and *American Atheists v. Port Authority* (2011), over the placement of cross-shaped steel beams called the "World Trade Center Cross" at the National September 11 Memorial and Museum.

American Civil Liberties Union

The American Civil Liberties Union (ACLU) is a nonpartisan, nonprofit organization formed to defend and preserve the individual rights and liberties of every person in America by the Constitution and laws of the United States. It was founded in 1920 and is headquartered in New York, claiming a national membership of 1.2 million as of 2017 and having an annual budget of more than $133 million and a staff of 300 attorneys as well as several thousand volunteer attorneys. It lobbies for policy positions that include opposition to the death penalty; support of same-sex marriage rights and the right of LGBT people to adopt; support of birth control and abortion rights; elimination of discrimination against women, minorities, and LGBT people; support of the rights of prisoners and opposition to torture; and opposition to government preference for religion over nonreligion or for particular faiths over others. The ACLU consists of two separate but closely affiliated nonprofits: the ACLU, a 501(c)(4) social welfare group, and the ACLU Foundation, a 501(c)(3) public charity. Both engage in civil rights litigation, advocacy, and education, but only the 501(c)(3) donations are tax deductible, and only the 501(c)(4) group can engage in unlimited political lobbying.

The ACLU often engages in cases supporting Native American rights and defense of Jehovah's Witnesses members (filing support in *Lovell v. City of Griffin*, *Martin v. Stuthers*, and *Cantwell v. Connecticut*). The ACLU supported Jehovah's Witnesses in a couple of flag-saluting cases, winning in *West Virginia State Board of Education v. Barnette* (1943). It led legal battles over the separation of church and state, including *Everson v. Board of Education* (1947), in which Justice Hugo Black wrote: "the First Amendment has erected a wall between church and state. . . . That wall must be kept high and impregnable." The ACLU prevailed in *McCullum v. Board of Education* (1948) and in *Engel v. Vitale* (1962). The ACLU participated in lobbying efforts to oppose the School Prayer Constitutional Amendment and the 1966 congressional vote on the proposed amendment that failed to obtain the required two-thirds majority. The ACLU challenged but lost cases on state laws requiring commercial businesses to close on Sunday.

Americans for Religious Liberty

Founded in 1981, the Americans for Religious Liberty (ARL) is a political organization supporting the constitutional principle of separation of church and state to guarantee religious and intellectual freedom, religiously neutral democratic public education, and individual freedom of conscience. It promotes its goals through publishing, litigation, coalition building, public speaking, and expert testimony before national and state legislative committees, and it regularly cooperates with a wide range of civil liberties, educational, religious, labor, and reproductive rights advocacy groups and organizations. The ARL is open to all who share its dedication to defending and advancing the separation of church and state. In 2016–2017, it lobbied against the Mexican border wall. It is headquartered in Silver Spring, Maryland, a suburb of Washington, D.C. In January 2015, it published a comprehensive analysis of school voucher and tuition tax credit plans detailing their harm to public education, religious freedom, and democratic values and institutions based on decades of research and involvement with the school voucher issue. In 2013, the ARL filed an amicus curiae brief with the Supreme Court in the case of *Town of Greece v. Susan Galloway* and *Linda Stephens*, which challenged as discriminatory the town practice of town council prayer. In 2012, it opposed any form of aid to faith-based private schools. As part of its public relations campaign, it publishes the journal/newsletter *The Voice of Reason*.

The ARL has been involved in 60 actions in the courts, regularly using amici curiae briefs in U.S. Supreme and lower courts, often working with other organizations in coalition briefs, for example, in *Lamont v. Woods* (1991), filed in the U.S. Second Court of Appeals in New York. *Lamont* involved a challenge to U.S. government aid to faith-based schools in other countries. Between 1983 and 1989, the U.S. Agency for International Development distributed more than $14 million to faith-based schools in the Philippines, Egypt, Israel, Jamaica, South Korea, and Micronesia. The Appeals Court found such aid unconstitutional and the Bush administration decided not to appeal. Other cases the ARL supported include *Gonzales v. O Centro Espirita Beneficente Uniao do Vegetal* (2006), *Cutter v. Wilkinson* (2005), and *Gonzales v. State of Oregon* (2005) in defense of Oregon's physician-assisted suicide. It was involved in a number of religion in public school cases: *Bauchman v. West High School* (1997), *Chaudari v. State of Tennessee* (1996), *Ingebretsen v. Jackson Public School District* (1994), *Lee v. Weisman* (1990), and *Board of Education of the Westside Community Schools v. Mergens* (1989). It supported briefs in a number of cases regarding religious displays in government buildings: *Van Orden v. Perry* (2004), *Freethought Society v. Chester County* (2002), and *Capitol Square Review and Advisory Board v. Pinette* (1994). It supported challenges to tax aid to faith-based schools (mostly various voucher plans) in such cases as *Bush v. Holmes* (2006), which successfully challenged the Florida school voucher plan, which the Florida Supreme Court ruled unconstitutional in 2006; *Zelman v. Simmons-Harris* (2001), challenging Ohio's school voucher plan; and *Agostini v. Felton* (1996), challenging tax aid to faith-based schools in New York.

Americans United for Separation of Church and State

Founded in 1947, the Americans United for Separation of Church and State (AU) is a broad coalition of religious, educational, and civic leaders first formed to oppose pending legislation in the U.S. Congress that would have extended government aid to private religious schools. It is headquartered in Washington, D.C., and has a professional staff of 40 full-time employees. The organization's leadership founded the group to activate a national focus pursuing goals on several fronts: education (lobbying) of members of Congress and state and local legislators on the importance of maintaining church and state separation. State and local chapters were formed to work at the grassroots level. AU began publishing a magazine, *Church and State*, to help educate the general public as well. These goals continue to the present as central to AU's activities. In the 1960s, AU supported the Supreme Court's rulings striking down state and local government-sponsored prayer and Bible reading in public school laws and defended the rulings in public, arguing that no government had the right to compel children to take part in religious worship and that truly voluntary student prayer remained legal.

When the religious right began to rise as a political force in American politics during the late 1970s, with such groups as Jerry Falwell's Moral Majority and its allied groups vigorously attacking the church and state separation principle in the halls of Congress and in federal courts, AU fought their efforts. The Moral Majority also targeted public schools for "takeover" campaigns to saturate the curriculum with fundamentalist theology. Again, AU fought their efforts.

By the 1980s, "education choice" advocates began their campaign for tax subsidies for religious education through school voucher programs and tuition tax credit plans. AU rallied to oppose those efforts and helped secure a string of court victories turning back the religious right and the pro-voucher allied groups. It organized Americans to speak out against the extreme and intolerant agenda of the religious right. In the 1990s, those forces regrouped under the leadership of TV evangelist Pat Robertson's Christian Coalition. The coalition focused heavily on local school board politics. The Coalition advocated an end to public education and the "Christianization" of American politics, arguing that the nation was founded as "a Christian nation." AU launched an in-depth media campaign exposing and opposing the radical agenda of the Christian Coalition.

AU soon was opposing other religious right organizations, like Focus on the Family, the Family Research Council, and the Alliance Defense Fund. AU continued opposing voucher plan initiatives at the state level and to block so-called faith-based initiatives in the federal government, although it failed to block the George W. Bush administration's efforts to establish such an office in the White House. AU continues to advocate that all Americans have the constitutionally protected right to practice the religion of their choice, or to refrain from taking part in any religion, as their individual conscience dictates, and to uphold the principle that government at all levels must remain neutral on religious matters.

Its current executive director is the Reverend Barry Lynn, a United Church of Christ minister, as well as a long-active civil rights and civil liberties attorney. Throughout its history, AU has enjoyed the participation of many clergy members, but it is officially a non-sectarian and nonpartisan organization. AU works with Christians, Jews, Muslims, Buddhists, Hindus, humanists, and those who profess religious beliefs or no belief. Its members are affiliated with Democrats, Republicans, Independents, and other political affiliations (e.g., Libertarians) who likewise espouse belief in the principle of religious liberty. AU continues to stress that the wall of separation must remain a high and firm barrier between the institutions of government and religion; that religious liberty is not secure when the government presumes to promote religion over nonreligion, or favors one faith over another; and that it is not secure when government uses public services intended for everyone, such as public schools, to indoctrinate or coerce participation in worship. AU stresses that religious liberty is not secure when federal or state taxes are used to forward someone's religion, or when the government appropriates and displays the symbols of faith that not everyone shares; that government-sponsored religion is dangerous, unnecessary, and bad for government and bad for religion; and that it is wrong for government to interfere in what must always remain a deeply personal matter.

Center for the Study of Law and Religion

Founded in 1982, the Center for the Study of Law and Religion (CSLR) is an organized center at Emory University dedicated to studying the religious dimensions of law, the legal dimensions of religion, and the interaction of religious and legal ideas in institutions, norms, customs, and practices.

The Center is founded on the assumptions that religion gives law its spirit and inspires adherence to ritual and justice and that law gives religion its structure and encourages its devotion to order and organization. The Center engages thousands of scholars and students each year through its courses, degree programs, fellowships, research projects, and public program-ming. The Center publishes, through Cambridge University Press, a leading periodical, *Journal of Law and Religion*, as well as two book series, Law and Christianity and Law and Judaism. It works in the fields of faith, freedom, and the family; legal and political theory; and the place of religious legal systems in modern democracies.

The Center is interdisciplinary in perspective, bringing re-ligious wisdom and traditions into greater conversation with law, public policy, and humane and social sciences. It is inten-tionally international in orientation, seeking to situate debates in America over interdisciplinary issues of law and religion within an emerging global discourse. Its claimed mission is to help peoples of the world learn how law and religion can bal-ance each other and stabilize society and politics. Its director is John Witte, Jr. and its associate director is Silas W. Allard.

The Center offers six degree programs, pursues multiyear re-search projects, and has produced more than 300 books, as well as hosting major international conferences and distinguished lecture series. In 1985, the Center's founder, Emory President James T. Laney, convinced Harvard Law School's Harold J. Berman to join Emory as the first Robert W. Woodruff Pro-fessor of Law, and John Witte, Jr., then a recent Harvard Law graduate and research assistant, who led the Emory's Law and Religion Program. In 1991, its conferences were launched into international prominence when 800 participants from 5 continents came together, and when the conference's key-note addresses were presented by former U.S. president Jimmy Carter and Anglican archbishop Desmond Tutu. By 2000, the Pew Charitable Trust solidified the program's status with a $3.2 million grant and it officially became a Pew Center of Excellence and renamed the Center for the Study of Law and Religion. In recent years it has added the study of law and Asian religions; law, religion, and immigration; and religion, state, and housing. It is supported with some $20 million in grant funding, as well as generous university endowment of the Center's general operations.

Council on American-Islamic Relations

The Council on American-Islamic Relations (CAIR)'s stated mission is to enhance understanding of Islam, encourage dialogue, protect civil liberties, empower American Muslims, and build coalitions to promote justice and mutual understanding. It is a grassroots civil rights and advocacy group, noted as the largest Muslim civil liberties organization, with national headquarters in Washington, D.C., on Capitol Hill, and with several regional offices. The CAIR began in 1994. Through media relations, government relations, education, and advocacy, it promotes an Islamic perspective to ensure the Muslim voice is represented and to empower the American Muslim community and encourage their participation in political and social activism.

Its stated core principles are as follows: (1) support for free enterprise, freedom of religion, and freedom of expression; (2) protection of civil rights of all Americans, regardless of faith; (3) support for domestic policies that promote civil rights, diversity, and freedom of religion; (4) opposition to domestic policies that limit civil rights and permit racial, ethnic, or religious profiling; (5) alliance with groups, religious or secular, that advocate justice and human rights in America and around the world; (6) support for foreign policies that help create free and equitable trade, encourage human rights, and promote representative government based on socio-economic justice; (7) belief that the active practice of Islam strengthens the social and religious fabric of America; (8) condemnation of all acts of violence against civilians by any individual, group, or state; (9) advocacy of dialogue between faith communities both in America and worldwide; and (10) support for equal and complementary rights and responsibilities for men and women.

Its civil rights department provides counsels, mediates and advocates on behalf of Muslims and others who have experienced religious discrimination, defamation, or hate crimes, and protects and defends the constitutional rights of American Muslims. Its government affairs department conducts and organizes lobby efforts on issues related to Islam and Muslims, monitors legislation and other government activities, and responds on behalf of the American Muslim community. Its representatives have testified before Congress and have sponsored activities to bring Muslim concerns to Capitol Hill. It issues action alerts to generate grassroots response to critical social, political, and media-related issues, providing an e-mail list to be a source of information and news for the American Muslim community.

CAIR's research team conducts empirical research studies relevant to the American Muslim community, gathering and analyzing data for its annual civil rights reports, and publishes the *North American Muslim Resource Guide: Muslim Community Life in the United States and Canada.* CAIR offers internships to students and other interested individuals to gain experience in media relations, political activism, or civil rights work.

It regularly sponsors conferences, seminars and workshops, and training seminars for government and law enforcement agencies, media professionals, and the academic community and provides training to the Muslim community for activists in media relations, public speaking, lobbying, and civil rights. It sponsors voter registration drives and participation in the political arena. It participates in ongoing outreach and interfaith relations.

Freedom from Religion Foundation

Freedom from Religion Foundation (FFRF) was founded in 1978. It is a nonprofit, 501(c)(3) educational organization whose purpose is to support the separation of church and state, non-theism, atheism, and secularism. It is headquartered in Madison, Wisconsin, and has chapters in all 50 states and claims more than 23,500 members. It is the largest national organization for non-theists. It educates the public on matters relating to atheism, agnosticism, and non-theism. It publishes a newspaper, *Freethought Today*, and since 2006 runs a Freethought Radio Network producing the *Freethought Radio* show.

It was cofounded by Anne Nicol Gaylor and her daughter, Annie Laurie, and was incorporated nationally in 1978. In 2011, it spent $200,000 in legal fees and services and more than $1 million on education, outreach, publishing, broadcasting, and sponsored events. Legal fees are primarily supporting amici curiae briefs for cases supporting separation of church and state that involve government entities, and it has a paid staff of 22, including 5 full-time attorneys and 2 legal fellows.

Since 2011, it supports "Hardship Grants" for clergy as they leave their faith. In 2013, it announced, in partnership with the Secular Student Alliance, an educational program for students on their religious rights and assistance in rectifying violations. In 2015, it began a new charitable arm, NonBelief Relief, Inc., as a humanitarian agency for atheists, agnostics, freethinkers, and their supporters seeking to remediate conditions of human suffering on a global scale, whether the result of natural disasters, human actions, or adherence to religious dogma. In 2004, it challenged the constitutionality of the White House Office of Faith-Based and Community Initiatives (OFBCI); in 2007, the Supreme Court in *Hein v. Freedom from Religion* (551 U.S. 587, 2007) ruled, 5–4, that taxpayers do not have the right to challenge the constitutionality of expenditures made by the executive branch.

In 2007, FFRF won a suit challenging an Indiana Family and Social Services Administration program that hired a Baptist minister at an annual salary of $60,000, and the program was ended. It backed cases challenging aid to faith-based programs in health care and the use of chaplains to treat patients in drug and alcohol treatment programs as violations of the Establishment Clause. In 2004 and 2005, it supported successful challenges to state education programs holding weekly Bible classes. It has brought or supported cases challenging criminal justice programs, religion in the public sphere, employment issues, prayer in government schools; tax exemptions and cases against the IRS and Federal Elections Commission (FEC) for not enforcing electioneering laws in violation of the First Amendment. In 2013, it won a Florida case and was allowed to hang a banner at the capitol after a nativity scene was placed by a private group. It won cases in Illinois, Washington, Wisconsin, Rhode Island, and Texas over plaques and signs placed in state capitols.

Heritage Foundation

The Heritage Foundation was founded in 1973 as a "think tank" supporting research and education that has grown to the largest such conservative institution. Roughly a half-million persons are dues-paying members supporting the organization's attempts to promote "freedom, prosperity, opportunity and civil society." It is a public policy advocacy organization that formulates and promotes conservative public policies based on the principles of free enterprise, limited government, individual freedom, traditional American values, and a strong national defense. It funds timely research on key policy issues; funds effective marketing of its findings to primary audiences; and advocates conservative policies. Members believe in what they hold are the principles and ideas of the Founding, that such principles are worth conserving and renewing. As policy entrepreneurs, they promote what they believe are the most effective solutions consistent with "Founding" ideas and principles.

They back primary candidates (to date only in Republican Party politics, often to challenge "establishment Republicans"), lobby the Congress, and influence key congressional staff members and policy makers in the executive branch, national news media, and academic and policy communities. Their staff, with years of experience in business, in government, in communications, and on Capitol Hill, lobby effective communication of rigorously conservative policy research and policy proposals to the Congress, the Executive Branch, and the American public.

The Heritage Foundation is governed by a 22-member Board of Trustees, currently chaired by Thomas Saunders.

Jehovah's Witnesses

The Jehovah's Witnesses is a millenarian restorationist Christian denomination with non-trinitarian beliefs distinct from mainstream Christianity. Jehovah's Witnesses claims membership of about 8.5 million members in 240 lands and just over 20 million attendance at their annual memorials of Christ's death. They meet in roughly 120,000 congregations and have held more than 10 million home Bible courses.

Their headquarters are in Warwick, New York, and their governing body establishes all doctrines based on their reading and interpretation of the Bible and their own translation, the *New World Translation of the Holy Scriptures*. As a millenarian movement, they believe the destruction of the world at Armageddon is imminent and that the establishment of God's kingdom over earth is the only solution for the problems that humanity faces. It was begun in the 1870s by Charles Taze Russell, who formed the Zion's Watch Tower Tract Society, and was changed organizationally and doctrinally under the leadership of Joseph Franklin Rutherford, under whom they adopted the name Jehovah's Witnesses in 1931.

They are noted for their aggressive door-to-door preaching, distributing literature (the *Watchtower* and *Awake*), and for refusing military service and blood transfusions. They consider secular society corrupt and under the influence of Satan and limit their social interaction with non-Witnesses. Similar to the Old Order Amish, they use congregational disciplinary action including "disfellowshipping," their term for formal expulsion and shunning. Their conscientious objection to military service and their refusal to salute the flag has engendered the most conflict of Jehovah's Witnesses with governments, mostly at the local or state levels. In 1917, the Watch Tower Society's legal representative, Joseph Rutherford, was elected Jehovah's Witnesses president.

They have been involved in numerous Supreme Court cases challenging state and local laws on the basis of the Establishment Clause and the Free Exercise Clause. Even in cases they lost, their legal challenges have helped shape jurisprudence with respect to the First Amendment and freedom of religion matters and free speech matters.

Moral Majority

The Moral Majority was a prominent American political organization of the Christian right and the Republican Party begun in 1976 and formally founded by Baptist minister Jerry Falwell and his associates in June 1979. It was dissolved in the late 1980s. It played a key role in the development of the Christian right political movement and especially in Republican presidential politics throughout the 1980s (Allitt 2008; Liebman and Wuthnow 1983; Martin 1996; Utter and True 2004; Wilcox 1992). The name was coined by cofounder Paul Weyrich. It was a predominately Southern-oriented organization of the Christian right that grew to 18 chapters by 1980. Headquartered in Lynchburg, Virginia, where Falwell was the presiding minister of the nation's largest Baptist church, its advisory board became the primary leadership of the Moral Majority. It was made up of conservative political action committees, and they believed the Christian conception of moral law represented the opinion of the majority of Americans. At its height, it claimed four million members with over two million donors. In 1985, it was incorporated into the Liberty Federation. Jerry Falwell resigned as its formal head in 1987. It effectively dissolved in 1989. At its height, it sought to mobilize conservative Americans to become politically active on "moral" issues. It developed direct-mail campaigns, telephone hotlines, rallies, and religious television broadcasts. Its major issues included promotion of traditional vision of family life; opposition to media that it claimed promoted an anti-family agenda; opposition to the Equal Rights Amendment and strategic arms limitation talks; opposition to state recognition or acceptance of homosexual acts; prohibition of abortion with no exceptions; support for Christian prayers in public schools; and marketing to Jews and other non-Christians for conversion to conservative Christianity.

It was comprised of four distinct organizations: Moral Majority, Inc., its lobbying division; Moral Majority Foundation, its educational component; Moral Majority Legal Defense Fund, its legal instrument, used primarily to challenge the ACLU and secular humanists in court; and Moral Majority Political Action Committee, its arm to support the political candidacy of persons who supported the Moral Majority's values. It was an early and strong supporter of Ronald Reagan, who sought input from its leadership and who appointed its first executive director as his campaign's religious advisor. The last presidential election in which the Moral Majority was an active organization was in 1988. Fellow evangelist Reverend Pat Robertson sought the endorsement of the Moral Majority, but it in fact endorsed George H. W. Bush instead, highlighting the deep rivalry between Falwell and Robertson as televangelists and the fundamentalist tradition of Falwell versus the charismatic tradition of Pat Robertson (Wilcox 1992). Falwell disbanded the organization in 1989. In 2004, he revived the Moral Majority name for a new organization, the Moral Majority Coalition. Jerry Falwell died on May 15, 2007.

Seventh-day Adventists

The Seventh-day Adventists is a Protestant Christian denomination founded in 1863 in Battle Creek, Michigan, by Joseph Bates, James and Ellen White, and John Nevins Andrews. It is a branch of the Millerite movement. It claims just more than 20 million members in 81,500 churches and 70,000 companies organized into 13 world divisions from 200 countries. It runs 175 hospitals and 136 nursing homes and a humanitarian aid organization, the Adventist Development and Relief Agency. It runs more than 5,000 primary schools and 2,000 secondary schools. It proudly proclaims itself as a denomination "sola scriptura"—believing that the Bible is the only standard of faith and practice for Christians. It espouses 28 fundamental beliefs organized into 6 categories, adopted at its General Conference in 1980, with an 11th belief added in 2005. It is distinguished by its observance of Saturday as the Sabbath and by its belief in the imminent Second Coming of Jesus Christ (His advent). It grew out of the Millerite movement and was formally organized in 1863. It is also known for its emphasis on diet and health, its "holistic" understanding of the person, promotion of religious liberty, and conservative principles and lifestyle.

The Seventh-day Adventists is the largest of several Adventist groups emerging from the Millerite movement in upstate New York in the 1840s, a phase of the Second Great Awakening. As the early Adventist movement coalesced in its beliefs, the question of the biblical day of rest and worship arose in the movement. Joseph Bates was the foremost advocate that Sabbath keeping should be stressed and should be the biblical day of rest—Saturday, rather than Sunday. It was formally established as a church in Battle Creek, Michigan, in 1863, and moved to Takoma Park, Maryland, until 1989, then to its current location in Silver Spring, Maryland.

By the 1870s, it turned to missionary work and the holding of revivals, and it had grown rapidly by 1900. It supports 2 colleges, a medical school, a dozen academies, 27 hospitals, and 13 publishing houses. It espouses Trinitarian Protestant theology with a premillennial and Arminian emphasis. Seventh-day Adventists are considered evangelical and believe in baptism by full immersion and in creation having taken place in six literal (24-hour) days. The modern Creationist movement was started by Adventist George McCready Price, inspired by a vision of Ellen White. Aspects of its beliefs as distinctive doctrines are as follows: the Law of God is "embedded in the Ten Commandments," which bind Christians today; that the Sabbath should be observed on the seventh day of the week, from Friday sunset to Saturday sunset; that Jesus Christ will return to earth after a time of trouble and that the Second Coming will be followed by a millennial reign of the saints in heaven; that humans are an indivisible unity of body, mind, and spirit; that humans do not possess an immortal soul and that there is no consciousness after death (referred to as "soul sleep"); and that the wicked will not suffer eternal torment in hell but instead will be permanently destroyed. They believe in the Great Controversy—the struggle between Jesus Christ and Satan and that evil began in heaven when an angelic being (Lucifer) rebelled against the Law of God.

Seventh-day Adventist Church has been involved in a number of Supreme Court cases involving the Establishment and Free Exercise Clauses.

People

Many hundreds of people are involved in major ways in the politics of religious freedom in America. Space constraints limit discussion in this chapter to 21, organized into governmental actors (15) and nongovernmental people (6), each briefly profiled here. All such actors in the politics of religious freedom in America can be viewed as "stakeholders"—that is, persons with an interest or concern in something, especially in a business or political organization

Warren Burger (1907–1995)

Warren Burger was the 15th chief justice of the U.S. Supreme Court and the longest serving chief justice of the 20th century (1969–1986). He was appointed by President Richard Nixon. During his term as chief justice, 21 cases involving religious freedom questions were ruled on, and Burger wrote the majority opinion on 10 of them and assigned the justice who wrote the majority opinion for the other 11. He strove for achieving comfortable margins or consensus on the bench, and during his tenure as chief justice, only 9 of those 21 cases were decided 5–4. He disappointed President Nixon, who expected him to reverse the decisions of the Court under Chief Justice Earl Warren. Burger voted with the majority, for example, in the 1973 decision *Roe v. Wade*, which established women's constitutional right to have abortions.

Warren Burger was born in St. Paul, Minnesota, in 1907. He attended the University of Minnesota and the St. Paul College of Law, earning his JD magna cum laude in 1931. He married Elvera Stormberg, a fellow UMN student, and they had two children, a boy and a girl.

Warren Burger was an early and effective supporter of Dwight David Eisenhower for president, and upon his election as president, in 1952, Eisenhower appointed Burger as assistant attorney general, Civil Rights Division, of the DOJ. Burger was appointed to the U.S. Court of Appeals for the District of Columbia by President Dwight D. Eisenhower, in 1965, and served there until his appointment to the Supreme Court in 1969. He was conservative, and advocated the literal, strict-constructionist reading of the Constitution; the Court under his leadership delivered many conservative decisions, but a few liberal decisions as well, on abortion, capital punishment, religious establishment, and school desegregation.

Notably, Chief Justice Burger led the Court to a 9–0 decision in *United States v. Nixon* (1974). He was not a popular chief justice among his colleagues, as described in the thinly disguised John Grisham legal thriller novel *The Brethren* (2000).

Burger retired in 1986, and in 1988 received the prestigious Presidential Medal of Freedom. He died of a heart attack on June 25, 1995, at the age of 86.

George W. Bush (1946–)

George W. Bush served as the nation's 43rd president (2001–2009). He was transformed into a wartime president in the aftermath of the terrorist attacks on September 11, 2001. The attacks put on hold some of his domestic agenda, in which he had promised to promote "compassionate conservatism." One of the key domestic policies of his campaign promises was his establishment by Executive Order in January 2001 of the OFBCI. The initiative sought to strengthen faith-based community organizations and expand their capacity to provide federally funded social services. The ACLU was strongly critical of the OFBCI, asserting that it violated the Establishment Clause by using tax money to fund religion. The White House formulated certain restrictions on the use of such funds to avoid violations of the Establishment Clause.

President Bush was born in New Haven, Connecticut, in 1946, while his father was attending Yale University after service in World War II. The family moved to Texas, where George H. W. Bush entered the oil business. George W. Bush graduated from Yale and received a business degree from Harvard, before returning to Texas, where he, too, entered into the oil business. He married Laura Welch, a teacher and librarian, and they had twin daughters. Where George H. W. Bush served in World War II and was a decorated veteran, George W. Bush was able to avoid serving in the Vietnam War by joining the Texas National Guard as a pilot.

When George W. Bush became president, it was only the second time in American history that a president's son went on to the office. (Previously, John Quincy Adams was the sixth president, in 1824, the son of John Adams, the second president.) George W. Bush won the office in 2000, in which he lost the popular vote to Vice President Al Gore but was awarded the contested Electoral College votes of Florida by the Supreme Court in a 5–4 ruling along strictly partisan lines (*Bush v. Gore*, 531 U.S. 98, 2000).

President Bush's impact on freedom of religion issues was also significant by several post–September 11 actions. In 2001, he pushed for and Congress passed the USA PATRIOT Act of October 26, 2001. The act gave the federal government sweeping powers to combat terrorism, including "enhanced interrogation," that critics contend were used against Muslims. Even more sweeping was the Homeland Security Act of 2002. As discussed earlier, the DHS has been embroiled in many actions and policies that critics contend involve racial and ethnic profiling against Muslim Americans and the current controversial travel bans against immigrants and refugees from Muslim countries. Finally, President Bush has also indirectly impacted freedom of religion through his appointment, in 2005, of John Roberts as chief justice of the Supreme Court.

Jimmy Carter (1924–)

President Jimmy Carter served as the 39th president of the United States from 1977 to 1981. He is one of only four presidents awarded the Nobel Peace Prize (in 2002) in recognition of his tireless efforts to end international conflicts, to advance democracy and human rights, and to promote economic and social development.

He was born in Plains, Georgia, in 1924. He managed a family peanut farm, became involved in politics, and was a devout Baptist—a lifetime Sunday school teacher—and is perhaps the most notably and openly religious of all the presidents, certainly of any of the modern presidents. He graduated from the Naval Academy in 1946. He married Rosalynn Smith, and they have three sons and a daughter. After serving seven years as a naval officer, in 1970, Carter was elected governor of Georgia, emphasizing ecology, efficiency in government, and the removal of racial barriers. Before entering electoral politics, he practiced community service as a member of Lions Clubs International, rising to the rank of district governor.

He announced his candidacy for the presidency in December 1974 (for the 1976 election), a decided dark horse candidate who nonetheless went on to secure the Democratic Party's nomination. Jimmy Carter selected Senator Walter Mondale (D-MN) as his running mate. They defeated Republican president Gerald Ford, winning 297 Electoral College votes to Ford's 241. Carter won the electoral support of the evangelicals before that movement became firmly conservative Republican in its presidential politics.

Carter established the Department of Education (which was subsequently involved in several Supreme Court cases challenged on First Amendment freedom of religion or

Establishment Clause grounds), bolstered the Social Security System, and appointed a record number of women, blacks, and Hispanics to federal government jobs.

In 1977, he created the Department of Energy. The Department of Education and the Department of Energy have both resulted in policy implementation that have been challenged in the courts for conflict with Native American Indian religious rights and with the evangelical Christian right's campaigns over prayers in school and religious holiday practices, in cases such as *McDaniel v. Paty* (1978) and *Committee for Public Education and Religious Liberty v. Regan* (1980).

Ted Cruz (1970–)

Potentially any member of Congress can have an impact on freedom of religion issues through the legislation they sponsor. Space limitations here are such that Senator Ted Cruz is being profiled to exemplify the role that senators can play in the issue, in part because Senator Cruz is an avowed advocate of the religious right and Senate champion of their views and positions.

Senator Cruz, in private practice for five years, led the large firm's Supreme Court and National Appellate Litigation practice and authored more than 80 U.S. Supreme Court briefs and argued 43 oral arguments, nine of which were before the Supreme Court. As solicitor general of Texas (2003–2008), appointed by then attorney general of Texas Greg Abbott, he was the state's youngest and first Hispanic solicitor general. He successfully defended U.S. sovereignty against the United Nations in *Medellin v. Texas*, the Second Amendment right to keep and bear arms, the constitutionality of the Texas Ten Commandments monument, the constitutionality of the words "under God" in the Pledge of Allegiance, the constitutionality of Texas's Sexually Violent Predator Civil Commitment law, and the Texas congressional redistricting plan. He drafted the amicus curiae brief for *District of Columbia v. Heller*, winning 5–4; the *Van Orden v. Perry* (2005) case; and *Elk Grove Unified School District v. Newdow* (2004).

Ted Cruz was born in 1970, in Calgary, Canada, of Cuban descent. He married Heidi Cruz, née Nelson, in 2001 and they have two daughters. Ted earned a BA from Princeton University, from which he graduated cum laude, and a JD from Harvard University, in 1995, graduating magna cum laude, having served as editor of the *Harvard Law Review*. He clerked for Chief Justice William Rehnquist, where he worked on matters relating to the National Rifle Association and helped prepare testimony for the impeachment proceedings against President William Clinton.

Ted Cruz was elected the 34th senator from Texas, in 2012. In 2012, he served as vice chair of the National Republican Senatorial Committee. In the Senate, he serves on the Committee on the Judiciary and on its Subcommittee on Immigration, Refugees and Border Security. He is notably strongly pro-life and has pushed to defund Planned Parenthood. He opposes same-sex marriage as well as civil unions. With the support of the Alliance Defense Fund and its "Pulpit Freedom Initiative," Senator Cruz has sponsored a bill in the U.S. Senate to repeal the Johnson Amendment (which, as noted earlier, has been significantly diluted by President Donald Trump's Executive Order).

He was a candidate for the presidential nomination of the Republican Party in 2016, being backed by the religious right and several evangelical PACs. He lost to Donald Trump, being the last of Trump's opponents to withdraw from the race.

He is the author of the 2015 book *A Time for Truth: Reigniting the Promise of America* (Harper/Collins).

Ruth Bader Ginsburg (1933–)

Ruth Bader Ginsburg was appointed to the U.S. Supreme Court in August 1993 by President William Jefferson Clinton, filling the seat vacated by Justice Byron White. She is the unquestioned leader of the Court's liberal bloc, regularly joined by Justices Stephen Breyer, Sonia Sotomayor, and Elena Kagan.

Since her appointment to the Court, Justice Ginsburg has participated in 14 decisions on religious freedom cases, 8 of which were 5–4 votes in which she voted with the minority. Throughout her long legal career, she has been notably an advocate against gender discrimination, serving for example, as the first female member of the *Harvard Law Review*. She wrote the dissenting opinion in the *Ledbetter v. Goodyear Tire and Rubber Company* (550 U.S. 618, 2007, 5–4 decision).

In her dissent, she called on Congress to undo the "improper interpretation of the law" and was vindicated when Congress passed and President Obama signed into law, as the very first act he signed, the Lilly Ledbetter Fair Pay Act of 2009.

Justice Ginsburg earned her BS from Cornell, attended Harvard Law, and received her LLB from Columbia Law School, where she graduated first in her class. She clerked for Edmund Palmieri, judge of the U.S. District Court for the Southern District of New York, 1959–1961. From 1961 to 1963, Ginsburg was a research associate and then associate director of the Columbia Law School Project on International Procedure, living abroad in Sweden to do research for her book on Swedish civil procedure. In 1963, she became a professor at Rutgers University Law School. In 1972, she began teaching at Columbia Law, the first female to earn tenure there. She directed the Women's Rights Project for the ACLU, successfully arguing six landmark cases before the U.S. Supreme Court. In 1977–1978, she was a fellow at the Center for Advanced Study in the Behavioral Sciences at Stanford University. In 1980, President Jimmy Carter appointed Justice Ginsburg to the U.S. Court of Appeals for the District of Columbia, and she served on the court until President Clinton appointed her to the Supreme Court in 1993.

Ruth Bader was born in Brooklyn, New York, in 1933. She married Martin Ginsburg in 1954, and they have two children, a daughter and a son. He battled cancer in 1956, during her first year of law school. He passed away in 2010. Although she disagreed with Justice Scalia on virtually every case, they were friends in their personal lives, sharing a love for the opera. They did vote together on four religious freedom decisions: *Church of the Lukumi Babalu v. City of Hialeah* (1993), *Elk Grove v. Newdow* (2004), *Gonzales v. U.D.V.* (2006), *Hosanna-Tabor v. E.E.O.C.* (2012).

Alberto Gonzales (1955–)

Alberto Gonzales served as the 80th attorney general of the United States, the first Hispanic appointed to the office, serving from 2005 to 2007. He was involved in four U.S. Supreme Court cases, two of which he won, two of which he lost. *Gonzales v. Raich* (545 U.S. 1, 2005), involved the federal government's power to regulate, in this case to ban, the use of medical marijuana. The Court ruled 6–3 for the attorney general. In *Gonzales v. Oregon et al.* (546 U.S. 243, 2006), the Court decided 6–3 against the attorney general in a case where the Court ruled the federal government could not prohibit doctors from prescribing drugs for use in physician-assisted suicide. In *Gonzales v. O Centro Espirita Beneficente Uniao do Vegetal* (546 U.S. 418, 2006), the Court decided 8–0 against the attorney general, ruling the government failed to meet its burden under the Religious Freedom Restoration Act (1993) and the Controlled Substances Act (1970), to ban the importation and use of hoasca, a hallucinogenic tea, in religious ceremonies. In *Gonzales v. Carhart* (550 U.S. 124, 2007), the Court ruled 5–4 in favor of the government upholding the partial-birth abortion ban.

Alberto Gonzales was born in 1955. He was educated at the Air Force Academy and Rice University (a BA degree in 1979) and earned his JD from Harvard Law School in 1982. He practiced corporate law in Texas and taught law as an adjunct professor at the University of Houston Law Center. He served as Texas's 100th secretary of state, from 1997 to 1999. He served as general counsel to then Texas governor George W. Bush and as a justice of the Supreme Court of Texas in 1999. President

Bush appointed him White House counsel in 2001. In 2005, President Bush appointed him U.S. attorney general. He was at the time the first attorney general of Hispanic heritage and became the highest-ranked Hispanic in the federal government at the time.

By 2007, Gonzales faced scrutiny by the Senate Judiciary Committee over his firing of several U.S. attorneys on purely political grounds and for his defense of President Bush's domestic eavesdropping program. In August 2007, he was forced to resign as attorney general. Alberto and his wife Rebecca have three sons.

Thomas Jefferson (1743–1826)

Thomas Jefferson was one of the Founding Fathers, the principal author of the Declaration of Independence, the nation's first secretary of state (1789–1794), second vice president (1797–1801), and third president (1801–1809). He was an early advocate of the total separation of church and state and author of the Virginia Statute for Religious Liberty. He was Virginia's representative to the Second Continental Congress in 1775.

Thomas Jefferson was born in Virginia in 1743 and died there (at Monticello) on July 4, 1826. He married Martha Jefferson, née Wayles, with whom he had three daughters. He attended William and Mary College and as draftsman of the Declaration of Independence was known as the "Apostle of Liberty."

As president, he was responsible for the Louisiana Purchase (1803, from France), which essentially doubled the territory of the United States and added a significant population of Catholics (from the Spanish and the French colonies) to the American population at a time when Catholics were still highly suspected as to their loyalty and often discriminated against by the nation's Protestant majority.

In his writings, he popularized the language and the principle of the "wall of separation" between church and state (Butler 2006; Dreisbach 2002; Jefferson 1977; Lambert 2003).

Lyndon B. Johnson (1908–1973)

Lyndon B. Johnson, then vice president, became the 36th president on November 22, 1963, upon the assassination of President John F. Kennedy. His impact on religious freedom issues was twofold. In 1954, then U.S. senator from Texas and Senate majority leader Lyndon Johnson sponsored what came to be known as the "Johnson Amendment." It made significant changes to the IRS tax code. The Amendment essentially prohibited tax-exempt religious organizations from either endorsing or opposing candidates for political office. The Amendment affected churches and other 501(c) tax-exempt organizations. Eventually, the religious right launched a vigorous and concerted attempt to repeal the Johnson Amendment, to date without success. Critics of the Amendment, however, note that the IRS has been extraordinarily lax in the enforcement of the ban. President Donald Trump signed an Executive Order that greatly limited the IRS in using the prohibition.

As president, Johnson appointed Abe Fortas as associate justice of the Supreme Court. Fortas served from 1965 to 1969. Justice Fortas wrote the majority opinion in *Epperson v. Arkansas* (393 U.S. 97, 1968), a 7–2 ruling that banned creationism from public school science curricula (see Table 5.3).

Johnson was born in 1908, in Texas, not far from Johnson City, which his family founded. He worked his way through Southwest Texas State Teachers College and taught students of Mexican descent. In 1934, he married Claudia "Lady Bird" Taylor. In 1937, he was elected to the U.S. House of Representatives. With the outbreak of World War II, Johnson left the Congress to serve in the U.S. Navy. He was a Navy lieutenant commander in the South Pacific and the recipient of a Silver Star. After the war, Johnson was elected to the U.S. Senate, in 1948.

In 1960, he was elected vice president, and became president when Kennedy was assassinated. He ran for the office and won by a landslide in 1964, defeating Republican nominee

Senator Barry Goldwater (R-AZ), with 61 percent of the popular vote. As elected president who could claim a mandate, Johnson proposed a package of bills he called "The Great Society" and strove to achieve an FDR-like first 100 days. Johnson urged passage of a new civil rights bill (the Civil Rights Act of 1965), a tax cut, and enactment of the 1965 Immigration Act, a Voting Rights Act, and the 1965 Medicare Amendment to the Social Security Act, and finally, the Fair Housing Act of 1968 (82 Stat. 73), which dealt with racial discrimination in housing.

As the Vietnam war heated up, President Johnson approved a massive escalation of military forces. The subsequent intense political controversy over the war led Johnson to withdraw as a candidate for reelection. He died suddenly of a heart attack on January 22, 1973.

Anthony Kennedy (1936–)

Associate Justice Anthony M. Kennedy was appointed to the Supreme Court by President Ronald Reagan, in 1988. In many respects, Justice Kennedy has replaced Justice O'Connor in the role as the swing voter on the Court between the conservative and liberal wings. He participated in 21 cases involving religious freedom issues. He wrote the majority opinion in five of those cases: *Lee v. Weisman* (1992), *Church of the Lukumi Babalu v. City of Hialeah* (1993), *Rosenberger v. W.VA.* (1995), *Arizona Christian School v. Winn* (2011), and *Town of Greece v. Galloway* (2014). His was the swing vote in four cases: *Zobrest v. Catalina Foothills* (1993), *Rosenberger v. U.Va.* (1995), *Arizona Christian School v. Winn* (2011), and *Town of Greece v. Galloway* (2014).

Kennedy graduated with honors at Stanford University and in his senior year studied at the London School of Economics. He earned his LLB from Harvard Law School. He went into private practice in California in 1961–1975, during which time he worked as a lobbyist for the Republican Party of California with Ed Meese, through whom he met then governor Ronald

Reagan. He taught constitutional law at the McGeorge School of Law, University of the Pacific. Kennedy served on the board of the Federal Judicial Center, 1987–1988, and on two committees of the Judicial Conference of the United States, including chairing the Committee on Pacific Territories from 1982 to 1990. Through Reagan, he was recommended to President Gerald Ford and was appointed to the U.S. Court of Appeals for the Ninth Circuit in 1975, making him at the time the youngest federal appellate judge. After President Reagan's failed attempt to name Robert H. Bork to the Supreme Court, President Ronald Reagan nominated Anthony Kennedy as associate justice of the Supreme Court, and he was unanimously confirmed by the Senate. Kennedy was sworn in on February 18, 1988, filling the seat of Justice Lewis Powell, Jr. On the Court, he soon established himself as a proponent of individual rights. He cowrote the majority opinion in *Planned Parenthood of Southeastern Pennsylvania v. Casey*, which upheld the right to abortion under *Roe v. Wade*.

He wrote the majority opinion in *Romer v. Evans*, which invalidated a provision of the Colorado Constitution denying homosexuals the right to bring local discrimination claims. In *Lawrence v. Texas* (2003), he wrote the majority opinion declaring unconstitutional a Texas law that criminalized sodomy between two consenting adults of the same sex. He soon became known as the swing vote between the liberal and conservative camps of the other eight justices. He voted to guarantee the right to same-sex marriage and wrote the majority opinion in the 5–4 landmark decision in *Obergefell v. Hodges* (2015), despite his being a devout Roman Catholic. He voted to uphold the Affordable Care Act, in 2010, in the Court's 6–3 ruling in the case.

Kennedy was born in 1936, in Sacramento, California. As a young man, he served as a page in the California State Senate. From 1961 to 1962, he served in the California Army National Guard. He married Mary Davis in 1963, and they have two sons and a daughter.

Barack Obama (1961–)

Barack H. Obama served as the 44th president of the United States. He was born in Honolulu, Hawaii, in 1961. He is the first African American to serve as president. He was educated at Occidental College, at Columbia University (BA), and at Harvard University Law School (JD) and was the first African American editor of the prestigious *Harvard Law Review.* His father was from Kenya and his mother from Kansas, and he was raised by his maternal grandparents.

A devout Christian, Barack Obama attended the Trinity United Church of Christ. During his presidency, he continued the OFBCI begun by President Bush, renaming it the White House Office of Faith-Based and Neighborhood Partnerships and appointing within it an Advisory Council composed of religious and secular leaders and scholars.

In terms of impact on religious freedom, Obama notably appointed two associate justices of the U.S. Supreme Court: Sonia Sotomayor (2009) and Elena Kagan (2010). He emphasized LGBT rights, same-sex marriage, and ended the Defense of Marriage Act, all of which drew harsh criticism and opposition from the religious right.

Sandra Day O'Connor (1930–)

Sandra Day O'Connor is notable as the first woman appointed to the U.S. Supreme Court. Throughout her judicial career, she was considered to be a moderate conservative and on the Supreme Court (1981–2006) often provided the swing vote between the conservative and progressive (liberal) blocs. She participated on 33 decisions dealing with religious freedom cases. She wrote the majority opinion in two cases: *Lyng v. Indiana County* (1988) and *Westside v. Mergens* (1990). Importantly, Justice O'Connor provided the swing vote on six cases: *Lee v. Weisman* (1992), *Rosenberger v. University of Virginia* (1995), *Mitchell v. Helms* (2000), *Zelman v. Simmons-Harris* (2002), *McCreary County v. ACLU* (2005), and *Van Orden v.*

Perry (2005). She also provided the swing vote in a case upholding the abortion rights ruling in *Roe v. Wade* (1973).

Sandra (née Day) O'Connor was born in El Paso, Texas, in 1930. She married John Jay O'Connor III in 1952, and they have three sons. O'Connor received her BA and LLB from Stanford University.

She was elected to two terms in the Arizona State Senate. She served as deputy county attorney of San Mateo County, California, from 1952 to 1953, and as a civilian attorney for Quartermaster Market Center, Frankfurt, Germany from 1954 to 1957. From 1958 to 1960, she was in private practice in Maryvale, Arizona. O'Connor served as the assistant attorney general of Arizona (1965–1969) and was appointed to the Arizona State Senate in 1959, then reelected to two terms. In 1975, O'Connor was elected judge of the Maricopa County Superior Court in 1975 and served in that capacity until 1979, when she was appointed to the Arizona Court of Appeals. President Ronald Reagan appointed her as associate justice of the Supreme Court in 1981, where she served for 24 years until she retired in January 2006. Since her retirement from the Supreme Court, Justice O'Connor has continued her judicial service by hearing cases in the U.S. Courts of Appeals. In 2009, President Obama awarded her with the nation's highest civilian honor, the Presidential Medal of Freedom.

William Rehnquist (1924–2005)

William Rehnquist served on the U.S. Supreme Court for 33 years, as associate justice, 1972–1986, and as chief justice, 1986–2005. During his years as associate justice, he often wrote dissenting opinions, sometimes solo dissents. As chief justice, he often wrote the majority opinion and impacted the Court by managing its docket. On religious freedom, he wrote: "just because an action is religiously motivated, does not make it consequence-free for society, and should not make it consequence-free under society's laws." A consistently conservative voice on the Court, he supported the death penalty and opposed gay rights. In 1973, he opposed the decision in *Roe v. Wade.*

As chief justice, William Rehnquist managed the Court over 18 decisions involving freedom of religion cases. He wrote the majority opinion in four decisions that were decided by 5–4 votes: *Stone v. Graham* (1980), *Bowen v. Kendrick* (1988), *Zobrest v. Catalina Foothills School District* (1993), and *Zellman v. Simmons-Harris* (2002).

As associate justice, in 1985, Rehnquist dissented in *Wallace v. Jeffree*, contending that the Founders' intent to erect a "wall of separation" between church and state was misguided. He wrote several majority opinions in close (5–4) religious freedom cases: *Valley Forges and People Christian Colleges v. Americans United for Separation of Church and State* (1982), *Mueller v. Allen* (1983). He was a "swing" vote in *Committee for Public Education and Religious Liberty v. Nyquist* (1971) and in *Meek v. Pittenger* (1975).

William Rehnquist was born in Milwaukee, Wisconsin, in 1924. He married Natalie Cornell in 1953. He graduated from Harvard University (BA and MA in political science) and earned his JD from Stanford Law School, graduating in the same law class as Sandra Day O'Connor. He served in the U.S. Army Air Forces during World War II.

As chief justice, he presided over the impeachment trial (in the U.S. Senate) of President Bill Clinton and the *Bush v. Gore* election decision. He died in September 2005 of thyroid cancer.

John Roberts (1955–)

John Roberts, Jr., was appointed chief justice of the United States by President George W. Bush in 2005. In the six religious freedom cases where he presided as chief justice, four were decided 5–4; in two, he wrote the majority opinions, in *Gonzales v. U.D.V.* (8–0, 2006) and in *Hosanna-Tabor v. E.E.O.C.* (9–0, 2012).

Chief Justice Roberts attended Harvard College (AB in 1976) and Harvard Law School (JD, 1979). He was a law clerk for Associate Justice William Rehnquist in 1980. He was special assistant to the attorney general, DOJ, from 1981 to 1982, and served as associate counsel to President Ronald Reagan, White House Counsel's Office, from 1982 to 1986. He was principal deputy solicitor general, DOJ, from 1989 to 1993. He practiced law in Washington, D.C. He served on the U.S. Court of Appeals, 2003, appointed by President George W. Bush, before being appointed to the U.S. Supreme Court by President Bush and confirmed as chief justice in 2005.

John Roberts was born in Buffalo, New York, in 1955. His family moved to Long Beach, Indiana. He attended Notre Dame Elementary School there and La Lumiere boarding school in La Porte, Indiana, where he excelled as a wrestler, becoming regional champion while there. He married Jane Sullivan in 1996, and they have two children, a boy and a girl.

As chief justice, John Roberts ruled on two landmark legislative cases: reaffirming the legality of the Affordable Care Act by siding with the liberal wing of the Supreme Court, along with the swing vote of Associate Justice Anthony Kennedy. He voted his conservative views in the minority on the issue of same-sex marriage, which decision made same-sex marriage legal in all 50 states. It has been roundly opposed by the religious right but is supported by a majority of Americans in post-decision public opinion polls.

Antonin Scalia (1936–2016)

Associate Justice Antonin Scalia was unquestionably the leading voice of the conservative bloc on the Supreme Court. He participated in 24 decisions on religious freedom cases. He wrote the majority opinion in several: *Employment Division v. Smith* (1990), *R.A.V. v. City of St. Paul* (1992), *Capitol Square v. Pinette* (1995). He was the forceful articulator of the judicial principle of "original interpretation" or "strict construction" and argued forcefully against what he labeled judicial activism, yet he was an activist on several decisions in which his conservative philosophy outweighed judicial precedent, Court tradition, or any language in the Constitution and cases in which the justices voted 5–4 along political party lines: *Gore v. Bush, 531 U.S. 98* (2000), *Citizens United v. F.E.C., 558 U.S. 310* (2010).

Antonin Scalia was born in New Jersey in 1936. He married Maureen McCarthy, with whom he had nine children. He was a lifelong devout Roman Catholic. He earned his AB from Georgetown University and the University of Fribourg, Switzerland, and his LLB from Harvard Law School. Justice Scalia served as a Sheldon fellow of Harvard University, 1960–1961. Upon graduating from Harvard Law, he went into private practice in Cleveland, Ohio, for several years, before becoming a professor of law at the University of Virginia, 1967–1971. He went on to teach law as a professor of law at the University of Chicago, 1977–1982, and as a visiting professor of law at Georgetown University and Stanford University. Justice Scalia was chair of the American Bar Association's Section on Administrative Law (1981–1982) and the Conference Section Chair (1982–1983). In the federal government, Justice Scalia was general counsel of the Office of Telecommunications Policy (1971–1972), chair of the Administrative Conference of the United States (1972–1974), and assistant attorney general for the Office of Legal Counsel (1974–1977). In 1982, President Ronald Reagan appointed Scalia judge of the U.S. Court of Appeals for the District of Columbia Circuit (the Appeals Court from which the most justices have moved up to the Supreme Court). In 1986, President Reagan appointed him associate justice of the Supreme Court and he took his seat in September 1986.

Justice Antonin Scalia died suddenly of a heart attack on February 13, 2016.

Donald Trump (1946–)

Donald J. Trump was elected the 45th president of the United States in 2016 and sworn in to the office in January 2017. It is early in his presidency to assess his impact on freedom of religion issues, but early actions, within his first 100 days, indicate it may be significant in tilting policy toward the conservative right. He nominated a hard-right conservative justice, Neil Gorsuch, to the Supreme Court to fill the seat vacated by the untimely death of Antonin Scalia; Gorsuch will be an associate justice hearing several religious freedom cases currently on the Court's docket. Significantly, also, Trump has issued two Executive Orders attempting to enforce a Muslim ban, both of which have been ruled unconstitutional in two federal district courts, and the ban is likely to be appealed to the U.S. Supreme Court. President Trump issued Executive Orders to relax the IRS restrictions on the political activities of tax-exempt religious organizations, greatly modifying the Johnson Amendment.

Donald Trump was born in New York City in 1946, the son of a multimillionaire real estate tycoon. He graduated from the New York Military Academy, attended Fordham University, and the Wharton School of the University of Pennsylvania. He has been married three times and has five children from those unions. He has built a real estate empire, claiming billionaire status, and became a television celebrity (*The Apprentice*).

Trump ran a decidedly unorthodox campaign for the presidency and surprised most analysts by winning the Electoral College vote despite losing the popular vote to Secretary Hillary Clinton (D-NY) by nearly three million votes. He selected Indiana Republican governor Mike Pence as his running mate, further appealing to the conservative religious right.

Nongovernmental Stakeholders

Any one of dozens of nongovernmental activists on the issue of freedom of religion in American politics could be profiled. Space considerations limit the profiles here to six: two representing the religious right movement and the pro–freedom of expression side of the conflict, two representing atheism and the freedom from religion and upholding the Establishment Clause, and two representing the middle and the think tank and academic perspective on the matter.

James Dobson (1936–)

James Dobson founded Focus on the Family in 1977 and led the organization until 2003; he then led Family Talk, since 2010, a radio talk show broadcast with over 300 stations nationwide. In the 1980s, Dobson was considered to be the conservative social movement leader and the most influential evangelical leader, often considered to be the successor to Jerry Falwell and Pat Robertson.

Dobson is a psychologist with a PhD from Southern California University (1967). In the 1980s, he produced Focus on the Family as a daily radio program broadcast to over 7,000 stations and in a dozen languages, with a claimed audience of 220 million. In the 1980s, it was carried on about 60 television stations daily. He resigned as president and CEO of Focus on the Family in 2003, citing philosophical differences with his successor, Jim Daly. Dobson is a strong proponent of traditional marriage, with the husband as the breadwinner and the wife as homemaker and mother, and recommends women with children remain focused on mothering until any children are 18. He is adamantly opposed to same-sex marriage.

In 1981, he founded the Family Research Council, the political arm of the social conservative movement; he exercised considerable political influence lobbying and in Republican presidential politics. He opposed Senator John McCain in 2008 for not being conservative enough. He supports "intelligent design" and opposes evolution. He was criticized for hijacking the National Day of Prayer. He supports the formal, congressional repeal of the Johnson Amendment.

Dobson is the author or coauthor of 36 books. He married his wife, Shirley, in 1960, and they have raised two children, a girl and a boy.

Madalyn Murray O'Hair (1919–1995)

Once known as the "Pope of Atheism" and called "the most hated woman in America," Madalyn Murray O'Hair was the litigant in the Supreme Court case of *Murray v. Curlett* and its consolidated case *Abington School District v. Schempp* (232 Md 368 and 374 U.S. 203, 1963), in which the Court, in its 8–1 decision, ruled that required Bible reading and recitation of the Lord's Prayer in public schools violated the Establishment Clause of the First Amendment. She became the nation's most famous atheist.

Madalyn Murray O'Hair founded American Atheists in 1963 and remained its leading spokesperson for 30 years, appearing on radio and television and authoring three books, *What on Earth Is an Atheist?* (American Atheist Press, 1969), *Freedom under Seige* (J.P. Tarcher, 1974), and *An Atheist Epic* (Atheist Press, 1989).

She was born in 1919, in Pennsylvania. She died in September 1995, murdered along with her two children. She was married twice: to Richard O'Hair and to John Roths. She earned a BA from Ashland College and a JD from South Texas College of Law. In 2013, the first "atheist monument" was erected and it contained quotes from Benjamin Franklin, Thomas Jefferson, and Madalyn O'Hair.

She disappeared in 1995, in San Antonio, Texas, along with $500,000 in American Atheist funds; a note was found saying she and her two adult children would be away temporarily. For a time, it was suspected that she stole the funds and fled to New Zealand, but, eventually, police arrested David Waters, an ex-convict who worked for the American Atheist organization. He and an accomplice kidnapped Madalyn, John Garth Murray, and Robin Murray O'Hair, forcing her to withdraw the funds and then killing and burying them. He led authorities to their grave site in 2001.

An avowed atheist and champion for the separation of church and state, she was also a notable feminist.

Ron Reagan (1958–)

Ron Reagan is an avowed atheist and public spokesperson for the Freedom from Religion Foundation. In his radio and television ads, Ron Reagan describes himself as "an unabashed atheist, not afraid of burning in hell." He is the son of conservative Republican president Ronald Reagan and Nancy Reagan.

Politically, Ron is registered as an independent and is a radio host on the Air America radio network. He is a frequent political commentator/consultant for MSNBC, including a stint in 2005 as cohost of the talk show *Connected: Coast to Coast with Monica Crowly*. He briefly hosted a late-night television talk show, *The Ron Reagan Show* (2008–2010). He is on the board of the Creative Coalition, a politically active organization founded in 1989 that mobilizes entertainers and artists to advocate for First Amendment rights and causes as a 501(c)(3) nonprofit public charity. He spoke at the 2004 Democratic National Convention and in 2008 endorsed and worked for Barack Obama's presidential bid. In the 2016 presidential primaries, he endorsed Vermont senator Bernie Sanders.

Ron authored a book *My Father at 100: A Memoir* (Penguin/Random House, 2010). In it, he addresses his father's Alzheimer's disease.

Ron was born in 1958 in Los Angeles, California, the son of Ronald Reagan and Nancy Davis Reagan. He declared his atheism to his parents at age 12. He attended Yale University but dropped out to become a ballet dancer, joining the Joffrey Ballet Company.

He married Doria Palmieri, a clinical psychologist, in 1980. She died in 2014 from a neuromuscular disease. They had no children.

The Freedom from Religion Foundation named him to its Honorary Board of distinguished achievers. He is an outspoken opponent of conservative Christian right movement's attempts to repeal the Johnson Amendment and their support of school voucher programs to provide public financial aid to religious-based schools.

Ralph Reed (1961–)

Ralph Reed is the founder and chairman of the Faith and Freedom Coalition, a former advisor to the Bush-Cheney campaigns of 2000 and 2004 and a leading voice of the conservative Christian right movement. He is credited with founding and serving as the CEO of the Christian Coalition in 1989–1997, widely considered one of the most successful public policy lobbying organizations.

The Faith and Freedom Coalition is primarily a fund-raising and political contribution organization supporting conservative Republicans and emphasizing a religious freedom agenda. It claims over one million members. It was founded in 2009 by Ralph Reed, who also established the Faith and Freedom Foundation, a 501(c)(3) organization that promotes political lobbying to enact legislation favorable to the religious right and political activism.

Reed was born in Virginia in 1961. He earned his AB from the University of Georgia (1985) and his PhD from Emory University (1989), majoring in history for both degrees. He started and led the Georgia College Republicans. He married JoAnne Young in 1987, and they have four children.

In the early 1980s, he moved to Washington, D.C., and along with Jack Abramoff and Grover Norquist, formed a "triumvirate" of political activists and became a born-again Christian activist in 1983. He led Students for America, a conservative activist group before founding the Christian Coalition, which organized Pat Robertson supporters. In 1996, the FEC brought enforcement actions against the Coalition for violating federal campaign laws, and Reed resigned as its executive director. In 2005, he became embroiled in the Abramoff Indian Gaming scandal.

Reed ran for the Georgia Republican Party chairmanship in 2001, and he led the party to electoral success in 2002. He ran unsuccessfully for lieutenant governor of Georgia in 2006.

Reed is CEO of Century Strategies, LLC, a public relations and public affairs firm, as well as executive director of the Faith and Freedom Coalition.

Ralph Reed is the author of seven books: three political thriller novels and four nonfiction books: *After the Revolution* (Word Publishing, 1996), *Politically Incorrect: The Emerging Faith Factor in American Politics* (Word Publishing, 1996), *Active Faith: How Christians Are Changing the Face of America* (Free Press, 1996), and *Awakening: How America Can Turn From Moral and Economic Destruction Back to Greatness* (Worthy Publishing, 2014).

Melissa Rogers (Not Known)

Melissa Rogers is a nonresident senior fellow in governance studies at the Brookings Institution and previously served as executive director of the Pew Forum on Religion and Public Life. She served as special assistant to the president, in the White House Office of Faith-Based and Neighborhood Partnerships under President Barack Obama. She also served as the inaugural chair of its Advisory Council.

Melissa Rogers earned her BA from Baylor University and her JD from the University of Pennsylvania Law School. She coauthored a book on religion and law for Baylor University Press, *Freedom and the Supreme Court* (2008).

Rogers directed the Center for Religion and Public Affairs at Wake Forest University Divinity School. She was the executive director of the Pew Forum on Religion and Public Life. She also served as the general counsel of the Baptist Joint Committee for Religious Liberty.

Her area of expertise at the Brookings Institution includes the First Amendment's religion clauses, religion in American public life, and the interplay of religion, policy, and politics. She well exemplifies the activist in religious freedom from the think tank perspective.

John Witte, Jr. (1959–)

John Witte, Jr., is another good example of a freedom of religion stakeholder representing the think tank approach to the issue. He is director of the Center for the Study of Law and Religion at Emory University, the Robert F. Woodruff professor of law, and a McDonald distinguished professor at Emory. His areas of expertise include American legal history, human rights, law and religion, legal history, marriage and family law, and religious liberty. A prolific scholar, he has authored 230 articles, 15 journal symposia, and 30 books.

Witte was born in 1959 in Canada. He earned his BA from Calvin College in 1982 and his JD from Harvard University Law in 1985. He was selected 12 times by Emory Law students as the Most Outstanding Professor. He married Eliza Ellison, a theologian and trained mediator, and they have two daughters.

He has given the McDonald Lecture at Emory University on the topic "Separation of Church and State: There Is No Wall." Among his hundreds of articles of special note to this topic are "The Legal Challenges of Religious Polygamy in the USA," "Lift High the Cross? Religion in Public Spaces," "Sex May Be Free, but Children Come with a Cost," "Keeping the Commandments," and "Can America Still Ban Polygamy?"

Among his 30 books, some recent, published since 2010, are *Christianity and Human Rights: An Introduction* (Cambridge University Press, 2010), *Religion and Human Rights: An Introduction* (Oxford University Press, 2012), *From Sacrament to Contract: Marriage, Religion, and Law in the Western Tradition* (Westminster John Knox Press, 2nd ed., 2012), *No Establishment of Religion: America's Original Contribution to Religious Liberty* (Oxford University Press, 2012), *The Western Case for Monogamy over Polygamy* (Cambridge University Press, 2015), and *Texts and Contexts in Legal History: Essays in Honor of Charles Donahue* (The Robbins Collection, 2016).

References

Allitt, Patrick. 2008. *Religion in America since 1945: A History.* New York: Columbia University Press.

Butler, Jon. 2006. *Religion in Colonial America.* New York: Oxford University Press.

Dreisbach, Daniel. 2002. *Thomas Jefferson and the Wall of Separation of Church and State.* New York: New York University Press.

Jefferson, Thomas. 1977. Merrill Peterson, ed. *The Portable Thomas Jefferson.* New York: Penguin Books.

Lambert, Frank. 2003. *The Founding Fathers and the Place of Religion in America.* Princeton, NJ: Princeton University Press.

Liebman, Robert, and Robert Wuthnow. 1983. *The New Christian Right.* New York: Aldine Publishing.

Martin, William. 1996. *With God on Our Side: The Rise of the Religious Right in America.* New York: Broadway Books.

Utter, Glenn, and James L. True. 2004. *Conservative Christians and Political Participation: A Reference Handbook.* Santa Barbara, CA: ABC-CLIO.

Wilcox, Clyde. 1992. *God's Warriors.* Baltimore, MD: The Johns Hopkins University Press.

Introduction

Public policy related to religious freedom in America is advanced by enactment of laws, presidential actions, and especially Supreme Court cases. This chapter presents a synopsis of critical actions, both legislative and judicial, that collectively set national policy on the matter. In its first section, this chapter presents data on religious freedom in America. This is followed by a documents section that presents excerpts from some key legislative actions, a letter from James Madison on the topic, an excerpt from a state governor's order of extermination of Mormons, excerpts from several landmark Supreme Court decisions, and some federal legislation pertaining to the topic. The documents are presented in chronological order.

Data

In terms of religious affiliations, America is a richly diverse nation—arguably the most religiously diverse country in the world. Table 5.1 presents data on the religious affiliation of the American population as found by self-proclaimed affiliation, in the 2010 census, and in a study of religious affiliation by the Pew Research Center.

A nativity scene is seen through an 8-and-a-half foot tall letter "A," which stands for Atheist or Agnostic, erected by the Wisconsin-based Freedom From Religion Foundation at the annual Christmas market in Chicago's Daley Plaza on December 12, 2013. Members of the group say it's meant to send a message that they believe that religious displays on public property are a violation of the separation of church and state. (AP Photo/Kiichiro Sato)

Table 5.1   Religions in the United States (2010 Census)

Religious Group	Number in 2010	Percentage in 2010
Self-Proclaimed Affiliation (2010 Census)		
Total U.S. population	308,745,538	100.0
Evangelical Protestant	50,013,107	16.2
Mainline Protestant	22,568,258	7.3
Black Protestant	4,877,067	1.6
Catholic	20,800,000	23.0
Mormon	10,600,000	2.9
Jehovah's Witnesses	800,000	0.02
Eastern Orthodox	500,000	0.016
Other Christian	400,000	0.012
Jewish	6,141,325	2.0
Muslim	2,600,000	0.08
Buddhist	2,000,000	0.07
Hindu	400,000	0.01
PEW Religious Landscape Study		
Christian		70.6
Evangelical Protestant		25.4
Mainline Protestant		14.7
Historically Black Protestant		6.5
Catholic		20.8
Mormon		1.6
Orthodox Christian		0.5
Jehovah's Witnesses		0.8
Other Christian		0.4
Non-Christian Faiths		6.9
Jewish		1.9
Muslim		0.9
Buddhist		0.7
Hindu		0.7
Other World Religions		1.5
Unaffiliated (Religious "Nones")		22.8
Atheist		3.1
Agnostic		4.1
Nothing in particular		15.8

Source: Data from 2010 Census and the Pew Research Center, Religious Landscape Study. Retrieved from www.pewforum.org/religious-landscape-study

To help put American religious affiliations in context, Figure 5.1 presents a pie chart detailing the major world religions by percentage their adherents' share of total world population.

Table 5.2 lists the major Supreme Court cases dealing with religious freedom issues. The cases are organized by those dealing with challenges based on the Establishment Clause and then those based on the Freedom of Expression Clause. Within each category, cases are listed by the nature of the problem at issue in the case.

The Equal Employment Opportunity Commission (EEOC) collects statistics on the number of cases filed and resolved alleging religion-based discrimination, under Title VII of the Civil Rights Act (see Table 5.3), which prohibits discrimination based on sex, race, color, national origin, and religion.

Hate crimes are often inspired by religious-related animosity. The Federal Bureau of Investigation publishes annual statistics of hate-crime data. Table 5.4 presents those data for 2015 (the latest year available), identifying the number of incidents, the religion

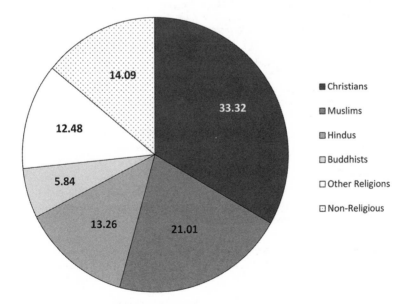

Figure 5.1   World Religions (by Percentage)
Source: CIA World Factbook, 2010.

Table 5.2   Religious Freedom Supreme Court Cases

Establishment Clause Cases

Religions Involved

Anglican, Congregational, Roman Catholic, Evangelical, Church of Jesus Christ of Latter-day Saints

Cases:

1. Aid to Church-Related Schools: *Pierce v. Society of Sisters* (268 U.S. 510, 1925); *Cochran v. Louisiana State Board of Education* (281 U.S. 370, 1930); *Everson v. Board of Education* (330 U.S. 1, 1947); *Abington School District v. Schempp* (374 U.S. 203, 1963); *Board of Education v. Allen* (392 U.S. 236, 1968); *Lemon v. Kurtzman* (403 U.S. 602, 1971); *Tilton v. Richardson* (403 U.S. 672, 1971); *Committee for Public Education and Religious Liberty v. Nyquist* (413 U.S. 756, 1971); *Meek v. Pittenger* (421 U.S. 349, 1975); *Roemer v. Board of Public Works of Maryland* (426 U.S. 736, 1976); *Wolman v. Walter* (433 U.S. 229, 1977); *Committee for Public Education and Religious Liberty v. Regan* (413 U.S. 473, 1980); *Mueller v. Allen* (463 U.S. 388, 1983); *Aguilar v. Felton* (473 U.S. 402, 1985); *Grand Rapids School District v. Ball* (473 U.S. 373, 1985); *Zobrest v. Catalina Foothills School District* (509 U.S. 1, 1993); *Zelman v. Simmons-Harris* (536 U.S. 639, 2002); *Arizona Christian School Tuition Organization v. Winn* (563 U.S. 125, 2011).

2. Religion in Public Education: *McCullum v. Board of Education* (330 U.S. 203, 1948); *Zorach v. Clauson* (343 U.S. 306, 1952); *Engel v. Vitale* (370 U.S. 421, 1962); *Abington School District v. Schempp* (374 U.S. 203, 1963); *Epperson v. Arkansas* (393 U.S. 97, 1968); *Stone v. Graham* (449 U.S. 39, 1980); *Rosenberger v. University of Virginia* (515 U.S. 819, 1995); *Agostini v. Felton* (473 U.S. 402, 1997); *Mitchell v. Helms* (530 U.S. 783, 2000).

3. Government-Sponsored Religious Displays: *Lynch v. Donnelly* (465 U.S. 668, 1984); *Board of Trustees of Scarsdale v. McCreary* (471 U.S. 83, 1985); *County of Allegheny v. ACLU Greater Pittsburgh Chapter* (492 U.S. 573, 1989); *McCreary County v. ACLU of Kentucky* (545 U.S. 844, 2005); *Van Ordern v. Perry* (545 U.S. 677, 2005).

4. Prayers in Public Schools: *Wallace v. Jaffree* (472 U.S. 38, 1985); *Lee v. Weisman* (505 U.S. 577, 1992); *Santa Fe Independent School District v. Doe* (530 U.S. 290, 2000); *Elk Grove Unified School District v. Newdow* (542 U.S. 1, 2004).

5. Sabbatarian Laws (a.k.a. Blue Laws): *McGowan v. Maryland* (366 U.S. 420, 1961); *Braunfeld v. Brown* (366 U.S. 599, 1961); *Gallagher v. Corwin Kosher Super Market of Massachusetts, Inc.* (366 U.S. 617, 1981); *Thorton v. Caldor* (472 U.S. 703, 1963).

6. Religious Institutions Functioning as Government Agency: *Larkin v. Grendel's Den* (459 U.S. 116, 1982); *Bowen v. Kendrick* (487 U.S. 589, 1988); *Board of Education of Kiryas Joel Village School v. Grumet* (512 U.S. 687, 1994).

7. Tax Exemption to Religious Institutions: *Walz v. Tax Commission of the City of New York* (397 U.S. 664, 1970); *Bob Jones University v. United States* (461 U.S. 574, 1983); *Texas Monthly, Inc. v. Bullock* (489 U.S. 1, 1989).

   Legislative Chaplains/Prayers: *Marsh v. Chambers* (463 U.S. 783, 1984); *Town of Greece v. Galloway* (572 U.S. _____, 2014)

8. Standing to Sue: *Flast v. Cohen* (392 U.S. 83, 1968); *Valley Forges and People Christian College v. Americans United For Separation of Church and State* (454 U.S. 464, 1982).

9. Teaching Creationism in Public Schools: *Edwards v. Aguillard* (482 U.S. 578, 1987).

10. Unequal Government Treatment of Religious Groups: *Larson v. Valente* (456 U.S. 228, 1982).

Free Exercise Clause

Religions Involved

Amish/Mennonites, Jehovah's Witnesses, Church of Jesus Christ of Latter-day Saints

Cases:

1. Solicitation by Religious Groups: *Cantwell v. Connecticut* (310 U.S. 296, 1940); *Minersville School District v. Gobitis* (310 U.S. 586, 1940); *Cox v. New Hampshire* (312 U.S. 569, 1941); *Jones v. City of Opelika-I* (316 U.S. 584, 1942); *Marsh v. Alabama* (326 U.S. 501, 1942); *Murdock v. Pennsylvania* (319 U.S. 105, 1943); *Jones v. City of Opelika-II* (319 U.S. 103, 1943); *West Virginia State Board of Education v. Barnette* (321 U.S. 158, 1943); *Prince v. Massachusetts* (321 U.S. 158, 1944); *Heffron v. International Society for Krishna Consciousness* (452 U.S. 640, 1981).

2. Religious Tests for Public Benefits/Services: *Chaplinsky v. New Hampshire* (315 U.S. 568, 1942); *Toracaso v. Watkins* (376 U.S. 488, 1961); *McDaniel v. Paty* (435 U.S. 618, 1978); *Thomas v. Review Board of the Indiana Employment Division* (450 U.S. 707, 1981); *Goldman v. Weinberger* (475 U.S. 503, 1986); *Bowen v. Roy* (476 U.S. 693, 1986).

3. Free Exercise and Public Education: *Wisconsin v. Yoder* (406 U.S. 205, 1972); *Widmar v. Vincent* (454 U.S. 263, 1981); *Board of Education of the Westside Community Schools v. Mergens* (496 U.S. 266, 1990); *Lamb's Chapel v. Center Moriches Union Free School District* (508 U.S. 384, 1993); *Rosenberger v. Rector and Visitors of the University of Virginia* (515 U.S. 819, 1995).

4. Religion versus the Right to Work: *Sherbert v. Verner* (374 U.S. 398, 1963); *Trans World Airlines v. Hardison* (432 U.S. 63, 1977); *Ohio Civil Rights Commission v. Dayton Christian Schools* (477 U.S. 619, 1986); *Corporation of the Presiding Bishop of the Church of Jesus Christ of Latter-day Saints v. Amos* (483 U.S. 327, 1987); *Employment Division v. Smith* (494 U.S. 872, 1990).

(continued)

Table 5.2   (*continued*)

Free Exercise Clause

Religions Involved

5. Government Intrusion into Church Controversies: *United States v. Ballard* (322 U.S. 78, 1944); *Kedroff v. Saint Nicholas Cathedral* (344 U.S. 94, 1952); *Presbyterian Church v. Hall Church* (393 U.S. 440, 1969); *Jones v. Wolf* (443 U.S. 595, 1979); *Hosanna-Tabor Evangelical Lutheran Church and School v. EEOC* (565 U.S. _____, 2012).

6. Free Exercise versus Eminent Domain: *Lyng v. Northwest Indian Cemetery Protective Association* (485 U.S. 439, 1988); *City of Boerne v. Flores* (521 U.S. 507, 1997).

7. Free Exercise versus Freedom of Speech: *R.A.V. v. City of St. Paul* (505 U.S. 377, 1992); *Gonzales v. O Centro Espirita Beneficente Uniao do Vegetal* (546 U.S. 418, 2006).

8. Polygamy: *Reynolds v. United States* (98 U.S. 145, 1878); *Davis v. Beason* (133 U.S. 333, 1890).

9. Ritual Sacrifice of Animals: *Church of Lukumi Babalu Aye v. City of Hialeah* (508 U.S. 520, 1993).

Table 5.3   **Charges of Religion-Based Discrimination (1997 to 2016)**

Year	Number of Complaints Received	"No Reasonable Cause"	"Reasonable Cause"
1997	1,709	1,265	95
1998	1,786	1,363	147
1999	1,811	1,269	155
2000	1,939	1,343	208
2001	2,127	1,349	227
2002	2,572	1,729	212
2003	2,532	1,744	205
2004	2,466	1,672	172
2005	2,340	1,442	201
2006	2,541	1,524	137
2007	2,880	1,498	194
2008	3,273	1,705	172
2009	3,386	1,805	136

2010	3,790	2,309	314
2011	4,151	2,737	303
2012	3,811	2,800	300
2013	3,721	2,558	168
2014	3,549	2,327	116
2015	3,502	2,542	139
2016	3,825	2,706	121

Note: *EEOC total workload includes charges carried over from previous fiscal years, new charge receipts, and charges transferred to EEOC from Fair Employment Practice Agencies (FEPAs). Resolution of charges each year may therefore exceed receipts for that year because workload being resolved is drawn from a combination of pending, new receipts and FEPA transfer charges rather than from new charges only.*

Source: Religion-Based Charges, FY 1997 to FY 2016. U.S. Equal Employment Opportunity Commission. Retrieved from https://www.eeoc.gov/eeoc/statistics/enforcement/religion.cfm

Table 5.4   Religious-Related Hate Crime Statistics (2015)

	Incidents	Offenses	Victims	Known Offenders
Religion				
Anti-Jewish	664	695	731	387
Anti-Catholic	53	59	60	29
Anti-Protestant	37	47	48	18
Anti-Islamic	257	301	307	228
Anti-Other Religion	96	104	107	53
Anti-Multiple Religions	51	57	58	30
Anti-Mormon	8	8	8	8
Anti–Jehovah's Witnesses	1	1	1	1
Anti-Orthodox	48	50	50	36
Anti-Other Christian	15	18	18	16
Anti-Buddhist	1	1	1	1
Anti-Hindu	5	5	5	2
Anti-Sikh	6	6	6	4
Anti-Atheist	2	2	2	0

(continued)

Table 5.4 *(continued)*

	Incidents	Offenses	Victims	Known Offenders
Sexual Orientation				
Anti-Gay (Male)	664	758	786	803
Anti-Lesbian	136	168	170	142
Anti-LGBT	203	235	248	218
Anti-Heterosexual	19	23	24	19
Anti-Bisexual	31	35	35	39
Gender Identity				
Anti-Transgender	73	75	76	114
Anti-Gender, Non-Conforming	41	43	46	43

Source: Data from FBI Statistics. 2015. Retrieved from https://ucr.fbi.gov/hate-crime/2015/tables-and-data-declarations-1table

targeted, the number of victims involved in those incidents, and the number of known perpetrators. The data show that a significant number of incidents are the result of religious hatred harbored by less than 2,000 individual offenders. Data for hate crimes targeting victims based on sexual identity and gender identification are included because often the offenders are motivated against the "other" related to sexual orientation in part because of the offender's perceptions that are related to religious belief: that the others practice a sinful lifestyle and are deserving of hell and similar religious intolerance.

Documents

The Maryland Toleration Act (1649)

The Maryland Toleration Act of 1649 was enacted to protect the Catholic minority in the Maryland colony from the Protestant majority. While it only lasted a short time, it is important in that it provided modest protection for the Catholic minority and set a precedent to which other religious minorities, other colonies, and ultimately the United States in its First Amendment freedoms, could refer.

Forasmuch as in a well governed and Christian Commonwealth, matters concerning Religion and the honour of God ought in the first place to be taken into serious consideration and endeavored to be settled,—Be it therefore ordained and enacted by the Right Honourable Cecilius, Lord Baron of Baltimore, absolute Lord and Proprietary of this Province, with the advice and consent of this General Assembly that whatsoever person or persons within this province and the islands thereunto belonging, shall from henceforth blaspheme God, that is curse His, or shall deny Our Saviour Jesus Christ to be the Son of God, or shall deny the Holy Trinity, the Father, Son & Holy Ghost, or the Godhead of any of the said three persons of the Trinity, or the unity of the Godhead, or shall use or utter any reproachful speeches, words or language concerning the Holy Trinity, or any of the said three persons thereof, shall be punished with death, and confiscation or forfeiture of all his or her land and goods to the Lord Proprietary and his heirs.

And be it also enacted by the authority and with the advice and assent aforesaid: That whatsoever person or persons shall from henceforth use or utter any reproachful words or speeches concerning the Blessed Virgin Mary, the Mother of our Saviour, or the holy Apostles or Evangelists, or any of them, shall in such case for the first offence forfeit to the said Lord Proprietary, and his heirs, Lords and Proprietaries of this Province, the sum of £5 sterling, or the value thereof, to be levied on the goods and chattels of every such person so offending: but in case such offender or offenders should not then have goods and chattels sufficient for the satisfying of such forfeiture, or that the same be not otherwise speedily satisfied, that then such offender or offenders shall be publicly whipped and be imprisoned during the pleasure of the Lord Proprietary or the Lieutenant or chief governor of this Province for the time being; and that every such offender or offenders for every such second offence shall forfeit £10 sterling, or the value thereof to be levied as aforesaid or in case such offender or offenders shall not then have goods and chattels within this Province sufficient for that purpose, then to be publicly and severely whipped and imprisoned as before is expressed; and that every person or persons before mentioned offending herein the third time, shall for such third offence forfeit all his lands and goods, and be forever banished and expelled out of this province.

And be it also further enacted by the same authority, advice and assent, that whatsoever person or persons shall from henceforth upon any occasion of offence or otherwise, in a reproachful manner or other way, declare, call, or denominate any person or persons whatsoever inhabiting, residing, trafficing, trading or commercing, within this Province, or within any the ports, harbours, creeks or havens to the same belonging, an Heretic, Schismatic, Idolator Puritan, Presbyterian, Independent, Popish Priest, Jesuit, Jesuited Papist, Lutheran, Calvinist, Anabaptist, Brownist, Antinomian, Barrowist, Roundhead, Separatist, or other name or term in a reproachful manner, relating to matters of religion, shall for every such offence forfeit and lose the sum of 10s. sterling or the value thereof to be levied on the goods and chattels of every such offender or offenders, the one-half thereof to be forfeit and paid to the person or persons of whom such reproachful words are or shall be spoken or uttered, and the other half thereof to the Lord Proprietary and his heirs, lords and proprietaries, but if such person or persons who shall at any time utter or speak any such reproachful words or language, shall not have goods or chattels sufficient and overt within this province to be taken to satisfy the penalty aforesaid, or that the same be not otherwise speedily satisfied, then the person or persons so offending shall be publicly whipped, and shall suffer imprisonment without bail or mainprise, until he, she or they respectively, shall satisfy the party offended or grieved by such reproachful language, by asking him or her, respectively forgiveness publicly for such his offence before the magistrate or chief officer or officers of the town or place where such offence shall be given.

And be it further likewise enacted by the authority and consent aforesaid, that every person and persons within this Province, that shall at any time hereafter profane the Sabbath or Lord's Day, called Sunday, by frequent swearing, drunkenness, or by any uncivil, or disorderly recreation, or by working on that day when absolute necessity doth not require, shall for every such first offence forfeit 2s. 6d. sterling or the value thereof, and for the second offence 5s. sterling or the value thereof and for the third offence, and for every time he shall offend in like manner afterwards 10s. sterling or the value thereof; and in case such offender or offenders shall not have sufficient goods or chattels within this Province to satisfy any of the said penalties respectively hereby imposed for profaning the Sabbath or Lord's Day called Sunday as aforesaid, then in every such case the party so offending, shall for the first and second offence in that kind be imprisoned until he or she shall publicly in open Court, before the Chief Commander, judge or magistrate of that county, town or precinct wherein such offence shall be committed, acknowledge the scandal and offence he hath in that respect given against God, and the good and civil government of this Province; and for the third offence and for every time after shall also be publicly whipped. And whereas the enforcing of the conscience in matters of religion hath frequently fallen out to be of dangerous consequence in those Commonwealths where it has been practised, and for the more quiet and peaceable government of this Province, and the better to preserve mutual love and amity amongst the inhabitants here,—Be it therefore also, by the Lord Proprietary, with the advice and assent of this Assembly, ordained and enacted, except as in this present Act is declared and set forth, that no person or persona whatsoever within this Province or the Islands, ports, harbours, creeks or havens thereunto belonging, professing to believe in Jesus Christ, shall from henceforth be anyways troubled, molested or discountenenced, for or in respect of his or her religion, nor in the free exercise thereof, within this Province or the Islands thereunto belonging, nor anyway compelled to the belief or exercise of any other religion against his or her consent, so as they be not unfaithful to the Lord Proprietary or molest or conspire against the civil government, established or to be established in this Province under him or his heirs; and that all and every person or persons that shall presume contrary to this Act, and the true intent and meaning thereof, directly or indirectly, either in person or estate, wilfully to wrong, disturb or trouble, or molest any person or persons whatsoever within this Province, professing to believe in Jesus Christ, for or in respect of his or her religion, or the free exercise thereof within this Province, otherwise than is provided for in this Act, that such person or persons so offending shall be compelled to pay treble damages to the party so wronged or molested, and for every such offence shall also forfeit 20s. sterling in money or the value thereof, half thereof for the use of the Lord Proprietary and his heirs, Lords and Proprietaries of this Province, and the other half thereof for the use of the party so wronged or molested as aforesaid; or if the party so offending as aforesaid shall refuse or be unable to recompence the party so wronged or to satisfy such fine or forfeiture, then such offender shall be severely punished by public whipping and imprisonment during the pleasure of the Lord Proprietary, or his lieutenant or chief Governor of this Province for the time being, without bail or mainprise.

And be it further also enacted by the authority and consent aforesaid, that the sheriff or other officer or officers from time to time be appointed and authorized for that purpose of the county, town or precinct where every particular offence, in this present Act contained, shall happen at any time to be committed, and whereupon there is hereby a forfeiture, fine or penalty imposed, shall from time to time distrain, and seize the goods and estates of every such person so offending as aforesaid against this present Act or any part thereof, and sell the same or any part thereof for the full satisfaction of such forfeiture, fine or penalty as aforesaid, restoring to the party so offending the remainder or overplus of the said goods and estate after such satisfaction so made as aforesaid.

Source: *Maryland: The Land of Sanctuary: A History of Religious Toleration in Maryland from the First Settlement until the American Revolution* by William Thomas Russell (1863–1927), J.H. Furst Company, 1907.

The Virginia Statute for Religious Freedom (1786)

Virginia was the first state to enact a law for religious freedom. The law was drafted by Thomas Jefferson in 1777, introduced into the Virginia General Assembly in 1779, and enacted into the state's law in 1786. It served as a model for the First Amendment and for subsequent states when they disestablished their official state religions.

[Sec. 1] Where as Almighty God hath created the mind free; that all attempts to influence it by temporal punishments or burthens, or by civil incapacitations, tend only to beget habits of hypocrisy and meanness, and are a departure from the plan of the Holy author of our religion, who being Lord both of body and mind, yet chose not to propagate it by coercions on either, as it was in his Almighty power to do; that the impious presumption of legislators and rulers, civil as well as ecclesiastical, who being themselves but fallible and uninspired men, have assumed dominion over the faith of others, setting up their own opinions and modes of thinking as the only true and infallible, and as such endeavouring to impose them on others, hath established and maintained false religions over the greatest part of the world, and through all time; that to compel a man to furnish contributions of money for the propagation of opinions which he disbelieves, is sinful and tyrannical; that even the forcing him to support this or that teacher of his own religious persuasion, is depriving him of the comfortable liberty of giving his contributions to the particular pastor, whose morals he would make his pattern, and whose powers he feels most persuasive to righteousness, and is withdrawing from the ministry those temporary rewards, which proceeding from an approbation of their personal conduct, are an additional incitement to earnest and unremitting labours for the instruction of mankind; that our civil rights have no dependence on our religious opinions, any more than our opinions in physics or geometry; that therefore the proscribing any citizen as unworthy the public confidence by laying upon him an incapacity of being called to offices of trust and emolument, unless he profess or renounce this or that religious opinion, is depriving him injuriously of those privileges and advantages to which in common with his fellow-citizens he has a natural right; that it tends only to corrupt the principles of that religion it is meant to encourage, by bribing with a monopoly of worldly honours and emoluments, those who will externally profess and conform to it; that though indeed these are criminal who do not withstand such temptation, yet neither are those innocent who lay the bait in their way; that to suffer the civil magistrate to intrude his powers into the field of opinion, and to restrain the profession or propagation of principles on supposition of their ill tendency, is a dangerous fallacy, which at once destroys all religious liberty, because he being of course judge of that tendency will make his opinions the rule of judgment, and approve or condemn the sentiments of others only as they shall square with or differ from his own; that it is time enough for the rightful purposes of civil government, for its officers to interfere when principles break out into overt acts against peace and good order; and finally, that truth is great and will prevail if left to herself, that she is the proper and sufficient antagonist to error, and has nothing to fear from the conflict, unless by human interposition disarmed of her natural weapons, free argument and debate, errors ceasing to be dangerous when it is permitted freely to contradict them:

[Sec. 2] Be it enacted by the General Assembly, That no man shall be compelled to frequent or support any religious worship, place, or ministry whatsoever, nor shall be enforced, restrained, molested, or burdened in his body or goods, nor shall otherwise suffer on account of his religious opinions or belief; but that all men shall be free to profess, and by argument to maintain, their opinion in matters of religion, and that the same shall in no wise diminish enlarge, or affect their civil capacities.

[Sec. 3] And though we well know that this assembly elected by the people for the ordinary purposes of legislation only, have no power to restrain the acts of succeeding assemblies, constituted with powers equal to our own, and that therefore to declare this act to be irrevocable would be of no effect in law; yet we are free to declare, and do declare, that the rights hereby asserted are of the natural rights of mankind, and that if any act shall be hereafter passed to repeal the present, or to narrow its operation, such act shall be an infringement of natural right.

Source: W. W. Hening, ed., *Statutes at Large of Virginia*, vol. 12 (1823): 84–86.

Constitutional Provisions

The U.S. Constitution, in Article VI, and in the First and Fourteenth Amendments, establishes the fundamental principles of freedom of religion. Those key provisions are cited here in their entirety. Emphasis has been added.

Article VI (1787)

All Debts contracted and Engagements entered into, before the Adoption of this Constitution, shall be as valid against the United States under this Constitution, as under the Confederation.

This Constitution, and the Laws of the United States which shall be made in Pursuance thereof; and all Treaties made, or which shall be made, under the Authority of the United States, shall be the supreme Law of the Land; and the Judges in every

State shall be bound thereby, any Thing in the Constitution or Laws of any State to the Contrary notwithstanding.

The Senators and Representatives before mentioned, and the Members of the several State Legislatures, and all executive and judicial Officers, both of the United States and of the several States, shall be bound by Oath or Affirmation, to support this Constitution; *but no religious Test shall ever be required as a Qualification to any Office or public Trust under the United States.*

First Amendment (1789)

Congress shall make no law respecting an establishment of religion, or prohibiting the free exercise thereof; or abridging the freedom of speech, or of the press; or the right of the people peaceably to assemble, and to petition the Government for a redress of grievances.

Fourteenth Amendment (1868)

Section 1. All persons born or naturalized in the United States, and subject to the jurisdiction thereof, are citizens of the United States and of the State wherein they reside. *No State shall make or enforce any law which shall abridge the privileges or immunities of citizens of the United States; nor shall any State deprive any person of life, liberty, or property, without due process of law; nor deny to any person within its jurisdiction the equal protection of the laws.*

Section 5. The Congress shall have the power to enforce, by appropriate legislation, the provisions of this article.

Source: Charters of Freedom, National Archives.

Letter from James Madison to Edward Livingston (1822)

James Madison, who along with Thomas Jefferson is the principal author of the Bill of Rights, wrote a letter in July 1822, to Edward

Livingston, about the latter's Report to the Legislature of the State (Louisiana) on the subject of a penal code. In his letter, excerpted here to its main points about freedom of religion, Madison expounds on his own thoughts on that lofty principle.

To Edward Livingston
Montpellier, July 10, 1822

Dear Sir,

I was favored some days ago with your letter of May 19, accompanied by a copy of your Report to the Legislature of the State on the subject of a penal Code.

I should commit a tacit injustice if I did not say that the Report does great honor to the talents and sentiments of the author. It abounds with ideas of conspicuous value, and presents them in a manner not less elegant than persuasive.

The reduction of an entire code of criminal jurisprudence into statutory provisions, excluding a recurrence to foreign or traditional codes, and substituting for technical terms more familiar ones, with or without explanatory notes, cannot but be viewed as a very arduous task. I sincerely wish your execution of it may fulfil every expectation.

I cannot deny, at the same time, that I have been accustomed to doubt the practicability of giving all the desired simplicity to so complex a subject without involving a discretion, inadmissible in free Government, to those who are to expound and apply the law. The rules and usages which make a part of the law, though to be found only in elementary treatises, in respectable commentaries, and in adjudged cases, seem to be too numerous and too various to be brought within the requisite compass; even if there were less risk of creating uncertainties by defective abridgments, or by the change of phraseology.

This risk would seem to be particularly incident to a substitution of new words and definitions for a technical language, the meaning of which had been settled by long use and authoritative expositions. When a technical term may express a very simple idea, there might be no inconveniency, or rather an advantage, in exchanging it for a more familiar synonyme, if a precise one could be found. But where the technical terms and phrases have a complex import, not otherwise to be reduced to clearness and certainty than by practical applications of them, it might be unsafe to introduce new terms and phrases, though aided by brief explanations. The whole law expressed by single terms, such as "trial by jury, evidence, &c., &c.," fill volumes, when unfolded into the details which enter into their meaning.

I hope it will not be thought by this intimation of my doubts I wish to damp the enterprise from which you have not shrunk. On the contrary, I not only wish that you may overcome all the difficulties which occur to me, but am persuaded that if complete success should not reward your labors, there is ample room for improvements in the criminal jurisprudence of Louisiana, as elsewhere, which are well worthy the exertion of your best powers, and will furnish useful examples to other members of the Union. Among the advantages distinguishing our compound Government, it is not the least that it affords so many opportunities and chances in the local Legislatures for salutary innovations by some, which may be adopted by others; or for important experiments, which, if unsuccessful, will be of limited injury, and may even prove salutary as beacons to others. Our political system is found, also, to have the happy merit of exciting a laudable emulation among the States composing it, instead of the enmity marking competitions among powers wholly alien to each other.

I observe with particular pleasure the view you have taken of the immunity of Religion from civil jurisdiction, in every case where it does not trespass on private rights or the public peace. This has always been a favorite principle with me; and it was not with my approbation that the deviation from it took place in Congress, when they appointed chaplains, to be paid from the National Treasury. It would have been a much better proof to their constituents of their pious feeling if the members had contributed for the purpose a pittance from their own pockets. As the precedent is not likely to be rescinded, the best that can now be done may be to apply to the Constitution the maxim of the law, *de minimis non curat.*

There has been another deviation from the strict principle in the Executive proclamations of fasts and festivals, so far, at least, as they have spoken the language of injunction, or have lost sight of the equality of all religious sects in the eye of the Constitution. Whilst I was honored with the Executive trust, I found it necessary on more than one occasion to follow the example of predecessors. But I was always careful to make the Proclamations absolutely indiscriminate, and merely recommendatory; or, rather, mere *designations* of a day on which all who thought proper might *unite* in consecrating it to religious purposes, according to their own faith and forms. In this sense, I presume, you reserve to the Government a right to *appoint* particular days for religious worship. I know not what may be the way of thinking on this subject in Louisiana. I should suppose the Catholic portion of the people, at least, as a small and even unpopular sect in the U. States, would rally, as they did in Virginia when religious liberty was a Legislative topic, to its broadest principle. Notwithstanding the general progress made within the two last centuries in favour of this branch of liberty, and the full establishment of it in some parts of our Country, there remains in others a strong bias towards the old error, that without some sort of alliance or coalition between Government and Religion neither can be duly supported. Such, indeed, is the tendency to such a coalition, and such its corrupting influence on both the parties, that the danger cannot be too carefully guarded against. And in a Government of opinion like ours, the only effectual guard must be found in the soundness and stability of the general opinion on the subject. Every new and successful example, therefore, of a perfect separation between ecclesiastical and civil matters, is of importance; and I have no doubt that every new example will succeed, as every past one has done, in shewing that religion and Government will both exist in greater purity the less they are mixed together. It was the belief of all sects at one time that the establishment of Religion by law was right and necessary; that the true religion ought to be established in exclusion of every other; and that the only question to be decided was, which was the true religion. The example of Holland proved that a toleration of sects dissenting from the established sect was safe, and even useful. The example of the Colonies, now States, which rejected religious establishments altogether, proved that all sects might be safely and advantageously put on a footing of equal and entire freedom; and a continuance of their example since the Declaration of Independence has shewn that its success in Colonies was not to be ascribed to their connection with the parent Country. If a further confirmation of the truth could be wanted, it is to be found in the examples furnished by the States which have abolished their religious establishments. I cannot speak particularly of any of the cases excepting that of Virginia, where it is impossible to deny that religion prevails with more zeal and a more exemplary priesthood than it ever did when established and patronised by public authority. We are teaching the world the great truth, that Governments do better without kings and nobles than with them. The merit will be doubled by the other lesson: that Religion flourishes in greater purity without, than with the aid of Government.

My pen, I perceive, has rambled into reflections for which it was not taken up. I recall it to the proper object, of thanking you for your very interesting pamphlet, and of tendering you my respects and good wishes.

Source: *Letters and Other Writings of James Madison*, vol. 3. 1865. Philadelphia: J.B. Lippincott & Co. 273–276.

Order of Extermination, Missouri Executive Order 44 (1838)

A black stain on religious tolerance in America is the Missouri Executive Order 44, of Governor Lilburn W. Boggs, the Order of Extermination, in which, pursuant to the order, hundreds of Mormon civilians were, as applicable, attacked, lynched, looted, tarred, raped, and murdered. The order is presented here verbatim and in its entirety.

Headquarters of the Militia
City of Jefferson, Oct. 27, 1838

General John B. Clark:

Sir, Since the order of this morning to you, directing you to cause four hundred mounted men to be raised within your division, I have received by Amos Reese, Esq., of Ray county, and Wiley C. Williams, Esq., one of my aids, information of the most appalling character, which entirely changes the face of things, and places the Mormons in the attitude of an open and avowed defiance of the laws, and of having made war upon the people of this state. Your orders are, therefore, to hasten your operation with all possible speed. The Mormons must be treated as enemies, and must be exterminated or driven from the state if necessary for the public peace—their outrages are beyond all description. If you can increase your force, you are authorized to do so to any extent you may consider necessary. I have just issued orders to Maj. Gen. Willock, of Marion County, to raise five hundred men, and to march them to the northern part of Daviess, and there unite with Gen. Doniphan, of Clay, who has been ordered with five hundred men to proceed to the same point for the purpose of intercepting the retreat of the Mormons to the north. They have been directed to communicate with you by express, you can also communicate with them if you find it necessary. Instead therefore of proceeding as at first directed to reinstate the citizens of Daviess in their homes, you will proceed immediately to Richmond and then operate against the Mormons. Brig. Gen. Parks of Ray, has been ordered to have four hundred of his brigade in readiness to join you at Richmond. The whole force will be placed under your command.

I am very respectfully,
Your ob't serv't, L. W. Boggs, Commander-in-Chief

Source: Mormon War Papers. 1837–1841. Office of Secretary of State, Record Group 5, Missouri State Archives, Jefferson City. Courtesy of the Missouri State Archives.

Lemon v. Kurtzman (1971)

In 1971, the Supreme Court decided the landmark case of Lemon v. Kurtzman, *overturning as unconstitutional establishment a Pennsylvania state law supporting the non-public (i.e., parochial) religious-based studies passed through the Non-public Elementary and Secondary Education Act of 1968. This case set the precedent of the* Lemon *test, a three-part test the Supreme Court stipulated for states and for guidance to lower courts, to use when assessing a law being challenged on the grounds of the Establishment Clause of the First Amendment.*

Syllabus

Rhode Island's 1969 Salary Supplement Act provides for a 15% salary supplement to be paid to teachers in nonpublic schools at which the average per-pupil expenditure on secular education is below the average in public schools. Eligible teachers must teach only courses offered in the public schools, using only materials used in the public schools, and must agree not to teach courses in religion. A three-judge court found that about 25% of the State's elementary students attended nonpublic schools, about 95% of whom attended Roman Catholic affiliated schools, and that to date about 250 teachers at Roman Catholic schools are the sole beneficiaries under the Act. The court found that the parochial school system was "an integral part of the religious mission of the Catholic Church," and held that the Act fostered "excessive entanglement" between government and religion, thus violating the Establishment Clause. Pennsylvania's Nonpublic Elementary and Secondary Education Act, passed in 1968, authorizes the state Superintendent of Public Instruction to "purchase" certain "secular educational services" from nonpublic schools, directly reimbursing those schools solely for teachers' salaries, textbooks, and instructional materials. Reimbursement is restricted to courses in specific secular subjects, the textbooks and materials must be approved by the Superintendent, and no payment is to be made for any course containing "any subject matter expressing religious teaching, or the morals or forms of worship of any sect." Contracts were made with schools that have more than 20% of all the students in the State, most of which were affiliated with the Roman Catholic Church. The complaint challenging the constitutionality of the Act alleged that the church-affiliated schools are controlled by religious organizations, have the purpose of propagating and promoting a particular religious faith, and conduct their operations to fulfill that purpose. A three-judge court granted the State's motion to dismiss the complaint for failure to state a claim for relief, finding no violation of the Establishment or Free Exercise Clause.

Held: Both statutes are unconstitutional under the Religion Clauses of the First Amendment, as the cumulative impact of the entire relationship arising under the statutes involves excessive entanglement between government and religion.

. . .

MR. CHIEF JUSTICE BURGER delivered the opinion of the Court . . .

The language of the Religion Clauses of the First Amendment is, at best, opaque, particularly when compared with other portions of the Amendment. Its authors did not simply prohibit the establishment of a state church or a state religion, an area history shows they regarded as very important and fraught with great dangers. Instead, they commanded that there should be "no law respecting an establishment of religion." A law may be one "respecting" the forbidden objective while falling short of its total realization. A law "respecting" the proscribed result, that is, the establishment of religion, is not always easily identifiable as one violative of the Clause. A given law might not establish a state religion, but nevertheless be one "respecting" that end in the sense of being a step that could lead to such establishment, and hence offend the First Amendment.

In the absence of precisely stated constitutional prohibitions, we must draw lines with reference to the three main evils against which the Establishment Clause was intended to afford protection: "sponsorship, financial support, and active involvement of the sovereign in religious activity."

Every analysis in this area must begin with consideration of the cumulative criteria developed by the Court over many years. Three such tests may be gleaned from our cases. First, the statute must have a secular legislative purpose; second, its principal or primary effect must be one that neither advances nor inhibits religion; finally, the statute must not foster "an excessive government entanglement with religion."

Inquiry into the legislative purposes of the Pennsylvania and Rhode Island statutes affords no basis for a conclusion that the legislative intent was to advance religion. On the contrary, the statutes themselves clearly state that they are intended to enhance the quality of the secular education in all schools covered by the compulsory attendance laws. There is no reason to believe the legislatures meant anything else. A State always has a legitimate concern for maintaining minimum standards in all schools it allows to operate.

Source: *Lemon v. Kurtzman*, 403 U.S. 602 (1971).

Committee for Public Education and Religious Liberty v. Nyquist (1973)

Among the most contentious and controversial issues dealt with by the Supreme Court is the issue of government aid to religious schools. In the 1970s, the Court was particularly skeptical of such aid. One of the Court's landmark decisions consisted of rejecting government efforts to provide aid to private sectarian schools in the Nyquist *case of 1971. Significant details of the* Nyquist *decision are excerpted here.*

Syllabus

Amendments to New York's Education and Tax Laws established three financial aid programs for nonpublic elementary and secondary schools. The first section provides for direct money grants to "qualifying" nonpublic schools to be used for "maintenance and repair" of facilities and equipment to ensure the students' "health, welfare and safety." A "qualifying" school is a nonpublic, nonprofit elementary or secondary school serving a high concentration of pupils from low income families. The annual grant is $30 per pupil, or $40 if the facilities are more than 25 years old, which may not exceed 50% of the average per-pupil cost for equivalent services in the public schools. Legislative findings concluded that the State "has a primary responsibility to ensure the health, welfare and safety of children attending . . . nonpublic schools"; that the "fiscal crisis in nonpublic education . . . has caused a diminution of proper maintenance and repair programs, threatening the health, welfare and safety of nonpublic school children" in low income urban areas; and that "a healthy and safe school environment" contributes "to the stability of urban neighborhoods." Section 2 establishes a tuition reimbursement plan for parents of children attending nonpublic elementary or secondary schools. To qualify, a parent's annual taxable income must be less than $5,000. The amount of reimbursement is $50 per grade school child and $100 per high school student so long as those amounts do not exceed 50% of actual tuition paid. The legislature found that the right to select among alternative educational systems should be available in a pluralistic society, and that any sharp decline in nonpublic school pupils would massively increase public school enrollment and costs, seriously jeopardizing quality education for all children. Reiterating a declaration contained in the first section, the findings concluded that "such assistance is clearly secular, neutral and non-ideological." The third program, contained in §§ 3, 4, and 5 of the challenged law, is designed to give tax relief to parents failing to qualify for tuition reimbursement. Each eligible taxpayer-parent is entitled to deduct a stipulated sum from his adjusted gross income for each child attending a nonpublic school. The amount of the deduction is unrelated to the amount of tuition actually paid, and decreases as the amount of taxable income increases. These sections are also prefaced by a series of legislative findings similar to those accompanying the previous sections. Almost 20% of the State's students, some 700,000 to 800,000, attend nonpublic schools, approximately 85% of which are church-affiliated. While practically all the schools entitled to receive maintenance and repair grants "are related to the Roman Catholic Church and teach Catholic religious doctrine to some degree," institutions qualifying under the remainder of the statute include a substantial number of other church-affiliated schools. The District Court held that § 1, the maintenance and repair grants, and § 2, the tuition reimbursement grants, were invalid, but that the income tax provisions of §§ 3, 4, and 5 did not violate the Establishment Clause.

Held:

1. The propriety of a legislature's purpose may not immunize from further scrutiny a law that either has a primary effect that advances religion or fosters excessive church-state entanglements.

2. The maintenance and repair provisions of the New York statute violate the Establishment Clause because their inevitable effect is to subsidize and advance the religious mission of sectarian schools. Those provisions do not properly guarantee the secularity of state aid by limiting the percentage of assistance to 50% of comparable aid to public schools. Such statistical assurances fail to provide an

adequate guarantee that aid will not be utilized to advance the religious activities of sectarian schools.

3. The tuition reimbursement grants, if given directly to sectarian schools, would similarly violate the Establishment Clause, and the fact that they are delivered to the parents, rather than the schools, does not compel a contrary result, as the effect of the aid is unmistakably to provide financial support for nonpublic, sectarian institutions.

   (a) The fact that the grant is given as reimbursement for tuition already paid, and that the recipient is not required to spend the amount received on education, does not alter the effect of the law.

   (b) The argument that the statute provides "a statistical guarantee of neutrality," since the tuition reimbursement is only 15% of the educational costs in nonpublic schools and the compulsory education laws require more than 15% of school time to be devoted to secular courses, is merely another variant of the argument rejected as to maintenance and repair costs.

   (c) The State must maintain an attitude of "neutrality," neither "advancing" nor "inhibiting" religion, and it cannot, by designing a program to promote the free exercise of religion, erode the limitations of the Establishment Clause.

4. The system of providing income tax benefits to parents of children attending New York's nonpublic schools also violates the Establishment Clause because, like the tuition reimbursement program, it is not sufficiently restricted to assure that it will not have the impermissible effect of advancing the sectarian activities of religious schools.

5. Because the challenged sections have the impermissible effect of advancing religion, it is not necessary to consider whether such aid would yield an entanglement with religion. But it should be noted that, apart from any administrative entanglement of the State in particular religious

programs, assistance of the sort involved here carries grave potential for entanglement in the broader sense of continuing and expanding political strife over aid to religion.

Source: *Committee for Public Education v. Nyquist*, 413 U.S. 756 (1973).

The American Indian Religious Freedom Act (1978)

On August 11, 1978, the Congress enacted the American Indian Religious Freedom Act to preserve and protect the American Indians' right to believe and express their native religious traditions. The two key sections of that law are provided here in their entirety.

Section 1

On and after August 11, 1978, it shall be the policy of the United States to protect and preserve for American Indians, their inherent right of freedom to believe, express, and exercise the traditional religions of the American Indian, Eskimo, Aleut, and Native Hawaiians, including but not limited to access to sites, use and possession of sacred objects, and the freedom to worship through ceremonials and traditional rites.

Section 2

The President shall direct the various Federal departments, agencies, and other instrumentalities responsible for administering the relevant laws to evaluate their policies and procedures in consultation with native traditional religious leaders in order to determine appropriate changes necessary to protect and preserve Native American religious cultural rights and practices. Twelve months after August 11, 1978, the President shall report back to the Congress the results of his evaluation, including any changes which were made in administrative policies and procedures, and any recommendations he may have for legislative action.

Note: One of the changes in administrative policy and procedure was Executive Order 13007, Indian Sacred Sites.

Source: Federal Historic Preservation Laws, Act of August 11, 1978, 95–341, 42 U.S.C., 1996 and 1996a.

Denial of Equal Access Prohibited (1984)

In 1984, Congress added to the U.S. Code provisions prohibiting the denial of equal access to open, public forums and spaces in public schools on the basis of religious, political, philosophical, or other speech content. This document presents, in their entirety, those added provisions.

(a) Restriction of Limited Open Forum on Basis of Religious, Political, Philosophical, or Other Speech Content Prohibited.

It shall be unlawful for any public secondary school which receives Federal financial assistance and which has a limited open forum to deny equal access or for opportunity to, or discriminate against, any students who wish to conduct a meeting within that open forum on the basis of the religious, political, philosophical or other content of speech at such meeting.

(b) "Limited Open Forum" Defined

A public secondary school has a limited open forum whenever such school grants an offering to or opportunity for one or more noncurriculum related student groups to meet on school premises during noninstructional time.

(c) Fair Opportunity Criteria

Schools shall be determined to offer a fair opportunity to students who wish to conduct a meeting within its limited open forum if such school uniformly provides that (1) the meeting is voluntary and student-initiated; (2) there is no sponsorship of the meeting by the school, the government, or its agents or employees; (3) employees or agents of the school or government are present at religious meetings only in a non-participatory capacity; (4) the meeting does not materially and substantially interfere with the orderly conduct of educational activities within the school; and (5) nonschool persons may not direct, conduct, control, or regularly attend activities of student groups.

(d) Construction of Subchapter with Respect to Certain Rights

Nothing in this subchapter shall be construed to authorize the United States or any State or political subdivision thereof—(1) to influence the form or content of any prayers or other religious activity; (2) to require any person to participate in prayer or other religious activity; (3) to expend public funds beyond the incidental costs of providing the space for such student-initiated meetings; (4) to compel any school or agent employee to attend a school meeting if the content of the speech at the meeting is contrary to the beliefs of the agent or employees; (5) to sanction meetings that are otherwise unlawful; (6) to limit the rights of groups of students which are not of a specified numerical size; or (7) to abridge the constitutional rights of any person.

(e) Federal Financial Assistance to Schools Unaffected

Notwithstanding the availability of any other remedy under the Constitution or the laws of the United States, nothing in this subchapter shall be construed to authorize the United States to deny or withhold Federal financial assistance to any school.

(f) Authority of Schools With Respect to Order, Discipline, Well-being, and Attendance Concerns

Nothing in this subchapter shall be construed to limit the authority of the school, its agents or employees, to maintain order and discipline on school premises, to protect the well-being of students and faculty, and to assure that attendance of students at meetings is voluntary.

Source: 20 U.S. Code §4071.

Edwards v. Aguillard (1987)

In 1987, the Supreme Court handed down a 7–2 decision in Edwards v. Aguillard, *a case that challenged a Louisiana "Creationism Act" on the basis of violating the Establishment Clause of the First Amendment.*

Syllabus

Louisiana's "Creationism Act" forbids the teaching of the theory of evolution in public elementary and secondary schools unless accompanied by instruction in the theory of "creation science." The Act does not require the teaching of either theory unless the other is taught. It defines the theories as "the scientific evidences for [creation or evolution] and inferences drawn from those scientific evidences." Appellees, who include Louisiana parents, teachers, and religious leaders, challenged the Act's constitutionality in Federal District Court, seeking an injunction and declaratory relief. The District Court granted summary judgment to appellees, holding that the Act violated the Establishment Clause of the First Amendment. The Court of Appeals affirmed.

Held:

1. The Act is facially invalid as violative of the Establishment Clause of the First Amendment because it lacks a clear secular purpose.

   (a) The Act does not further its stated secular purpose of "protecting academic freedom." It does not enhance the freedom of teachers to teach what they choose, and fails to further the goal of "teaching all the evidence." Forbidding the teaching of evolution when creation science is not also taught undermines the provision of a comprehensive scientific education. Moreover, requiring the teaching of creation science with evolution does not give schoolteachers a flexibility that they did not already possess to supplant the present science curriculum with the presentation of theories, besides evolution, about the origin of life. Furthermore, the contention that the Act furthers a "basic concept of fairness" by requiring the teaching of all of the evidence on the subject is without merit. Indeed, the Act evinces a discriminatory preference for the teaching of creation science and against the teaching of evolution by requiring that curriculum guides be developed and resource services supplied for teaching creationism, but not for teaching evolution, by limiting membership of the resource services panel to "creation scientists," and by forbidding school boards to discriminate against anyone who "chooses to be a creation scientist" or to teach creation science, while failing to protect those who choose to teach other theories or who refuse to teach creation science. A law intended to maximize the comprehensiveness and effectiveness of science instruction would encourage the teaching of all scientific theories about human origins. Instead, this Act has the distinctly different purpose of discrediting evolution by counterbalancing its teaching at every turn with the teaching of creationism.

(b)   The Act impermissibly endorses religion by advancing the religious belief that a supernatural being created humankind. The legislative history demonstrates that the term "creation science," as contemplated by the state legislature, embraces this religious teaching. The Act's primary purpose was to change the public school science curriculum to provide persuasive advantage to a particular religious doctrine that rejects the factual basis of evolution in its entirety. Thus, the Act is designed either to promote the theory of creation science that embodies a particular religious tenet or to prohibit the teaching of a scientific theory disfavored by certain religious sects. In either case, the Act violates the First Amendment.

2. The District Court did not err in granting summary judgment upon a finding that the appellants had failed to raise a genuine issue of material fact. Appellants relied on the "uncontroverted" affidavits of scientists, theologians, and an education administrator defining creation science as "origin through abrupt appearance in complex form" and alleging that such a viewpoint constitutes a true scientific theory. The District Court, in its discretion, properly concluded that the postenactment testimony of these experts concerning the possible technical meanings of the Act's terms would not illuminate the contemporaneous purpose of the state legislature when it passed the Act. None of the persons making the affidavits produced by the appellants participated in or contributed to the enactment of the law.

Source: *Edwards v. Aguillard*, 482 U.S. 578 (1987).

Native American Graves Protection and Repatriation Act (1990)

This document presents portions of the Native American Graves Protection and Repatriation Act.

SEC 3. OWNERSHIP. (a) NATIVE AMERICAN HUMAN REMAINS AND OBJECTS.—The ownership or control of Native American cultural items which are excavated or discovered on Federal or tribal lands after the date of enactment of this Act shall be (with priority given in the order listed)—

(1) in the case of Native American human remains and associated funerary objects, in the lineal descendants of the Native American; or

(2) in any case in which such lineal descendants cannot be ascertained, and in the case of unassociated funerary objects, sacred objects, and objects of cultural patrimony—

(A) in the Indian tribe or Native Hawaiian organization on whose tribal land such objects or remains were discovered;

(B) in the Indian tribe or Native Hawaiian organization which has the closest cultural affiliation with such remains or objects and which, upon notice, states a claim for such remains or objects; or

(C) if the cultural affiliation of the objects cannot be reasonably ascertained and if the objects were discovered on Federal land that is recognized by a final judgment of the Indian Claims Commission or the United States Court of Claims as the aboriginal land of some Indian tribe—

(1) in the Indian tribe that is recognized as aboriginally occupying the area in which the objects were discovered, if upon notice, such tribe states a claim for such remains or objects, or

(2) if it can be shown by a preponderance of the evidence that a different tribe has a stronger cultural relationship with the remains or objects than the tribe or organization specified in paragraph

(1), in the Indian tribe that has the strongest demonstrated relationship, if upon notice, such tribe states a claim for such remains or objects.

(b) UNCLAIMED NATIVE AMERICAN HUMAN REMAINS AND OBJECTS.—Native American cultural items not claimed under subsection (a) shall be disposed of in accordance with regulations promulgated by the Secretary- in consultation with the review committee established under section 8,-Native American groups, representatives of museums and the scientific community.

(c) INTENTIONAL EXCAVATION AND REMOVAL OF NATIVE AMERICAN HUMAN REMAINS AND OBJECTS.—The intentional removal from or excavation of Native American cultural items from Federal or tribal lands for purposes of discovery, study, or removal of such items is permitted only if—

(1) such items are excavated or removed pursuant to a permit issued under section 4 of the Archaeological Resources Protection Act of 1979 (93 Stat. 721; 16 U.S.C. 470aa et seq.) which shall be consistent with this Act;

(2) such items are excavated or removed after consultation with or, in the case of tribal lands, consent of the appropriate (if any) Indian tribe or Native Hawaiian organization;

(3) the ownership and right of control of the disposition of such items shall be as provided in subsections (a) and (b); and

(4) proof of consultation or consent under paragraph (2) is shown.

(d) INADVERTENT DISCOVERY OF NATIVE AMER-ICAN REMAINS AND OBJECTS.—(1) Any person who knows, or has reason to know, that such person has discovered Native American cultural items on Federal or tribal lands-after the date of enactment of this Act shall notify, in writing, the Secretary of the Department, or head of any other agency or instrumentality of the United States, having primary management authority with respect to Federal lands and the appropriate Indian tribe or Native Hawaiian organization with respect to tribal lands, if known or readily ascertainable, and, in the case of lands that have been selected by an Alaska Native Corporation or group organized pursuant to the Alaska Native Claims Settlement Act of 1971, the appropriate corporation or group. If the discovery occurred in connection with an activity, including (but not limited to) construction, mining, logging, and agriculture, the person shall cease the activity in the area of the discovery, make a reasonable effort to protect the items discovered before resuming such activity, and provide notice under this subsection. Following the notification under this subsection, and upon certification by the Secretary of the department or the head of any agency or instrumentality of the United States or the appropriate Indian tribe or Native Hawaiian organization that notification has been received, the activity may resume after 30 days of such certification.

(2) The disposition of and control over any cultural items excavated or removed under this subsection shall be determined as provided for in this section.

(3) If the Secretary of the Interior consents, the responsibilities (in whole or in part) under paragraphs (1) and (2) of the

Secretary of any department (other than the Department of the Interior) or the head of any other agency or instrumentality may be delegated to the Secretary with respect to any land managed by such other Secretary or agency head.

(e) RELINQUISHMENT.—Nothing in this section shall prevent the governing body of an Indian tribe or Native Hawaiian organization from expressly relinquishing control over any Native American human remains, or title to or control over any funerary object, or sacred object.

Source: 104 Stat. 3048, Public Law 101–601, November 16, 1990.

Burwell v. Hobby Lobby Stores (2014)

In 2014, the Supreme Court, by a 5–4 vote, delivered its majority opinion written by Justice Alito, which overturned as unconstitutional regulations of the Department of Health and Human Services (DHHS), which required three closely held corporations to provide health insurance coverage for methods of birth control, deeming them violations of the Religious Freedom Restoration Act of 1993. The Court found that the owners of the corporation held religious beliefs against abortion and that those beliefs extended to four methods of birth control as abortifacients. The decision allows for-profit companies to deny contraceptive coverage to employees based upon the religious objections of the owners. It ruled against the DHHS under the Religious Freedom Restoration Act of 1993.

Justice Alito delivered the opinion of the Court.

We must decide in these cases whether the Religious Freedom Restoration Act of 1993 (RFRA), permits the United States Department of Health and Human Services (HHS) to demand that three closely held corporations provide health-insurance coverage for methods of contraception that violate the sincerely held religious beliefs of the companies' owners. We hold that the regulations that impose this obligation violate RFRA, which prohibits the Federal Government from taking any action that substantially burdens the exercise of religion unless that action constitutes the least restrictive means of serving a compelling government interest.

In holding that the HHS mandate is unlawful, we reject HHS's argument that the owners of the companies forfeited all RFRA protection when they decided to organize their businesses as corporations rather than sole proprietorships or general partnerships. The plain terms of RFRA make it perfectly clear that Congress did not discriminate in this way against men and women who wish to run their businesses as for-profit corporations in the manner required by their religious beliefs.

Since RFRA applies in these cases, we must decide whether the challenged HHS regulations substantially burden the exercise of religion, and we hold that they do. The owners of the businesses have religious objections to abortion, and according to their religious beliefs the four contraceptive methods at issue are abortifacients. If the owners comply with the HHS mandate, they believe they will be facilitating abortions, and if they do not comply, they will pay a very heavy price—as much as $1.3 million per day, or about $475 million per year, in the case of one of the companies. If these consequences do not amount to a substantial burden, it is hard to see what would.

Under RFRA, a Government action that imposes a substantial burden on religious exercise must serve a compelling government interest, and we assume that the HHS regulations satisfy this requirement. But in order for the HHS mandate to be sustained, it must also constitute the least restrictive means of serving that interest, and the mandate plainly fails that test. There are other ways in which Congress or HHS could equally ensure that every woman has cost-free access to the particular contraceptives at issue here and, indeed, to all FDA-approved contraceptives.

In fact, HHS has already devised and implemented a system that seeks to respect the religious liberty of religious nonprofit corporations while ensuring that the employees of these entities have precisely the same access to all FDA-approved contraceptives as employees of companies whose owners have no religious objections to providing such coverage. The employees of these religious nonprofit corporations still have access to insurance coverage without cost sharing for all FDA-approved contraceptives; and according to HHS, this system imposes no net economic burden on the insurance companies that are required to provide or secure the coverage.

Although HHS has made this system available to religious nonprofits that have religious objections to the contraceptive mandate, HHS has provided no reason why the same system cannot be made available when the owners of for-profit corporations have similar religious objections. We therefore conclude that this system constitutes an alternative that achieves all of the Government's aims while providing greater respect for religious liberty. And under RFRA, that conclusion means that enforcement of the HHS contraceptive mandate against the objecting parties in these cases is unlawful.

As this description of our reasoning shows, our holding is very specific. We do not hold, as the principal dissent alleges, that for-profit corporations and other commercial enterprises can "opt out of any law (saving only tax laws) they judge incompatible with their sincerely held religious beliefs." Nor do we hold, as the dissent implies, that such corporations have free rein to take steps that impose "disadvantages . . . on others" or that require "the general public [to] pick up the tab." And we certainly do not hold or suggest that "RFRA demands accommodation of a for-profit corporation's religious beliefs no matter the impact that accommodation may have on . . . thousands of women employed by Hobby Lobby." The effect of the HHS-created accommodation on the women employed by

Hobby Lobby and the other companies involved in these cases would be precisely zero. Under that accommodation, these women would still be entitled to all FDA-approved contraceptives without cost sharing.

Source: *Burwell v. Hobby Lobby*, 573 U.S. ___ (2014).

Executive Order Promoting Free Speech and Religious Liberty (2017)

On May 4, 2017, on the designated National Day of Prayer, President Donald Trump signed Executive Order 237888, the Religious Liberty order, allowing for broad exemptions for religious organizations in political speech as protected freedom of speech. The Executive Order relaxes the Internal Revenue Service enforcement of the ban, known as the Johnson Amendment, which prohibited churches from political speech activities (e.g., endorsing politicians from the pulpit). The Executive Order was applauded by many religious organizations and was opposed by groups that advocated for the strict separation of church and state.

By the authority vested in me as President by the Constitution and the laws of the United States of America, in order to guide the executive branch in formulating and implementing policies with implications for the religious liberty of persons and organizations in America, and to further compliance with the Constitution and with applicable statutes and Presidential Directives, it is hereby ordered as follows:

Section 1. Policy. It shall be the policy of the executive branch to vigorously enforce Federal law's robust protections for religious freedom. The Founders envisioned a Nation in which religious voices and views were integral to a vibrant public square, and in which religious people and institutions were free to practice their faith without fear of discrimination or retaliation by the Federal Government. For that reason, the United States Constitution enshrines and protects the fundamental right to religious liberty as Americans' first freedom. Federal law protects the freedom of Americans and their organizations to exercise religion and participate fully in civic life without undue interference by the Federal Government. The executive branch will honor and enforce those protections.

Sec. 2. Respecting Religious and Political Speech. All executive departments and agencies (agencies) shall, to the greatest extent practicable and to the extent permitted by law, respect and protect the freedom of persons and organizations to engage in religious and political speech. In particular, the Secretary of the Treasury shall ensure, to the extent permitted by law, that the Department of the Treasury does not take any adverse action against any individual, house of worship, or other religious organization on the basis that such individual or organization speaks or has spoken about moral or political issues from a religious perspective, where speech of similar character has, consistent with law, not ordinarily been treated as participation or intervention in a political campaign on behalf of (or in opposition to) a candidate for public office by the Department of the Treasury. As used in this section, the term "adverse action" means the imposition of any tax or tax penalty; the delay or denial of tax-exempt status; the disallowance of tax deductions for contributions made to entities exempted from taxation under section 501(c)(3) of title 26, United States Code; or any other action that makes unavailable or denies any tax deduction, exemption, credit, or benefit.

Sec. 3. Conscience Protections with Respect to Preventive-Care Mandate. The Secretary of the Treasury, the Secretary of Labor, and the Secretary of Health and Human Services shall consider issuing amended regulations, consistent with applicable law, to address conscience-based objections to the preventive-care mandate promulgated under section 300gg-13(a)(4) of title 42, United States Code.

Sec. 4. Religious Liberty Guidance. In order to guide all agencies in complying with relevant Federal law, the Attorney General shall, as appropriate, issue guidance interpreting religious liberty protections in Federal law.

. . .

Source: Executive Order 13798, 82 FR 21675, May 4, 2017.

Documents on the "Muslim Ban" (2017)

In early 2017, President Trump ordered a temporary ban on travel to the United States from seven (later six) predominantly Muslim nations. Three federal circuit court decisions placed a stay of those Executive Orders as unconstitutional actions by the executive branch. The case then moved to the Supreme Court where, after two policy revisions, the case was vacated since the temporary orders had expired.

President Trump's Executive Order 13769, entitled "Protecting the Nation from Foreign Terrorist Entry into the United States," was issued on January 27, 2017. It is excerpted below.

By the authority vested in me as President by the Constitution and laws of the United States of America, including the Immigration and Nationality Act (INS), 8 U.S. C. 1101 *et seq.*, and section 301 of title 3, United States Code, and to protect the American people from terrorist attack by foreign nationals admitted to the United States, it is hereby ordered as follows:

Section 1. Purpose. The visa issuance process plays a crucial role in detecting individuals with terrorist ties and stopping them from entering the United States. Perhaps no instance was that more apparent than the terrorist attacks of September 11, 2001, when State Department policy prevented consular officers from properly scrutinizing the visa applications of several of the 19 foreign nationals who went on to murder nearly 3,000 Americans. And while the visa-issuance process was reviewed and amended after the September 11 attacks to better detect would-be terrorists from receiving visas, these measures did not stop attacks by foreign nationals who were admitted to the United States. . . .

In order to protect Americans, the United States must ensure that those admitted to this country do not bear hostile attitudes toward it and its founding principles. The United States cannot, and should not, admit those who do not support the Constitution, or those who would place violent ideologies over American law. In addition, the United States should not admit those who engage in acts of bigotry or hatred (including "honor killings", other forms of violence against women, or the persecution of those who practice religions different from their own) or those who would oppress Americans of any race, gender, or sexual orientation.

Sec. 2. Policy. It is the policy of the United States to protect its citizens from foreign national who intend to commit terrorist attack in the United States; and to prevent the admission of foreign nationals who intend to exploit United States immigration laws for malevolent purposes.

Sec. 3. Suspension of Issuance of Visas and Other Immigration Benefits to Nationals of Countries of Particular Concern. (a) The Secretary of Homeland Security, in consultation with the Secretary of State and the Director of National Intelligence, shall immediately conduct a review to determine the information needed from any country to adjudicate any visa, admission, or other benefit under the INA (adjudications) in order to determine that the individual seeking the benefit is who the individual claims to be and is not a security or public-safety threat . . .

(c) Pursuant to section 212 (f) of the INA, 8 U.S.C. 1182 (f), I hereby proclaim that the entry of nationals from Syria as refugees is detrimental to the interests of the United States and thus suspend any such entry until such time as I have determined that sufficient changes have been made to the [United States Refugee Assistance Project] USRAP to ensure that admission of Syrian refugees is consistent with the national interest.

(d) Pursuant to section 212 (f) of the INA, 8 U.S.C. 1182 (f), I hereby proclaim that the entry of more than 50,000 refugees in fiscal year 2017 would be detrimental to the interests of the United States, and thus suspend any such entry until such time as I determine that additional admissions would be in the national interest.

Source: https://www.whitehouse.gov/the-press-office/2017/01/27/executive-order-protecting-the-nation-from-foreign-terrorist-entry-into-the-United-States. Accessed 9/5/2017.

Other documents relating to the travel ban can be found here:

State of Washington & State of Minnesota v. Trump, February 9, 2017, United States Courts for the Ninth Circuit, 17-35105. https://cdn.ca9.uscourts.gov/datastore/opinions/2017/02/09/17-35105.pdf

President Trump's Executive Order 13780: issued March 6, 2017, also entitled "Protecting the Nation from Foreign Terrorist Entry Into the United States" (replacing Executive Order 13769). https://www.whitehouse.gov/the-press-office/2017/03/06/executive-order-protecting-nation-foreign-terrorist-entry-united-states

State of Hawaii and Ismail Elshikh v. *Donald Trump et al.*, CV17-00050DKW-KSC. Filing 219, March 15, 2017. https://docs.justia.com/cases/federal/district-courts/hawaii/hidce/1:2017cv00050/132721/219

Presidential Proclamation Enhancing Vetting Capabilities and Processes for Detecting Attempted Entry Into the United States by Terrorists or Other Public-Safety Threats. Issued September 24, 2017 (third revision of the policy). https://www.whitehouse.gov/the-press-office/2017/09/24/enhancing-vetting-capabilities-and-processes-detecting-attempted-entry

The Supreme Court's dismissal of *Trump v. Hawaii*, **16-1540**. October 24, 2017. https://www.supremecourt.gov/orders/courtorders/102417zr_e29f.pdf

Introduction

This chapter lists and briefly annotates the major sources of information that the reader is encouraged to consult for further research and study on the topic of religious freedom in America. It begins with print resources, first discussing more than 100 scholarly books that are cited and annotated. Next, the major scholarly journals publishing original research articles and book reviews on the subject are covered and described. Finally, the chapter discusses feature-length films and videos available for viewing. These nonprint resources often dramatically depict the issues and people involved in religious freedom politics, putting real faces to the numbers and statistics.

Print Resources

Books

Abanes, Richard. 2002. *One Nation under God: A History of the Mormon Church*. New York: Four Walls Eight Windows.

Reverend Rob Schenck, president of Faith and Action, right, leads colleagues in prayer at the U.S. Supreme Court in Washington, as justices were releasing their decisions on the display of the Ten Commandments in public buildings and courthouses on June 27, 2005. Standing in opposition at rear is Ellen Johnson, president of American Atheists. A sharply divided Supreme Court upheld the constitutionality of showing the Ten Commandments on government land, especially when displayed in a historical context, but drew the line on certain renderings inside courthouses, saying they go too far in violating the doctrine of separation of church and state. (AP Photo/J. Scott Applewhite)

Abanes discusses the political agenda at the core of Mormonism (Church of Jesus Christ of Latter-day Saints [LDS]), its gradual transformation from a persecuted movement of radical zealots practicing polygamy and advocating a theocracy under a Mormon kingdom into a mainline Protestant denomination, and in doing so reevaluates its position on issues involving church and state relations.

Abrams, Paula. 2009. *Cross Purposes: Pierce v. Society of Sisters and the Struggle over Compulsory Education.* Ann Arbor: University of Michigan Press.

Constitutional law professor Abrams has written this definitive study of the *Pierce v. Society of Sisters* landmark Supreme Court case. The book is solidly researched; clearly written; blends law, politics, and history; and offers a captivating look at the clash between nationalism and religious pluralism.

Alley, Robert S. 1999. *The Constitution and Religion: Leading Supreme Court Cases on Church and State.* Amherst, NY: Prometheus Books.

This volume is a solid collection of original scholarly essays on the major Supreme Court cases dealing with church-state relations. It covers such issues as prayer in state legislatures, the Pledge of Allegiance, displays of the Ten Commandments in public buildings and public spaces, school prayer issues, vouchers for religious-based schools, and religion in science classes. It is an objective presentation of the Court's decisions.

Allitt, Patrick. 2008. *Religion in America since 1945: A History.* New York: Columbia University Press.

Allitt's book is a broad survey of American religion since 1945, in which he identifies major trends and critical moments with major, and a few minor, denominations and sects and traces how they have shaped—and in turn have been shaped by—the most important and often diverse events in American history since World War II, such as the Cold War, the civil rights movement, the Vietnam war, feminism and the sexual revolution, abortion rights, the anti-nuclear, and the environmental movements.

Amar, Akhil Reed. 1998. *The Bill of Rights.* New Haven, CT: Yale University Press.

This award-winning history by Amar, a Yale Law scholar and leading constitutional law scholar, provides deep insight into the impact, flexibility, and timeliness of the Bill of Rights that guarantees personal rights and shields society against authoritarianism. Amar emphasizes the counter-majoritarianism of the Bill of Rights and its impact over time, especially on state and local governments as the courts have incorporated the Bill of Rights by the Fourteenth Amendment.

Armstrong, Karen. 2000. *The Battle for God.* New York: Ballantine Books.

Armstrong examines the fear of modernity and the resulting contesting of the dominance of secular values by the fundamentalist strains in Judaism, Christianity, and Islam. She covers fundamentalist Protestantism in the United States, Orthodox Judaism in Israel, Sunni Islam in Egypt, and Shii Islam in Iran. Armstrong, a former Roman Catholic nun and Oxford University–educated scholar, has authored a couple of bestselling books on the topic.

Arrington, Leonard J., and Davis Bitton. 1992. *The Mormon Experience: A History of the Latter-day Saints,* 2nd ed. Urbana: University of Illinois Press.

The authors offer an excellent history of the LDS, which is aimed at the general audience. It has been referred to as the definitive history of Mormonism and its predominant and peculiar feature of plural marriage, or polygamy, as the major source of its conflict with majority society.

Baer, Hans. 1988. *Recreating Utopia in the Desert: A Sectarian Challenge to Modern Mormonism.* Albany, NY: State University of New York Press.

Baer's book is a major monograph on Mormonism, and it provides a brief history of the Church's struggle with modernity. It places the LDS within the context of other sects (the Jehovah's Witnesses, the Seventh-day Adventists, Christian Science, and Pentacostalism) emerging on American soil with the rise of millennialism. He shows how the LDS sees itself as the restoration of biblical priesthoods.

Bagby, Ihsan, Paul M. Perl, and Bryan T. Froehle. 2001. *The Mosque in America: A National Portrait.* Washington, DC: Council of American-Islamic Relations.

The authors present a comprehensive study of mosques in the United States, including extensive data gathered by some hundreds of interviews with mosque leaders, and it provides fascinating data about the mosques, the ethnic diversity of their attendees, inner-city versus suburban mosques, and differences among them in the role played in the mosque by the imam.

Bagley, Will. 2004. *Blood of the Prophets.* Norman: University of Oklahoma Press.

This is an award-winning book that provides an in-depth history of the Mountain Meadows massacre that took place on September 11, 1857. Bagley provides a riveting account of the attack on a wagon train by Mormons and a local militia that murdered 120 men, women, and children. He explains how the murders occurred, the involvement of Brigham Young, and the subsequent suppression and distortions of the event by the LDS to

protect the image of the Church during a politically critical time for it.

Baltzell, E. Digby. 1996. *Puritan Boston and Quaker Philadelphia.* New Brunswick, NJ: Transaction Publishers.

This study examines the biographies of 300 people in each
city to provide an historical analysis of the social character
in each city. Baltzell explores how the class authority and
leadership in the two cities are still related to the ethics of
the founders of the two cities.

Barrett, David, and Todd Johnson. 2001. *World Christian Encyclopedia.* 2 vols. New York: Oxford University.

Working for the World Evangelism Research Center, the
authors provide a reference volume that details the membership statistics for all the major and minor religions in
every country of the world. The two-volume set includes
historical data and projections—a global accounting of
the faiths and the faithful of religions in 238 nations and
territories. It is a comprehensive, thorough, and objective
reference work.

Beverly, James A. 2003. *Islamic Faith in America.* New York:
Facts on File.

This basic text explores the impact of Muslims on American culture, social issues, and politics. It provides a glimpse
into the lives of some of the most influential Muslims in
America. Like all Facts of Files books, this book introduces its readers to the basic beliefs and history of this
intricate religion.

Bilhartz, Terry D. 1986. *Urban Religion and the Second Great
Awakening.* Madison, NJ: Fairleigh Dickinson University Press.

Bilhartz explores the development of the Second Great
Awakening by concentrating on the Baltimore area and
examines the development and consequences of the
church system in Baltimore during the turbulent era

that played so prominent a role in the formation age for American religion. It is an award-winning book by the author of books on religion in America and on world religions.

Bonomi, Patricia U. 1986. *Under the Cope of Heaven: Religion, Society, and Politics in Colonial America.* New York: Oxford University Press.

Bonomi's book examines the role that religion played in American politics and economy, shaping early American life and values. She focuses on the middle and Southern colonies as well as on Puritan New England. She examines colonial clergy and church goers of diverse religious backgrounds and explores the relationship between religion and politics and the vital role religion played in the American Revolution.

Bowman, Robert M., Jr. 1992. *Understanding Jehovah's Witnesses.* Grand Rapids, MI: Baker Book House.

The author of a dozen books, and the executive director of the Institute for Religious Research, Bowman studies the Jehovah's Witnesses and how and why they read, interpret, and understand the Bible the way they do. In doing so, he explains the major doctrinal errors—from the Institute's perspective—of the Jehovah's Witnesses and how the Witnesses are distinguished from other Evangelicals.

Brinton, Henry G. 2012. *The Welcoming Congregation: Roots and Fruits of Christian Hospitality.* Louisville, KY: Westminster John Knox Press.

In this volume, Brinton, a pastor, studies the biblical basis for Christian hospitality and traces how it is practiced in congregations today. He acknowledges the challenges for the open embracing of all people in the life of the church and offers a guide for creating the hospitable congregation and how to welcome others through formation, reconciliation, and outreach. Each chapter includes discussion questions and action plans.

Brooks, Roy L. 1996. *Integration or Separation? A Strategy for Racial Equality.* Cambridge, MA: Harvard University Press.
  Brooks, a law professor, clearly and frankly admits that integration hasn't worked and possibly never will. But he casts equal doubt on total separation. His book proposes a strategy for a middle way—limited separation, what many scholars today term "segmented incorporation." His limited separation would promote cultural and economic integration, while promoting separate schooling, housing, and business enterprises. He envisions the African American schools, businesses, and communities redesigned to serve the enlightened self-interest of the individual.

Bushman, Claudia L., and Richard L. Bushman. 2001. *Building the Kingdom: A History of Mormonism in America.* New York: Oxford University Press.
  The authors provide a book within a series *Religion in American Life.* This volume introduces the readers to Mormon leaders like Joseph Smith and Brigham Young. It traces the Great Trek West, covers the skirmishes and battles, and the court conflict between Mormons and Gentiles (non-Mormons), other religions, the media, and the American government. It briefly explains the origins and history of the Latter-day Saints, with a balanced discussion of the difficult issues involved in that history and in the relations of Mormons to the broader American culture.

Butler, Jon. 2005. *Religion in Colonial America.* New York: Oxford University.
  Butler narrates the state of religious affairs in both the Old and the New Worlds during the era of colonial times, from the failure of John Winthrop's attempt to

establish "Puritan perfection" to the controversy over Anne Hutchinson, the evangelism of the ex-slave and Methodist preacher Absalom Jones, and to the spiritual resilience of the Catawba Indians. He explains how the meeting of these diverse groups produced an evolution of religious practice, including the birth of "revivals" and how they created a foundation for the First Amendment.

Byrd, James. 2013. *Sacred Scriptures, Sacred War: The Bible and the American Revolution.* New York: Oxford University Press.

Byrd presents a comprehensive analysis of how American revolutionaries defended their convictions through scripture; how many colonists saw the Bible as a book about war; and how God participated in combat, playing a decisive role on the battlefield. He details how, when war came, preachers and patriots alike turned to scripture for exhortations to fight. He shows how soldiers who died were given the halo of martyrdom and how a sense of divine providence was conferred on the revolutionary cause. The book describes how the Bible shaped the war, and how the war shaped Americans' view of the Bible.

Church of Jesus Christ of Latter-day Saints. 1989. *Church History in the Fullness of Time.* Salt Lake City, UT: The Church of the Latter-day Saints.

This book is the official church history of the Mormons. It covers the LDS from the time of Joseph Smith and Brigham Young to the current day. It was issued for use in Sunday school classes and is a volume of some 90 LDS publications hosted by Brigham Young University.

Colgrove, James. 2006. *State of Immunity: The Politics of Vaccination in Twentieth Century America.* Berkeley: University of California Press.

Colgrove offers a well-balanced, vivid, and comprehensive narrative history of the social and political aspects of vaccination and how dozens of vaccines were developed to immunize against a host of diseases. He considers how individual liberty must be balanced against the common welfare, how experts should act in the face of incomplete or inconsistent scientific information, and how the public should be involved in these decisions. He shows how the "anti-vaccination" movement took on religious freedom undertones.

Curtis, Edward E. 2002. *Islam in Black America.* Albany: State University of New York Press.

Curtis explores modern African American thought through the prism of Islamic history, stressing the question of universality versus particularity. He focuses on five notable African American Muslim figures. He shows how the tensions in African American Islam parallel those of Islam throughout its history. He concludes that the interplay of the universal and the particular interpretations of Islam can allow African American Muslims to embrace both a specific group of people and all people.

Daniels, Roger. 2002. *Coming to America: A History of Immigration and Ethnicity in American Life*, 2nd ed. New York: Perennial.

This volume is an updated, revised edition of an engrossing study of immigration to the United States from colonial times to the present, by an eminent immigration historian, written for the general reader. Daniels divides the book into three sections: Colonial America, the Century of Immigration (1820–1924), and Modern Times. He debunks the melting pot while showing xenophobia to be unfounded. The text includes tables, charts, and maps selected to bolster his case. Social science jargon creeps in enough to perhaps challenge some general readers and his eminent scholarly background shows and weakens the narrative power of his history.

Davies, Douglas J. 2000. *The Mormon Culture of Salvation.* New York: Ashgate Publishing.

Davies presents a comprehensive study of Mormonism, Mormon culture, and Mormon religious life, with an interdisciplinary perspective. He offers theories to explain the phenomenal growth of Mormonism. He describes Mormon belief, ritual, family life, history, the Mormon worldview, and how that view influences their relations with the broader culture. He details in their history their conflict with American government over religious freedom issues.

DeCarlo, Louis A., Jr. 1998. *Malcolm and the Cross.* New York: New York University Press.

DeCarlo explores how Christianity and Christians influenced Malcolm X, his spirituality, and his personal life as well as his career. He shows Malcolm X's complex relationship with the Nation of Islam and examines Malcolm X as an activist, journalist, orator, and revolutionist against the backdrop of his religious heritage. He depicts Malcolm X as a religious revolutionist and how cultic Islam, Christianity, and traditional Islam shape discussions of racism in the United States.

Dreisbach, Daniel. 2002. *Thomas Jefferson and the Wall of Separation of Church and State.* New York: New York University Press.

Jefferson has had the most profound influence on church-state law, policy, and discourse. His concept of a "wall of separation between church and state" is broadly accepted as a concise description of the U.S. Constitution's church-state arrangements. Dreisbach offers an in-depth examination of the origins, controversial uses, and competing interpretations of the concept in American public policy.

Feldman, Noah. 2005. *Divided by God.* New York: Farrar, Straus and Giroux.

Feldman offers an appraisal of the profound conflict between religiously devout value voters and secularists over church-state matters. He shows how that conflict is as old as the country and how that complex history of the nation's past struggle with church-state relations shows how it might be resolved in today's religiously diverse society of Muslims, Hindu, Buddhists, Catholics, Protestants, and Jews. Feldman covers how people resolved conflicts over the Bible, the Pledge of Allegiance, the teaching of evolution, and similar issues through the shared values of liberty, equality, and freedom of conscience. He tells the story of a long-running conflict that has made the American people who they are and proposes a solution to the current iteration of that conflict while respecting the long-running view that religion and state should not mix.

Fenn, Richard K. 1997. *The End of Time: Religion, Ritual, and the Forging of the Soul.* New York: Pilgrim Press.
A timely and topical study of how both societies and individuals cope with the meaning and passage of time. It shows that even in secular societies, religion remains an important source of attitudes and norms important to those who wish to explain human behavior. It is an interdisciplinary study by a leading sociologist of religion.

Fitzgerald, Frances. 2017. *The Evangelicals: The Struggle to Shape America.* New York: Simon and Schuster.
Pulitzer Prize–winning author Fitzgerald presents a sweeping history of evangelicalism and the conflict between modernists and traditionalists. Her book includes vivid portraits of Billy Graham, Jerry Falwell, Pat Robertson, Jim Bakker, James Dobson, Rick Warren, R. J. Rushdoony, and Francis Schaeffer. In this outsider's book, she argues that evangelicals lost their way when they became a white-male reactionary force about saving America by

electing Republican politicians and fighting the culture wars begun in the wake of massive social changes of the 1960s. She argues that the movement became an unholy marriage of top evangelical leaders to the Republican Party and conservative lobbyists and operatives. She concludes, however, that its influence is waning.

Flowers, Ronald, Stephen Green, and Mellisa Rogers. 2008. *Religious Freedom and the Supreme Court*, 8th ed. Waco, TX: Baylor University Press.

This is a revised and updated edition of a classic text on the subject, with a new introduction on how the Supreme Court delineates the idea of religious freedom on a case-by-case basis. Clearly written, the text is aimed at the undergraduate market. It covers cases up to 2006.

Gardner, Gerald. 1999. *Gardner Witchcraft Series: Witchcraft Today, The Meaning of Witchcraft*. New York: Mercury Publications, and Los Gatos, CA: Restivio Enterprises.

A reissue of the books that launched the Wicca religious movement in the twentieth century, which began in the United Kingdom in the 1950s. It includes *Witchcraft Today* and the *Meaning of Witchcraft*. It is an apologetic for pagan, polytheistic, nature-based religion that harkens back to the Druids of the ancient British Isles.

Gjerde, Jon, ed. 1998. *Major Problems in American Immigration and Ethnic History*. Boston: Houghton Mifflin.

This book is one within the series *Major Problems in American History*. This collection of essays and primary source documents explores the theme on political, economic, and cultural forces that cause immigration (including the search for religious freedom). Each chapter includes an introduction, source notes, and suggested readings. It is edited by the late University of California Berkeley historian.

Glenn, Charles L., Jr. 1988. *The Myth of the Common School.* Amherst: University of Massachusetts Press.

Glenn examines the historical development of the idea that the state should provide public education as a means to mold common loyalties and values among the citizenry to pursue the interest of national unity. That concept of public education is often rejected by parents and groups who do not accept the values of the state and its public educators. Glenn concludes with suggesting workable and tested solutions to this perennial dilemma of the clash of these basic values.

Green, Steven K. 2010. *The Second Disestablishment: Church and State in Nineteenth Century America.* New York: Oxford University Press.

Green posits that the nineteenth century was a critical period in the history of church-state separation despite the dominance of evangelical Protestantism during that century. Green's study focuses on the period between the ratification of the Constitution and the Supreme Court decision in *Everson v. Board of Education* (1947), which mandated that the Establishment Clause applied to the states via the Fourteenth Amendment.

Guastad, Edwin S. 1999. *Liberty of Conscience: Roger Williams in America.* Valley Forge: Judson Press.

Guastad explores the life of Roger Williams as the founder of the Rhode Island colony and the defender of religious freedom, as a person of deep convictions who passionately strove to achieve and preserve liberty of conscience. The book provides an illuminating examination of the life of one of history's elusive figures.

Guest, Kenneth. 2008. *God in Chinatown: Religion and Survival in New York's Evolving Immigrant Community.* New York: New York University Press.

This is a pathbreaking study of the largest wave of new immigrants to New York City's Chinatown. Guest explores the religious beliefs, practices, and deities they bring with them: Buddhists, Daoists, as well as Protestant and Catholic Christianity. An ethnographic study, it examines the role that religious communities play in the incorporation process in Chinatown's highly stratified ethnic enclave. He examines the transnational networks of religious communities in New York and in China, illuminating how these networks transmit religious and social dynamics to New York City.

Hall, Kermit, and James Ely, eds. 2009. *The Oxford Guide to United States Supreme Court Decisions.* New York: Oxford University Press.

The editors offer a collection of insightful accounts by eminent legal scholars of landmark cases before the Supreme Court, from *Marbury v. Madison* to the *Dred Scott* decision, to *Brown v. Board of Education*, and *Roe v. Wade.* It includes more than 400 cases, including more than 50 new landmark rulings, such as *Gonzales v. Planned Parenthood.*

Hartford Seminary/Hartford Institute for Religion Research. *The Encyclopedia of Religion and Society.* Hartford, CT: Alta Mira Press.

Hartford Seminary, a theological college in Hartford, Connecticut, traces its origins back to 1833. It publishes this extensive, multivolume encyclopedia of religion and society, which covers the field literally from A to Z (with an entry on Zoroastrianism), covering persons, ideas, religions, movements, sects, and policy and laws impacting religion.

Head, Tom. 2016. *The Religious Right in America: A Historical Encyclopedia.* Santa Barbara, CA: ABC-CLIO.

An encyclopedic approach that examines the political influence of the religious right movement and its often cult-like appeal that at times seems to stand the idea of religious freedom on its head.

Hoffman, Edward. 1991. *Despite All Odds: The Story of the Lubavitch.* New York: Simon and Schuster.
 Hoffman provides a moving, portrait of Rebbe, Rabbi Menachem Mendel Schneerson, who for more than 40 years led the Lubavitch sect of Hasidic Jews in New York. In an adulatory biography of the Libavicher Rebbe, Hoffman illuminates, as well, the ultra-orthodox conservative form of Judaism and its impact on the practice of Judaism and Jewish culture in New York and America.

Holmes, David R. 2006. *The Faith of the Founding Fathers.* New York: Oxford University Press.
 Religious historian David Holmes of the College of William and Mary provides this clear and concise examination of the religious beliefs of the Founding Fathers, the state of religious culture in the late colonial era, and an account of the religious groups found in each colony. His book enlightens the topic of the various forms of Deism that flourished in the American colonies and the impact their ideas had on the American Revolution and establishment of the nation, including the concept of freedom of religion as eventually espoused in the Constitution.

Hondagnev-Sotelo, Pierrette. 2008. *God's Heart Has No Borders: How Religious Activists Are Working for Immigrant Rights.* Berkeley: University of California Press.
 This volume provides a compelling account of the contribution to immigrant rights made by religious activists. It focuses upon the 1965–2001 period. It offers a close-up

of Muslim, Christian, and Jewish groups that worked together to counter xenophobia. It provides a context to religious fundamentalism and its capacity to incite violence.
The book revises our understanding of the role of religion
in social movements.

Hudson, Deal W. 2008. *Onward Christian Soldiers: The Growing Political Power of Catholics and Evangelicals in the United
States.* New York: Simon and Schuster.
    Hudson, an American conservative political activist and
    president of the Morley Institute for Church and Culture,
    provides an "insider's" view of the growing power of the
    Christian evangelical movement. It is a cultural history
    that spans 30 years and shows how evangelicals migrated
    to the Republican Party during those years.

Jacobson, Simon. 1995. *Towards a Meaningful Life: The Wisdom of the Rebbe.* New York: William Morrow.
    Chabad Hasidic writer Simon Jacobson's book explores
    the ideas of Chabad philosophy and elucidates the teach-
    ings of Rabbi Manachem Schneerson, the seventh Rebbe
    of the Chabad. The book explores the concept of the "soul"
    as the "flame of God," "faith" as the central component of
    the social order, and "charity" as the sanctifier of life.

Jefferson, Thomas. 1977. *The Portable Thomas Jefferson*, ed.
Merrill Peterson. New York: Penguin Books.
    This edited volume of Jefferson's writings includes his Sum-
    mary View of the Rights of British America, his Notes on
    the State of Virginia, 79 letters, his opinion on the "Con-
    stitutionality of the Central Bank," his proposal for the
    Virginia Statute on Religious Liberty, and other writings.

Jenkins, Philip. 2003. *The New Anti-Catholicism: The Last Acceptable Prejudice.* New York: Oxford University Press.
    Jenkins is a professor of history and religious studies
    at Pennsylvania State University. His book deals with

contemporary anti-Catholic bigotry, particularly in the United States. He argues that it is still possible to make hostile and vituperative public statements about Catholicism without fear of serious political repercussions. He examines anti-Catholicism stereotyping in academia, the media, politics, and the religious right.

Kaplan, Jeffrey. 1997. *Radical Religion in America: Millennium Movements from the Far Right to the Children of Noah*. Syracuse, NY: Syracuse University Press.
Kaplan focuses on the milieu of three religiously based apocalyptic movements, their radical doctrine, and their rejection of mainstream American culture: the Christian identity, Odinism and Asatru movement, and B'nai Noah. He examines millennialism in contemporary apocalyptic movements.

Kohut, Andrew, John C. Green, Scott Keeter, and Robert C. Toth. 2000. *The Diminishing Divide: Religion's Changing Role in American Politics*. Washington, DC: Brookings Institution.
This book, which examines the relationship between religion and politics, shows the blunt, direct role of religion in U.S. politics, drawing on the extensive research of the Pew Research Center, the National Election Studies, and other data sets. It examines the historical relationship between religion and politics, their changing role since the 1960s, and religious power in American political life in the 21st century.

Kraybill, Donald B., and Steven M. Nolt. 1995. *Amish Enterprises: From Plows to Profits*. Baltimore, MD: Johns Hopkins University Press.
This is the first book to examine how the development of 150 Amish cottage industries and microenterprises is reshaping Amish life and transforming Amish communities

across America. The authors trace the rise and impact of these businesses in recent decades, employing demographic and technological changes in Amish communities in and outside of Pennsylvania.

Kraybill, Donald B., and Marc A. Olshan, eds. 1994. *The Amish Struggle with Modernity.* Hanover, NH: University Press of New England.

An academic introduction to contemporary Amish culture, this book traces Amish history and their attempts to remain separate from the larger society. It examines the scale of the dilemma faced by some 140,000 Amish that arises when people devoted to plain living face the complexities of modern life in America.

Laderman, Gary, and Luis León, eds. 2014. *Religion and American Culture: Tradition, Diversity, and Popular Expression,* 2nd ed., 4 vols. Santa Barbara, CA: ABC-CLIO.

This revised and expanded edition of a four-volume work provides a detailed, multicultural survey of established and new American religions. It investigates the interactions between religion and ethnicity, gender, politics, regionalism, ethics, and popular culture in more than 140 essays that explore contemporary spiritual practices and cultures within an historical perspective.

Lambert, Frank. 2003. *The Founding Fathers and the Place of Religion in America.* Princeton, NJ: Princeton University Press.

Lambert examines how the colonies, founded on explicitly religious experiments, came to be the first modern nation-state committed to the separation of church and state, reflected in its Constitution. He explains why it happened through a synthesis of American history, from the Puritan's arrival to Jefferson's presidency. He locates the shift in mid-18th century in the wake of evangelical revivalism and the arrival of new immigrants.

Landes, Richard, ed. 2000. *Encyclopedia of Millennialism and Millennial Movements.* New York: Routledge.

Landes argues that all the major world religions, with the exception of Hinduism, began as millennialism movements and that they share a common form of social protest and a mechanism for societal change. This book is a comprehensive guide to a religious/social movement throughout history and around the world.

Landes, Richard. 2011. *Heaven on Earth: The Varieties of the Millennial Experience.* New York: Oxford University Press.

An American historian specializing in millennialism, Landes provides a revisionist argument about the significance of millennialism throughout history, focusing on millennialism across many religious and supposedly secular groups, demonstrating that the millennial movement is not exclusive to Judaism and Christianity.

Launius, Roger D., and Linda Thatcher, eds. 1994. *Differing Visions: Dissenters in Mormon History.* Urbana: University Press of Illinois.

Launius and Thatcher explore the dissenting traditions in Mormonism by presenting selections on 19 Mormon dissenters. The book focuses on the variety of religious sentiment within Mormonism and assesses factors encouraging divergent ideas from the early 1800s onward.

Lee, Jonathan, Fumitaka Matsuoka, Edmond Yee, and Ronald Nakasone, eds. 2015. *Asian American Religious Cultures.* 2 vols. Santa Barbara, CA: ABC-CLIO.

This is a two-volume encyclopedia of Asian American religious cultures. It demonstrates their widely diverse groups and with equality discusses their heterogeneous religious beliefs and traditions. It provides authoritative data on their various religious experiences and includes critical essays on the intersection of race and religion among Asian Americans.

LeMay, Michael C. 2009. *The Perennial Struggle*, 3rd ed. Upper Saddle River, NJ: Prentice-Hall.

This book integrates insights from all the social sciences to study ethnic and racial relations and how these groups interact in group politics in the United States. It intends its readers to better understand the history, contributions, and special problems of particular and exemplary minority groups in American society, including a host of religious minority groups.

LeMay, Michael C. 2013. *Transforming America: Perspectives on Immigration, vol. 1: The Making of a Nation of Nations: The Founding to 1865.* Santa Barbara, CA: Praeger.

This is the first of a three-volume set of edited collections that bring together essays by scholars from many disciplinary perspectives to explore the impact of immigrants on all aspects of American life, culture, economy, and politics.

Levy, Leonard W. 1994. *Establishment Clause and the First Amendment.* Chapel Hill: University of North Carolina Press.

Levy's classic work studies the circumstances leading to the writing of the Establishment Clause of the First Amendment. He argues that the Founders intended to prohibit government aid for religion even on an impartial basis. This edition incorporates new material and a discussion of Establishment Clause cases brought before the Supreme Court.

Levy, Leonard W. 1999. *Origins of the Bill of Rights.* New Haven, CT: Yale University Press.

In this history of the origins of the Bill of Rights, Levy offers a panoramic view of the liberties secured by the first ten amendments. He explores behind-the-scenes machinations, public rhetoric, and political motivations of James Madison and others. It is a terse and laconic study showing how the Bill of Rights evolved over time.

Liebman, Robert, and Robert Wuthnow. 1983. *The New Christian Right.* New York: Aldine Publishing.

> This book of original essays offers an objective and enlightening analysis of the emerging and changing forms of the new Christian right. It reexamines standard theories of social movements and the nexus between religion and politics in contemporary America. It uses personal interviews, survey data, and financial documents using nontechnical and non-jargonistic language.

Lincoln, C. Eric. 1994. *The Black Muslims in America,* 3rd ed. Trenton, NJ: Africa World Press.

> This edition of Lincoln's classic study of the Black Muslim movement focuses on Louis Farrakhan's movement as the true successor to the Nation of Islam founded by Elijah Muhammad.

Litt, Edgar. 1970. *Ethnic Politics in America.* Glenview, IL: Scott Foresman.

> Litt explores the persistence of ethnicity in political behavior, covering the strategies of accommodation, separatism, and radicalism. He covers a host of racial, ethnic, religious minority groups and their complex politics.

Lorentzen, Lois Ann. 2014. *Hidden Lives and Human Rights in the United States.* 3 vols. Santa Barbara, CA: Praeger.

> This three-volume set is a comprehensive collection of original essays on undocumented immigrants, covering a host of issues not often found elsewhere and featuring the latest research from the country's top immigration scholars.

Mapp, Alf. 2003. *The Faith of Our Fathers: What America's Founders Really Believed.* Lanham, MD: Rowman and Littlefield.

> Mapp's book cuts through the historical uncertainty to accurately portray the religious beliefs held by 11 of the

Founding Fathers, including John Adams, Benjamin Franklin, Thomas Jefferson, and James Madison. He shows that they were men with religious beliefs as diverse as their political opinions. These profiles shed light on their lives and times but also on the role of religion in public life throughout American history.

Marsh, Clifton E. 2000. *The Lost-Found Nation of Islam in America*. Lanham, MD: Scarecrow Press.
This book is an enlightening look at the Nation of Islam and Minister Louis Farrakhan from the ideological splits in the Nation of Island during the 1970s to its growth and expansion during the 1990s.

Martin, William. 1996. *With God on Our Side: The Rise of the Religious Right in America*. New York: Broadway Books.
Martin provides an insightful look at the rise of the religious right in United States' politics and culture. It is a balanced account of the impact of conservative Christianity on postwar politics. It presents an authoritative portrait of one of America's most powerful political interest groups.

Mauss, Armand. 1994. *The Angel and the Beehive: The Mormon Struggle with Assimilation*. Urbana: University of Illinois Press.
This classic study of Mormonism centers on the response of the LDS to societal changes, becoming first intermingled with its host society, then rejecting those changes in order to maintain its distinct identity. He symbolizes these contrasting ideas with the angel topping the LDS temple in Salt Lake City and the beehive sculpture crowning the former Utah hotel.

McGarvie, Mark Douglas. 2004. *One Nation under Law: America's Early National Struggle to Separate Church and State*. DeKalb: Northern Illinois University Press.

Using an innovative perspective, McGarvie argues that the separation of church and state principle emerged as a result of the contract clause of the Constitution, not the First Amendment, and that the original intent of the Framers was indeed separation. His book is a significant contribution to the vibrant scholarly debate on the subject.

Merriman, Scott. 2017. *When Religious and Secular Interests Collide: Faith, Law, and the Religious Exemption Debate.* Santa Barbara, CA: Praeger.
Merriman examines the countervailing arguments in the religious exemption debate and explains why it remains so heated and controversial a subject in modern politics. He uses up-to-date coverage as well as a full history of religious exemption cases from the 19th to the 21st centuries. The book explores the interplay between religion and law in the United States.

Middlekauff, Robert. 2005. *The Glorious Cause: The American Revolution, 1763–1789.* New York: Oxford University Press.
This critically acclaimed volume offers an unsurpassed history of the American Revolution and the birth of the Republic. Middlekauff traces the history from the French and Indian Wars through the election of President Washington, providing a compelling account of the key events and insightful portraits of key persons and groups.

Myers, Walter Dean. 2000. *Malcolm X: A Fire Burning Brightly.* New York: HarperCollins.
Award-winning author Walter Dean Myers provides a straightforward and compelling portrayal of one of America's most influential figures. His book is an evenhanded narrative that celebrates the man and his radical message to all people of color.

Nuovo, Victor. 2002. *John Locke: Writings on Religion.* New York: Oxford University Press.

Nuovo offers a comprehensive collection of Locke's writings on religion and theology that reveals Locke's deep religious motivation and its pervasive influence on his thought. They are key texts in intellectual history and had a profound impact on America's Founding Fathers.

Offitt, Paul A. 2015. *Bad Faith: When Religious Belief Undermine Modern Medicine.* New York: Basic Books.

Physician and author Offitt gives readers insight into the minds of those who medically martyr themselves, and sometimes their children, in the name of religion. He relates tales of Jehovah's Witnesses, Ultra-Orthodox Jews, Christian scientists, and others and their devastating experiences, which he chronicles with vivid storytelling, revealing complex and compelling characters.

Orsi, Robert. 2004. *Between Heaven and Earth: The Religious Worlds' People Make and the Scholars Who Study Them.* Princeton, NJ: Princeton University Press.

Orsi maintains that religion exists as a network of relationships between heaven and earth, involving people and the many sacred figures they hold dear. He then argues that many modern academic scholars marginalize the relationships that people have with these sacred figures by making dubious distinctions between "good" religious expressions and "bad" ones.

Penton, M. James. 1997. *Apocalypse Delayed: The Story of Jehovah's Witnesses.* Toronto: Toronto University Press.

Penton presents an overview of the Jehovah's Witnesses, from the perspectives of history, doctrine, and sociology. A former insider and now an observer at a distance from his subject, he presents a penetrating study. This edition considers changes in doctrine, practices, and governance on issues like medical treatment, higher education, apostates, and the apocalypse.

Peters, Shawn Francis. 2002. *Judging Jehovah's Witnesses: Religious Persecution and the Dawn of the Rights Revolution.* Lawrence: University Press of Kansas.

> Peters offers a complete account of the personalities, events, and institutions behind the First Amendment rights claims and cases of the Jehovah's Witnesses. He relates the persecution against them and how the American Civil Liberties Union (ACLU) and liberal clergy stepped in to defend them. He examines the strategies they used to combat that discrimination.

Peters, Shawn Francis. 2003. *The Yoder Case: Religious Freedom, Education, and Parental Rights.* Lawrence: University Press of Kansas.

> Peters tells the full story of the *Wisconsin v. Yoder* (1971) case. His book is a comprehensive, thoughtful, yet accessible examination of the events and personalities involved in the landmark case and the long battle of the Amish to secure their religious freedom rights.

Peterson, Merrill D., Robert C. Vaughan, and Robin Lovin, eds. 1988. *The Virginia Statute for Religious Freedom: Its Evolution and Consequences in American History.* Cambridge, England: Cambridge University Press.

> The editors present a collection of essays from a symposium at the University of Virginia that provides a comprehensive examination of one of the most important primary documents on the religious freedom doctrine.

Portman, Rob, and Cheryl Bauer. 2004. *Wisdom's Paradise: The Forgotten Shakers of Union Village.* Wilmington, OH: Orange Frazer Press.

> Senator Rob Portman (R-OH), a lifelong Shaker enthusiast, and freelance writer Cheryl Bauer coauthored this compelling story of the first western Shaker settlement, founded in 1805, as an attempt to create a utopian haven

community called Union Village. It chronicles their attempt at creating heaven on earth. It describes how they contended with hostile mobs, newspapers, and a state legislature, all of whom deemed them satanic.

Ragosta, John A. 2013. *Religious Freedom: Jefferson's Legacy, American Creed.* Charlottesville: University of Virginia Press.

A significant contribution to the extensive discourse on religious freedom, this is an engaging intellectual and legal history. Ragosta's core argument stands against both the preferentialist view and the view that the First Amendment was merely a jurisdictional mechanism to protect states' religious establishments. He makes a convincing case that Jefferson's strict separationist thought was and should remain at the center of the First Amendment.

Schaefer, Richard. 2014. *Racial and Ethnic Groups*, 14th ed. New York: Pearson.

This bestselling undergraduate sociology text provides readers with an accessible, comprehensive, and current introduction to the issues confronting racial and ethnic groups in the United States placed within a sociohistorical context. It covers the changing dynamic of the American population by incorporating the most current statistical data, including the 2010 census.

Sehat, David. 2011. *The Myth of American Religious Freedom.* New York: Oxford University Press.

In this historical review of religion in public life, Sehat traces the application of the First Amendment from the federal government to the states and local governments after 1940. He covers the culture wars of the last 50 years and the rise (and fall) of the Protestant establishment. Through a series of profiles of key actors, he questions the myths held by both the left and the right political belief in American politics.

Singer, David, and Lawrence Grossman, eds. 2007. *American Jewish Yearbook, 2006.* New York: American Jewish Committee. This is an annual record of the status of Judaism in the United States and around the world.

Singh, Robert. 1997. *The Farrakhan Phenomenon.* Washington, DC: Georgetown University Press. Singh presents for the general reader a critical analysis of Louis Farrakhan's rise to national prominence as a function of race and reaction in contemporary America. Using published and unpublished records, personal interviews, and Farrakhan's writings, Singh places Farrakhan within the "paranoid style" of reactionaries, arguing Farrakhan is an extreme conservative exploiting black-white divisions and conflicts within the black community.

Smith, Frank, ed. 2016. *Religion and Politics in America: An Encyclopedia of Church and State in American Life.* 2 vols. Santa Barbara, CA: ABC-CLIO. Organized alphabetically, this two-volume set offers insights into the contemporary controversies over religion and politics in America. Each entry places its topic in historical context and shows how religious beliefs and political ideals have always existed side by side and often clashed, from colonial times to the present.

Smith, Jane. 1999. *Islam in America.* New York: Columbia University Press. Smith introduces a richly textured portrait of Islam in the United States. Aimed at the general reader, she covers Islam's basic tenets, surveys a history of Islam in America, and profiles adherents' lifestyles, religious practices, and worldviews. She pays particular attention to the tensions felt by many Muslims as they attempt to live the faith, adhering to traditions while adapting to, from their perspective, an alien culture that is excessively secular and materialistic.

Spring, Joel. 2008. *The American School: From the Puritans to No Child Left Behind.* New York: McGraw-Hill.

This comprehensive history of American education offers critical analysis and alternative interpretations of each historical period, emphasizing the role of multiculturalism and cultural domination in shaping America's schools and the position of the school as one of many institutions that manage the distribution of ideas in society. He shows racism as a central issue in both American history and educational history and covers economic issues as important ones for understanding the evolution of schools in the United States.

Urofsky, Melvin. 2002. *Religious Freedom: Rights and Liberties under the Law.* Santa Barbara, CA: ABC-CLIO.

Urofsky addresses the question of what constitutes "legitimate" constitutionally protected religious practice as it has been debated throughout American history. He offers a thorough, responsible, and evenhanded analysis to provide readers with a solid grounding in the complex constitutional issues that lie behind the headlines associated with controversial court cases.

Utter, Glenn, and James L. True. 2004. *Conservative Christians and Political Participation: A Reference Handbook.* Santa Barbara, CA: ABC-CLIO.

The authors examine the involvement and influence of conservative Christians in American politics. They provide an historical overview of the interaction of religion and politics from colonial times to the present, exploring the demographics of conservative Christians, their major concerns, and their goals and the various political methods they employ to achieve them. It covers profiles of the major leaders and organizations of the movement.

Varsanyi, Monica, ed. 2010. *Taking Local Control: Immigration Policy Activism in U.S. Cities and States.* Stanford, CA: Stanford University Press.

Varsanyi analyzes the wide range of policies created by cities and states across the nation to address illegal immigration within their jurisdictions. These policies, both anti- and pro-immigrant in nature, run the gamut from California's Proposition 187, which sought to establish a state-run citizenship screening system, to cities and states who declare themselves as "sanctuaries" for undocumented immigrants who require access to their health care and social services. It is an important contribution to the body of literature on immigration that perhaps overfocuses on federal law and policy.

Vile, John R. 2015. *Encyclopedia of Constitutional Amendments, and Amending Issues, 1789–2015*, 4th ed. 2 vols. Santa Barbara, CA: ABC-CLIO.

In this fourth and updated edition, Vile presents a comprehensive review of Constitutional amendments and proposed amendments and discusses the critical issues they deal with from 1789 to the present. He covers each of the 27 amendments, as well as essays on proposed ones, and outlines proposals for more radical changes to the U.S. Constitution.

Vile, John R. 2015. *Founding Documents of America: Documents Decoded.* Santa Barbara, CA: ABC-CLIO.

In this volume in ABC-CLIO's popular *Documents Decoded* series, Vile offers historic documents key to the foundation of the national government with introductions that supply the background information and analysis that highlights key provisions and provides historical context. It covers the Declaration of Independence, the Constitution, the Bill of Rights, private diary entries, and political polemics organized chronologically into four sections: antecedents, revolutionary and confederal periods, calling and convening the Convention, and debating, ratifying, and implementing it. It covers more than

50 primary source documents. It is aimed at high school and college students.

Walters, Kerry S. 1992. *The American Deists: Voices of Reason and Dissent in the Early Republic.* Lawrence: University Press of Kansas.
Deism began in colonial America, flourishing by the American Revolution and dying by 1811. Walters presents a full analysis of Deism and rational religion in colonial and early America. He covers the works of six influential American Deists and provides a description of its roots, its major themes, its social and political implications, and the reasons for its eventual demise. He contends it offers insight of real significance today.

Weinstein, Allen, and David Rubel. 2002. *The Story of America: Freedom and Crisis from Settlement to Superpower.* New York: D.K. Publishing.
The authors present an insightful, informative, and entertaining book that covers American history aimed at the general reader as a story of twists and turns, heroes and villains, lovers and saints. It includes contributions from two-dozen eminent colleagues, several of whom are Pulitzer Prize winners. It shows how America became a world power and how its past impacts its present.

Wessinger, Catherine. 2000. *Millennialism, Persecution, and Violence: Historical Cases.* Syracuse, NY: Syracuse University Press.
In her cross-cultural and comparative book, Wessinger reveals three patterns with millennial groups that are not mutually exclusive: assaulted groups attacked by outsiders who feared and misunderstood them, fragile millennial groups that initiate violence to preserve their religious goals, and revolutionary millennial groups with an ideology that sanctions violence.

Wessinger, Catherine, ed. 2011. *The Oxford Handbook of Millennialism*. Oxford: Oxford University Press.

Wessinger presents original essays by 34 contributors that offer the general reader an in-depth look at the theoretical underpinnings of millennialism and how it has been manifested across history and in many different cultures.

Wilcox, Clyde. 1992. *God's Warriors: The Christian Right in Twentieth-Century America*. Baltimore, MD: Johns Hopkins University Press.

Wilcox assesses the Christian right's mass base and electoral appeal using social science theories to account for their origins. He provides an overview of the Christian right and the interaction of religion and politics using survey data and a review of the literature on the topic.

Wilder, Courtney. 2016. *Disability, Faith, and the Church: Inclusion and Accommodation in Contemporary Congregations*. Santa Barbara, CA: ABC-CLIO.

Wilder combines theoretical discussions with practical information for congregations to use, while exploring biblical texts and historical and theological issues of disability, and provides examples of successful minority people with disabilities.

Witte, John, Jr. 2012. *No Establishment of Religion: America's Original Contribution to Religious Liberty*. New York: Oxford University Press.

Witte provides an in-depth analysis of the meaning of the Establishment Clause as an American innovation in the relation of church and state. He presents 12 original essays.

Witte, John, Jr. 2012. *Religion and Human Rights: An Introduction*. New York: Oxford University Press.

This book is a comprehensive survey of religion and human rights, including both Eastern and Western traditions, and the category of indigenous religions. The book covers issues like environmental sustainability; conflict transformation; world peace; group rights; self-determination of religious communities; economic, social, and doctrinal rights; and the relationships between religion, culture, and ethnicity.

Wojcik, Daniel. 1997. *The End of the World as We Know It: Faith, Fatalism, and Apocalypse in America.* New York: New York University Press.

Wojcik examines doomsday scenarios and apocalyptic predictions of visionaries, televangelists, survivalists, and other end-times enthusiasts of popular culture, films, music, fashion, and humor. He explores contemporary apocalyptic beliefs and compares religious and secular apocalyptic speculations, showing how they have changed over time. He shows how apocalyptic ideas are today associated with UFOs and extraterrestrials.

Leading Scholarly Journals

Alabama Law Review has been published since 1980. It publishes original research from leading scholars as well as selected works from its own members and is the flagship legal journal in Alabama. It is a nationally recognized journal exploring issues of national, state, and local significance to scholars, journalists, and practitioners. It regularly publishes reviews of cases relating to freedom of religion and Establishment Clause cases. It is published quarterly.

American Journal of Sociology was established in 1895 and is the oldest academic journal of sociology in the United States. It is attached to the Department of Sociology at the University of Chicago and is published bimonthly. It is a leading voice in all areas of sociology, with an emphasis on theory building and innovative methods, and is open to interdisciplinary contributions, from anthropologists, economists, educators, historians, and political scientists, that often concern the sociological impact of religious freedom issues. It discusses and analyzes religious groups. It publishes book reviews and commissioned book review essays.

Biblical Higher Education Journal is the official journal of the Association for Biblical Higher Education, published annually with articles reflecting the wide diversity found across biblical higher education as well as book reviews. It regularly features the relation of freedom of religion issues and education.

Christian Apologetics Journal has been published by the Southern Evangelical Seminary since 1998, in the spring and fall of each year. It provides a forum for the presentation of articles contributing to the defense of the historic Christian faith, including occasional articles on the Free Exercise Clause, and supports the Religious Freedom Restoration Act.

Christian Education Journal is the leading evangelical journal in the field of education. It is edited and published by the faculty of the educational studies doctoral program at Talbot School of Theology. It is published biannually in the spring and fall. Each issue has approximately 60 contributors and has articles exploring the integration and application of social science theory and research to educational ministry, including the impact of the Religious Freedom Restoration Act of 1993 (RFRA). Published since 1980, it is published by Biola University, LaMirada, California.

Christian Higher Education is a journal published by the Taylor & Francis group, United Kingdom. It has been published annually since 2002 in five issues per year. It is a peer-reviewed archival journal by scholars and practitioners addressing issues of finance, innovation, teaching methods, higher education administration, curricular development, and issues of interest to higher education. It occasionally features articles on the Free Exercise Clause and the clause's impact on Christian higher education. It is an international, interdenominational, and interdisciplinary journal.

Christian Librarian is the official publication of the Association of Christian Librarians. It publishes articles, provides a forum, and encourages writings on issues related to the theory and practice of library science with a Christian interpretation, including occasional articles on the free exercise of religion issue. It contains bibliographic reviews and human interest articles. It is published twice per year, in June and December.

Christian Library Journal is a professional review publication that looks at books from a Christian worldview. It notes the values found in the text of the books, featuring books on the topics of the Free Exercise Clause and the Establishment Clause. It has been published since 1995.

Christian Periodical Index is a comprehensive electronic index to journal articles and book reviews from across the evangelical Christian perspective. It has been published quarterly since 1957 and it indexes 160 publications covering major doctrinal positions within the evangelical Christian perspective. It contains titles from a wide variety of disciplines that present a Christian viewpoint, including science, literature, medicine, music, philosophy, history, sociology, nursing, and education.

Christian Research Journal is aimed at Christian readers to provide information they need to discern doctrinal errors, evangelize people of other faiths, and defend Christian beliefs and ethics. It is most noted for its Evangelical Christian apologetics, which advocates for the RFRA and the ending of the Johnson Amendment. It is issued six times per year, published by the Christian Research Institute since 1960. Its new headquarters is located in Charlotte, North Carolina.

Christian Scholar's Review was established in 1970 as a medium for communication among Christians with an academic vocation. It publishes peer-reviewed articles of scholarship and research that are interdisciplinary and that advance the integration of faith from Christian scholars of all historical traditions. It aims to promote mutual understanding with other religious and academic communities. It is based at Hope College, Michigan. It is published in the spring and fall.

Christian School Education is a magazine published since 1997 by the Association of Christian Schools headquartered in Colorado Springs, Colorado. It is international in scope. It is published three times a year and addresses current and relevant education topics for the worldwide Christian school movement, including, of course, the rights of non-secular private schools to the free exercise of religion. Its articles are written by education professionals with a wealth of practical experience.

Christianity Today is an evangelical Christian periodical founded in 1956 by Billy Graham, with its headquarters in Carol Stream, Illinois. It has been called "evangelicalism's flagship magazine." It provides a biblical perspective on theology, church, ministry, and culture. It occasionally features articles on issues related to freedom of religion. It is published internationally and monthly.

Columbia Law Review has been published since 1901 and is a leading publication of legal scholarship. It is published in eight issues a year. It receives some 2,000 submissions per year and publishes 20 to 25 manuscripts annually. It has an online supplement, *Columbia Law Review Online*, published since 2008. It is edited by Columbia University Law School. It regularly reviews cases from state as well as federal courts that concern freedom of religion and Establishment Clause cases as well as book reviews pertinent to the subject.

Creation Research Society Quarterly is the official journal of the Creation Research Society. It is a peer-reviewed journal with an emphasis on original research and the reinterpretation of existing scientific data within a creationist framework. It carries both technical and popular articles in most scientific disciplines. It has been published since 1964. It has also published, since 1996, a bimonthly magazine, *Creation Matters*, which publishes "lighter" articles.

Ecumenical Review has been publishing for more than 60 years a variety of articles from Christian authors around the world. Founded with the World Council of Churches, it explores the potential and reality of Christian cooperation of faith and action, including political action to protect free exercise of religion and to uphold nondenominational Establishment Clause policy. It is a quarterly, peer-reviewed journal. Each issue is organized on a theme of current importance to the movement for Christian unity.

Emory International Law Review is a leading journal of international legal scholarship known for its excellence in scholarship, legal research, analysis, and professionalism. It publishes articles on a vast array of topics, from human rights to international intellectual property issues. It is published quarterly.

Emory Law Journal was founded in 1952 as the *Journal of Public Law*. It has been publishing academic, professional, and student-authored legal scholarship on the full range of legal subjects since 1978. Emory University hosts the Center for the Study of Law and Religion, and its articles often concern the religious rights protected by the First Amendment. It publishes six issues annually.

Ethics and Medicine is a peer-reviewed, international journal of bioethics published twice per year since 1984, first published in the United Kingdom, now in Michigan. It publishes articles from the Judeo-Christian worldview and its Hippocratic medical vision. It occasionally features articles concerning issues about refusing medical procedures on the basis of the patient's religious beliefs.

Evangelical Quarterly has been published since 1929 by Paternoster Press for Biblical Studies.org in London, print and online. It is an academic, peer-reviewed journal with articles on a wide variety of biblical and theological topics. On occasion, it contains articles about religious freedom issues. It is published quarterly.

Georgetown Journal of Legal Ethics was founded in 1987. It is published quarterly. It publishes interdisciplinary scholarship related to the future of the legal profession, issuing cutting edge articles on ethical issues from diverse practical areas. It frequently contains articles relevant to issues of free exercise and Establishment Clause–related cases.

Georgetown Law Review is headquartered at Georgetown University Law School in Washington, D.C. It has published more than 500 issues since its inception in 1912. It employs 100 law students. It publishes its *Annual Review of Criminal Procedure.* It publishes articles across the full spectrum of legal issues and cases, and, given the Catholic perspective of the University, it often has articles on the topic of religious freedom and Establishment Clause policy that impacts parochial education.

Harvard Law Review publishes eight regular annual issues of various legal articles by professors, judges, practitioners, law students, and leading case summaries. It is run by an independent student group at Harvard Law School. It also publishes an Online Harvard Law Review Forum. One of the nation's oldest law reviews, it has been published since 1887. It is one of the most prestigious law reviews and its alumni include former president Barack Obama, seven Supreme Court justices, and a host of federal court judges and other high-level federal government officials. It reviews all court cases that impact freedom of religion and the establishment of religion issues, particularly of policies of funding support by state and local governments.

Hastings Law Journal has been published since 1949. It is the flagship law review of the University of California-Hastings. It is published six times per year. Its scholarly articles span a wide variety of legal issues and are written by experts in the legal community. It also publishes an occasional law symposium issue on the subject of religious freedom and anti-establishment cases. It is run by 90 student members and it reaches a large domestic and international audience.

International Journal for Religious Freedom is the journal of the International Institute for Religious Freedom of the World Evangelical Alliance. Published since 2012, it is issued twice per year. It provides a platform for scholarly discourse on issues related to religious freedom in general and the persecution of

Christians in particular. It is an interdisciplinary, international, peer-reviewed scholarly journal with research articles, documents, book reviews, and academic news in each issue.

International Journal of Christianity and Education has been published for 20 years and is a platform for academic discussions on the relationship between Christianity and educational theory and practice in both formal and informal settings. It publishes articles from a wide range of educational contexts and all levels of educational institutions. It includes theological, philosophical, and sociological discussions using qualitative and quantitative empirical research, with articles related to religious freedom issues from the Christian perspective. It is a Sage publication.

Journal of Church and State is a quarterly peer-reviewed academic journal of religious studies and political science covering First Amendment issues. It is published by Oxford University Press for the J.M. Institute of Church-State Studies. It was established in 1959. It publishes constitutional, historical, philosophical, theological, and sociological studies on religion and the body politic in various countries of the world. Each issue covers 5 or more major articles, 35 to 40 book reviews, and occasional government or church documents, as well as laws and court cases.

Journal of Contemporary Theological Studies explores the connection between theology and practical ministry from a scholarly as well as practical perspective. It is a journal of Christian theology from a Scriptural perspective with articles written by both faculty and students. It began at Grace College of Divinity and since 2014 has been joined by New Hope Christian College in Oregon. Its occasional articles on the subject feature an emphasis on the Free Exercise Clause more so than the Establishment Clause.

Journal of Law and Religion is a peer-reviewed, interdisciplinary journal edited by the Center for the Study of Law and Religion at Emory University and published with collaboration of Cambridge University Press since 1982. It is one of the leading journals—if not *the* leading—publishing interdisciplinary and interfaith scholarship at the intersection of law and religion and thus regularly has articles dealing with both the Free Exercise and the Establishment Clauses of the First Amendment.

Journal of Religion is a quarterly, peer-reviewed academic journal publishing articles on theology, religion, and the ethics and philosophy of religion as well as on the role of religion in culture and society. Articles are written from a historical, sociological, psychological, linguistic, or artistic standpoint. It began in 1882 as *The Hebrew Student,* changed to *The American Journal of Theology* in 1897 and in 1921 to *The Journal of Religion.* It is published by the University of Chicago Press.

Journal of Religion, Spirituality, and Aging began in 1984 as the *Journal of Religion and Aging* and has been with its current title since 2005. It is a quarterly, peer-reviewed interdisciplinary and interfaith journal focusing on the aging constituencies. It balances theory and practice and informs secular professionals about developments in the field of religion, spirituality, and aging. It occasionally will feature articles on the Free Exercise Clause.

Journal of Research on Christian Education is an academic journal published since 1992 by Taylor & Francis (Routledge) for the scholarly interchange of research findings related to every level of Christian education with an emphasis on Christian schooling within the Protestant tradition. It is published twice per year for the School of Education at Andrews University, a Seventh-day Adventist institution. It is a peer-reviewed journal. As a Seventh-day Adventist–related journal, it reflects their tradition of being longtime advocates of the freedom of religion, especially as it pertains to the Free Exercise Clause. The Seventh-day Adventists have been involved in more than a dozen landmark Supreme Court cases on religious freedom issues.

Journal of the American Academy of Religion is a major academic journal in the field of religious studies. It is an international, interdisciplinary quarterly journal that covers the full range of world religious traditions and explores them with provocative studies of their methodologies. It has been published since 1967. It has a large, valuable book review section. It is published by Oxford University Press for the Department of Theological Studies at the Claremont Graduate University. Its articles occasionally are of particular interest to Establishment Clause issues from a philosophical viewpoint.

Liberty: A Magazine of Religious Freedom is a magazine founded in 1906 and published by the Seventh-day Adventist Church. It covers issues involving the separation of church and state and current events in politics. It has a circulation of 200,000. It is published bimonthly.

Mennonite Quarterly Review has been published since 1927 and is the quarterly journal devoted to Anabaptist-Mennonite history, thought, life, and affairs. It features articles on the radical reformation, Amish, Mennonite, and Hutterites. It is peer reviewed and is a cooperative publication of Goshen College, the Anabaptist Mennonite Biblical Seminary, and the Mennonite Historical Society. It features articles on the lengthy tradition of Amish and Mennonite conflict with majority society on freedom of religious practice, particularly as it relates to public education.

Northwestern University Law Review was founded in 1906 as the *Illinois Law Review*. It is published quarterly in print and online. It features articles on general legal scholarship. It is student operated with articles written by professors, judges, and legal practitioners as well as students. It hosts special symposium issues annually, such as *Ordering State-Federal Relations through Preemption Doctrine* (2007). The preemption doctrine directly relates to freedom of religion practices.

Notre Dame Law Review was founded in 1925 and was known as the *Notre Dame Lawyer* until 1982. It is student edited and fosters scholarly discourse within the legal community, mindful of its Catholic tradition. It is published quarterly and annually has a symposium issue on federal courts, practice, and procedure as a forum exploring civil practice and procedures in the federal courts. The forum issues occasionally directly relate to religious freedom issues and occasionally to the Establishment Clause.

Perspectives on Science and Christian Faith is an academic journal of the American Scientific Association, a network of Christians in the sciences. It has been published quarterly since 1949. It aims at promoting the study of the relationship between the facts of science and holy scripture and to disseminate the results of such studies. It includes divergent views and a nondoctrinal focus. It offers occasional articles on the creationism versus evolution topic.

Religion and American Culture is a semiannual publication by the University of California Press for the Center for the Study of Religion and American Culture. Since 1991, it has been publishing scholarly discussion of the nature, terms, and dynamics of religion in America, embracing a diversity of methodological approaches and theoretical perspectives. It concerns the interplay between religion and other spheres of American culture, including law and politics.

Review of Politics publishes articles primarily on political theory, interpretive studies of law, and historical analysis on all aspects of politics: institutions, techniques, literary reflections on politics, and constitutional theory and analysis. It has been published quarterly since 1939 and is published by Cambridge University Press for the University of Notre Dame. It occasionally offers articles on freedom of religion issues.

Social Work and Christianity publishes articles and book reviews related to the integration of faith and professional social work practices. It began publication in 1974. It is published quarterly and is the official publication of the National Association of Christians in Social Work. Its occasional articles on religious freedom issues touch on both the Free Exercise Clause and the Establishment Clause.

Stanford University Law Review is published both in print (since 1948) and online (since 2011). It fosters intellectual discourse among student members and contributes to legal scholarship by addressing important legal and social issues, with a focus on religious freedom issues at some regularity. It is published in six issues per year and its articles are contributed by Law Review members, other Stanford Law School students, professors, judges, and practicing attorneys.

Supreme Court Review is published by the University of Chicago Law School since it first appeared in 1910. It provides a sustained and authoritative survey of the Court's most significant decisions. It provides an in-depth critique of the Supreme Court and its work and of the ongoing reforms and interpretations of American law. It treats Supreme Court landmark cases related to freedom of religion issues and their impact on subsequent court cases that impact state and local courts and laws on the issue. It is written by and for legal academics, judges, political scientists, journalists, and sociologists. It is published annually, in the spring.

University of California Law Review is the preeminent legal publication of the University of California, Berkeley School of Law. It was founded in 1912. It is published six times annually, covering a wide variety of topics of legal scholarship, with freedom of religion issues appearing at some regularity. It is edited and published entirely by students at Berkeley Law. It publishes research by the Berkeley Law faculty, centers, students, judges, and legal practitioners.

University of Chicago Law Review was founded in 1933. It is edited by the Law School's students and is one of the most prestigious and often-cited law reviews. Its authors include a host of Supreme Court justices, federal court judges, state supreme court judges, and preeminent legal scholars. Its articles occasionally concern freedom of religion and often the nexus of the federal court system's impact on state and local courts as they pertain to religious freedom issues. It is published quarterly.

University of Minnesota Law Review has been published since 1917. It is solely student edited and its board of student editors number 39. It is published quarterly and covers the entire range of legal issues, including those related to the First Amendment's religious freedom protections. It also publishes an annual symposium issue, several of which have been on religious freedom.

University of Pennsylvania Journal of Constitutional Law provides a forum for the interdisciplinary study of and analysis of constitutional law. It cultivates legal scholarship, promotes critical perspectives, and reinvents the traditional study of constitutional law. Due to its focus on constitutional law, it touches on freedom of religion and Establishment Clause issues with some frequency. It has 20 student editors. It has been published quarterly since 1998.

University of Pennsylvania Law Review focuses on a wide range of legal issues. It was founded in 1852 and will publish its 165th volume in seven issues in the 2016–2017 academic year. It serves the legal profession, the bench, the bar, and the legal academy by providing a forum for publication of legal research. From about 2,000 submissions, it selects 12 articles in each volume and is cited with such peer organizations as Columbia, Harvard, and Yale. As do most law journals, it occasionally treats cases pertinent to freedom of religion concerns.

University of Virginia Law Review for more than 100 years has been one of the most prestigious publications in the legal profession. It was begun in 1913. The Virginia Law School was founded by Thomas Jefferson in 1819. The *Review* is published eight times annually. It covers law-related issues by and for judges, practitioners, teachers, legislators, students, and others interested in the law.

Yale Law Journal has been published since 1891. It has been at the forefront of legal scholarship and shapes discussion of the most important and relevant legal issues through rigorous scholarship. It is published eight times per year and its online companion has been published since 2005. It is one of the most widely cited law reviews in the nation. It often addresses legal cases and decisions that involve freedom of religion issues.

Nonprint Sources

Films

The Crucible

This 1996 film depicts a small group of girls in Salem, Massachusetts, who tell lies about how Satan invaded them. It is based on the award-winning play of Arthur Miller, who wrote the screenplay. It is inspired by the Salem Witchcraft trials. It was nominated for two Oscars. It runs 2 hours and 4 minutes and is a masterpiece of a film. It was produced by the 20th Century Fox film corporation and is available on IMDbPro.

Friendly Persuasion

This 1956 film depicts a family of pacifist Quakers who struggle with their pacifism during the Civil War. It depicts how the majority society pressured Quakers to abandon their pacifism to support the war and how it divided some Quaker families over the issue. It is set in Indiana in 1862. It stars Gary Cooper and Dorothy McGuire. It runs 137 minutes, in color. It is an Allied Artist picture that was nominated for six Oscars and won five. It is rated 7.5 stars on IMDbPro's 10 point rating scale.

Gangs of New York

This 2002 film stars Leonardo DiCaprio and Daniel Day-Lewis. It is directed by Martin Scorsese. In runs 2 hours 47 minutes, in color, and was nominated for 10 Oscars. Set in New York City's Manhattan in 1863, the film depicts the worst riot in U.S. history, when Protestant gangs terrorized Irish immigrants. It is a Miramax film. It is rated 7.5 on IMDbPro's 10-point rating scale.

Hacksaw Ridge

This 2016 film is a biography of the Seventh-day Adventist conscientious objector who served in World War II as an army medic. It is the true story of Desmond Doss, who saved the lives of 75 men during the battle of Okinawa. He is the only conscientious objector ever to win the Congressional Medal of Honor. The film is in color and runs 2 hours 19 minutes. It was directed by Mel Gibson and is a Cross Creek Pictures production. It was nominated for six Oscars and won two. It is rated 8.2 of 10 on IMDbPro's rating scale.

Inherit the Wind

This 1960 film stars Spencer Tracy and Gene Kelly. Tracy plays B. J. Cates, who is put on trial for teaching evolution. It is a thinly disguised depiction of the 1925 Scopes monkey trial. It runs 2 hours 8 minutes and is in black and white. It is a courtroom drama about evolution versus creationism. It was produced by MGM Studios and is available on DVD. It is rated 8.2 of 10 on the IMDbPro scale.

Ku Klux Klan: A Secret History

This 1998 movie is a documentary/biography crime film that depicts the history of the Ku Klux Klan in the United States. It vividly shows their anti-Catholicism and anti-Semitism, as well as their anti-black racial animus. Over its history, the Klan promoted itself as a defender of Christianity against non-Christian faiths. It appealed to a segment of the white Protestant population, particularly white Southern Baptists, who were especially anti-Catholic and anti-Semitic. It is in black and white and color. It is a Termite Art production, available on DVD and running 96 minutes. It rates 7.5 of 10 on the IMDbPro rating scale.

Malcolm X

This 1992 biographical feature film stars Denzel Washington as Malcolm X, for which he was nominated for the Academy Award for Best Actor, with Angela Bassett as his wife. It is in color and runs 3 hours 22 minutes. It shows Malcolm X's eloquent defense of Islam in black America and depicts his evolution from espousal of the Nation of Islam to his conversion to tradition Islam. It depicts how in his final years of life he increasingly stressed religious toleration, a position that played into his assassination by Nation of Islam followers, who viewed him as an apostate. The film was directed by Spike Lee. It is based on the autobiography of Malcolm X by Malcolm and Alex Haley. It was distributed by Warner Brothers. It is rated 7.7 of 10 on IMDb's ratings. It was distributed internationally by Largo International.

Mayflower: The Pilgrim's Adventure

This 1979 historical drama movie presents the story of the 1620 emigration of the Pilgrims to America, a journey of 103 religious "separatists." It depicts their religious persecution in England and journey to the Plymouth Colony. It runs 100 minutes, in color. It is rated 6.4 of 10 on IMDb ratings and is available on YouTube. It stars Anthony Hopkins and Richard Crenna. It was a Syzygy Productions film.

Monkey Trial

This is a 2002 PBS film, documentary/biography/historical drama, now available on TurnerClassicMovies.com. It is a depiction of the famous John Scopes monkey trial in 1925 and the epic court battle between science and religion. It is in both color and black and white. It was part of the PBS Series, the American Experience, and was broadcast in Season 14, as episode 9. It runs 1 hour and is on IMDbTV. It was produced by the Nebraska Etv Network. It rated 9.8 of 10 on IMDb.

Mormon Pioneers: The Great Trek West

This film is a docudrama dramatization of the history of the Mormon pioneers traveling west on their 1,000-mile trek across the then-western American wilderness.

It is in color and was produced in 1996 by the Latter-day Saints production company, Trek West Productions. It runs 1 hour 5 minutes. It is available on DVD (not rated on IMDbPro).

Salem

This television series from 2014 ran in 36 one-hour episodes. It is a drama/fantasy that explores what fueled the town's hysteria and infamous witch trials. It is distributed by 20th Television and WGN America. It is rated 7.2 of 10 on IMDb. It is available on DVD from Fox Home Entertainment for the first season and DVD Amazon, CreateSpace MOD Program, for the second season.

The Scarlet Letter

This 1995 film runs 2 hours 15 minutes in color and is a drama/romance film depicting life in 1666 Massachusetts Bay Colony, in which a young woman, who is presumed to be a widow, has an affair with a young Quaker pastor, with disastrous consequences. It vividly portrays the religious intolerance many colonial-era Quakers displayed. It stars Demi Moore and Gary Oldman. It is a film by Allied Stars Ltd., Cinergi Pictures Entertainment, and Hollywood Pictures. It rated 5.2 over 10 on the IMDb scale.

Witness

This 1985 film stars Harrison Ford, Kelly McGillis, and Lukas Haas. It was nominated for six academy awards and won two Oscars, for editing and writing. It is in color, a Paramount Picture production that runs 1 hour and 52 minutes. It is a gripping drama depicting a young Amish widow and her son who while changing trains in Philadelphia witness a murder. Detective Captain John Book (played by Ford) has to flee with them to protect them from fellow police officers who were the murderers. They flee to Amish country to hide. It is a good depiction of the Amish lifestyle and values. It illustrates the all-too-frequent religious intolerance experienced by the Amish, including how gangs of youngsters taunted and physically abused them for their religious beliefs. It illustrates the struggles of the Amish faithful to maintain their religious beliefs, which rejected modernity in a modern society that was so often intolerant of their insistence in maintaining their separatism. It was rated 7.4 of 10 on IMDb.

Videos

Alleged: The Scopes Monkey Trial

This video runs approximately 29 minutes. It is an accurate portrayal of the Scopes monkey trial of 1925 (using the trial manuscripts for its screen play). It stars Brian Dennehy as Clarence Darrow, Fred Thompson as William Jennings Bryan, and Colm Meaney as H. L. Mencken. It is available on DVD from Amazon.

Defining Religious Freedom in America

This is a video from the morning session of a day-long conference held by the First Amendment Center on March 18, 2013. The video runs 1 hour 38 minutes and aired on March 21, 2013. The video covers a panel of distinguished scholars on the topic, discussing it from their various legal and religious traditions, backgrounds, and perspectives (e.g., Christian, Hindu, ACLU, Jewish). It is available on YouTube.

Freedom of Religion: A History of God in America

This YouTube video features a lecture by Randall Niles as he looks at the truth underlying the First Amendment and tries to answer the question "where did the separation of church and state doctrine come from"?

God in America

This six-episode PBS Frontline series aired in October 2010 and is available on DVD and YouTube. Each episode runs about one hour.

A Nation Reborn

This fourth episode focuses on slavery and the conflict between abolitionists and slaveholders. It emphasizes President Lincoln's spiritual journey as he copes with the death of his young son and tries to make sense of the Civil War, showing how the war transformed his idea about God.

A New Adam

The first episode of the series explores the origins of Christianity in America and how the new world changed the faiths that settlers brought with them. It focuses on the alliance between Thomas Jefferson and evangelical Baptists and how that alliance served as the foundation of religious liberty.

A New Eden

This episode considers the origins of America's experiment in religious liberty and the competitive religious marketplace unleashed by religious liberty. It discusses how upstart denominations raced ahead of traditional faiths, the wave of religious revivals, and their fierce political struggle with Catholic immigrants.

A New Light

This episode covers 19th-century America and how forces of modernity challenged traditional faiths and drove a wedge between liberal and conservative believers.

The Soul of a Nation

This episode focuses on Evangelist Billy Graham's revivals that fused faith and patriotism. It covers the Reverend Dr. Martin Luther King, Jr., and his emergence as a modern-day prophet.

Of God and Caesar

The sixth episode discusses the moral crusade of evangelical conservatives and their efforts to change U.S. politics and culture. This episode reflects on the role of faith in public life in the country from the ongoing quest for religious liberty to the early idea of America as a "city on a hill" envisioned by the Puritans 400 years ago.

John Fea: Was America Founded as a Christian Nation?

In this video, Professor John Fea, of the History Department of Classics, Philosophy and Religion at the University of Mary Washington, lectures on his book of the same title. It aired August 31, 2012, as a Religious Freedom Lecture. It runs 1 hour 15 minutes. It is available on YouTube.

The Liberty Threat: Attack on Religious Freedom in America

This is a video of a lecture by James Tonkowich on his book *The Liberty Threat*. In it, he covers court cases arguing that the doctrine of the rigid separation of church and state has led to a nation hostile to true faith and calls for Christian activism to oppose it. It well illustrates the conservative religious right's views on the separation of church and state doctrine. It aired October 20, 2014, and runs approximately 35 minutes. In is available on YouTube.

The Pilgrims

This video is an Encyclopedia Britannica historical and educational documentary. It deals with the Pilgrims and their journey from England to Holland and then to the Plymouth Colony on the *Mayflower*. Its emphasis is on their search for religious freedom. It is in black and white and runs 22 minutes. It is available on YouTube and was rated 4.5 over 5.

Puritans and Religious Freedom

In this C-Span.org video, Professor Kevin Gooding, of the University of West Virginia, gives a talk about the Puritans in early colonial America and the idea of religious freedom and how the Puritans dealt (harshly) with those who dissented from their beliefs and codes. It runs one hour.

Religious Pacifists and the American Revolution

This C-Span video aired February 19, 2015. It covers Jared Burkholder, a Grace College professor, giving his lecture as part of C-Span's Lectures in History Series. It runs one hour. Burkholder speaks about religious pacifists during the American Revolution. He focuses on the diversity of responses to the war from Moravians, Mennonites, Brethren, and other "peace church" traditions rooted in Pietism.

7 Chronology

Below is a list of some of the major events impacting religious freedom in America.

1609 Dutch settlers emigrate to what becomes New York; Dutch Reformed religion is the established religion of the colony.

1620 Puritans flee England and establish the Plymouth colony in America.

1638 Swedes settle in southern part of New York and New Jersey area and establish Swedish Lutheran Church as its official religion.

1649 Maryland colony enacts the Maryland Act of Toleration.

1674 William Penn and the Quakers settle in New Jersey and establish colony as a holy experiment in religious tolerance.

1681 The Commonwealth of Pennsylvania established, with Pietists and Moravian communities. Religious tolerance, except for Catholics, is pronounced.

1691 Maryland's Charter revoked; it becomes a royal charter colony with its Act of Toleration revoked.

Faateha Syed listens to a roundtable discussion on religious freedom with the regional interfaith community at All Dulles Area Muslim Society (ADAMS) Mosque in Sterling, Virginia, on July 21, 2016. Syed's hajib, this one with the American flag symbol, is often a common trigger of anti-Muslim actions. Using a "flag-hajib" is a powerful antidiscrimination symbol. (AP Photo/Manuel Balce Ceneta)

1702   Maryland establishes the Anglican Church as its official religion.

1719   Dunkers, Church of the Brethren, move to Pennsylvania. King George II grants the Georgia colony, which seeks population to act as a buffer with Spanish and French colonies to its south; accepts various minority sects to freely practice their religion.

1734   Schwenckfelders emigrate as a large community to Pennsylvania.

1735   The Moravian Brethren immigrate to the Georgia colony.

1760   Old Order Amish and Mennonites move to Pennsylvania; start mother colony there.

1774   The Shaker Quakers move to New York to freely practice their faith.

1785   Protestant Episcopal Church of the United States established.

1786   Virginia disestablishes the Anglican Church as its official state faith; enacts Virginia Statute for Religious Freedom into the Virginia State Constitution.

1789   Constitution of the United States adopted; Bill of Rights with its First Amendment rights ratified.

1796   Treaty of Tripoli negotiated and ratified by the U.S. Senate with statement that the United States is not a Christian nation.

1798–1820   Second Great Awakening movement.

1803   President Thomas Jefferson's administration purchases the Louisiana Territory from France, roughly doubling the size of the United States and adding large numbers of Catholics to its population.

1812   War of 1812 (with England); heightens fear of foreigners and raises doubts about the allegiance and loyalty of Catholics.

1823   Mormon Church (Church of Jesus Christ of Latter-day Saints [LDS]) begun, formally established in 1830. Mormon versus "Gentile" wars begin. Massachusetts disestablishes its state church, last state of the original 13 to do so.

1836   Mormons move to Kirtland, Ohio.

1838   Battle of Crooked River (with Mormons); Missouri governor Lilburn Boggs issues Executive Order 44, "the extermination of Mormons" order.

1839   Mormons move to Nauvoo.

1840   Brigham Young travels to England; in 1841, brings some 10,000 converts to the New Zion in Nauvoo; Aaronic Order, Levite sect of LDS formed.

1843   Millerites Movement begun; formally becomes the Seventh-day Adventist Church in 1863.

1843   Smith brothers (Joseph and Hiram) martyred in Missouri.

1844   Seventh-day Adventist Church is officially formed.

1845   Nauvoo Charter revoked; sets off Mormons' Great Trek West.

1847   Mormons move to Nebraska, then to Salt Lake City area; Brigham Young begins long term (1847–1877) as president and prophet of LDS.

1848   Treaty of Guadalupe-Hidalgo signed, ending war with Mexico, adding huge territory to the United States, and giving citizenship to former Mexican nationals living in new U.S. territories, adding thousands of Catholic adherents to the U.S. population.

1848   Secret Order of the Star-Spangled Banner formed, anti-Catholic and anti-foreigners.

1848–1852   Approximately 1.2 Irish Catholic immigrants arrive on the "famine ships."

1858–1862   Union Army occupies Utah Territory.

1862   President Abraham Lincoln signs into law the Morrill Ant-Bigamy Act making polygamy illegal and limiting non-profit ownership of land in any territory of the United States to $50,000.

1870–1880   First wave of Hasidic Jews comes to the United States.

1872   Jehovah's Witnesses started by Charles Taze Russell.

1876   End of the LDS splinter group, Church of Christ.

1879   Supreme Court rules, in *Reynolds v. United States*, that polygamy law is constitutional. Establishment Clause bans government from regulation of belief, but allows it to regulate actions, like marriage.

1880–1900   Sunni Muslims come to America in first big wave.

1890   Supreme Court decides *Davis v. Beason*, again upholding the ban on polygamy.

1890   Mormon Manifesto published by LDS president Woodruff announcing an end to practice of polygamy as official doctrine.

1913   Self-declared prophet Noble Drew Ali, of Newark, New Jersey, starts Temple movement.

1919   Peace Mission Movement of Father Divine begins.

1925   Court issues ruling in *Pierce v. Society of Sisters* case that parochial schools are constitutional and legal.

1930   *Cochran v. Louisiana State Board of Education* decision.

1932   Ethiopian Pacific movement begun.

1932   Nation of Islam (NOI) started by W. Fard Muhammad.

1934   Fard Muhammad disappears and Elijiah (Poole) Muhammad takes over Nation of Islam. NOI begins Chicago Temple 2 as its headquarters.

1935   Supreme Court rules in *Lynch v. Massachusetts*.

1938   Supreme Court announces opinion in *Lovell v. Griffin*.

1940 Supreme Court issues ruling in *Cantwell v. Connecticut* that government cannot require permits to solicit for religious groups if not for secular ones; in *Minersville School District v. Gobitis*, Court upholds flag salute law. Lubavitch Hasidic Jewish sect moves to Crown Heights, Brooklyn, New York.

1941 The Supreme Court weighs in on religious solicitation in *Cox v. New Hampshire.*

1942 Supreme Court decides *Chaplinsky v. New Hampshire* and announces its "fighting words" doctrine; decides cases of *Jones v. City of Opelika,* and *Marsh v. Alabama.*

1943 The Supreme Court decides landmark case of *West Virginia State Board of Education v. Barnette* that overturns *Gobitis.*

1944 *United States v. Ballard* and *Prince v. Massachusetts* decisions.

1946 Supreme Court hands down its opinion in *Estep v. U.S.*

1947 *Everson v. Board of Education* decision announced; Court ruling provides Everson test about when aid to parochial schools is permissible.

1948 *McCullum v. Board of Education* case decided.

1952 Malcolm Little released from prison, during which time he had converted to Islam, joined NOI as Malcolm X. *Zorach v. Clauson* decision announced, as is *Kedroff v. Saint Nicholas Cathedral.*

1953 Supreme Court issues opinion in four major cases: *West Virginia v. Barnette*; *Murdock v. Commonwealth of Pennsylvania*; *Niemotkov v. Maryland*; *Fowler v. Rhode Island.*

1954 Wicca neo-pagan religion starts, comes to United States around 1960. U.S. senator Lyndon B. Johnson writes bill later called the Johnson Amendment that mandates Internal Revenue Service rules be changed; charitable religious nonprofit exemptions from federal taxes (the religious exemption for 501(c)(3) nonprofit organizations) are to be cancelled if the church advocates voting for a particular party or candidate from the pulpit and participates in the campaign in behalf of or against a candidate for public office.

1959   *Murray v. Curlett* opinion announced by Supreme Court.

1960   Malcolm X leaves NOI, founds Organization of Afro-American Unity. In *Braunfeld v. Brown* and *Gallagher v. Crown Kosher Super Market of Massachusetts, Inc.*, the Supreme Court hands down rulings on Sunday Blue Laws; decides case of *McCullum v. Maryland*; and in *Torcaso v. Watkins* declares Maryland law requiring swearing a religious oath for a public office as unconstitutional.

1962   American Atheists Organization formed. Landmark Supreme Court case of *Engle v. Vitale* decided that bans as unconstitutional officially required prayers in schools. *Thorton v. Caldor* decision announced by the Supreme Court.

1963   *Abington School District v. Schempp* rendered by Court banning officially required reading of the Bible in public schools; in *Sherbert v. Verner*, the Court overturns state law denying unemployment benefits to persons who refuse work on their Sabbath; decides case in *Murray v. Curlett*, another ban on school prayers.

1964   Malcolm X assassinated.

1965   Internal Revenue Service issues rule on Social Security exempting Old Order Amish and Mennonites.

1968   Supreme Court rules in *Board of Education v. Allen*; *Epperson v. Arkansas*, which bans state law forbidding the teaching of evolution; and *Flast v. Cohen*.

1969   Court decides for the Presbyterian national church in *Presbyterian Church v. Hall Church*.

1970   *Walz v. Tax Commission of the City of New York* decided.

1971   Court issues landmark decision in *Lemon v. Kurtzman*, which allows state aid to sectarian schools meeting a three-point test; decides *Tilton v. Richardson* and *Committee for Public Education and Religious Liberty v. Nyquist*.

1972 *Yoder v. Wisconsin* landmark Supreme Court decision ruling that states must provide exemptions from certain compulsory education attendance laws to Amish and Mennonites. U.S. Congress enacts the Indian Education Act.

1974 Congress passes the Indian Financing Act.

1975 Congress enacts the Indian Self-Determination and Education Assistance Act. Court reaches verdict in *Meek v. Pittenger.*

1975 Elijah Muhammad dies; his son, Wallace Dean Muhammad, succeeds him and moves from NOI to form American Society of Muslins and becomes a Sunni Immam.

1975–1990 Wave of Palestinian and Lebonese refugees arrive in United States.

1976 Minister Louis Farrakhan revives NOI. *Roemer v. Board of Public Works of Maryland* decision.

1977 *Wolman v. Walter* case decided, along with *Trans World Airlines v. Hardison.*

1978 Congress passes American Indian Religious Freedom Act; Tribally Controlled Community College Assistance Act; and the Indian Child Welfare Act; the Supreme Court decides *McDaniel v. Paty* that overturns state law banning clergy from serving in public office.

1979 Indian Archaeological Resources Protection Act passed by Congress. Supreme Court decides the case of *Jones v. Wolf.*

1980 *Committee for Public Education and Religious Liberty v. Regan* decision rendered by Supreme Court; in *Stone v. Graham,* it bans display of Ten Commandments in public schools as unconstitutional violation of the Establishment Clause.

1981 Court decides *Widmar v. Vincent; Thomas v. Review Board of Indiana Employment Security Division;* and *Heffron v. International Society for Krishna Consciousness.*

1982 *Larkin v. Grendel's Den* case decided, as are the *Valley Forges and People Christian College v. Americans United for*

Separation of Church and State; *Larson v. Valente*; and *Mueller v. Allen*. Court announces verdict in *Marsh v. Chambers*, allowing states to hire a chaplain to open legislative sessions; in *Bob Jones University v. United States*, the Court rescinds the university's tax-exempt status because of their racial discrimination policies.

1984   Congress passes Equal Access Act. *Lynch v. Donnelly* case decided, upholding nativity scene in a public park if among others to celebrate the holidays.

1985   *Aguillard v. Felton*; *Grand Rapids School District v. Ball*; *Board of Trustees of Scarsdale v. McCreary*; *Thorton v. Caldor*; *Wallace v. Jaffree* cases decided.

1986   *Ohio Civil Rights Commission v. Dayton Christian Schools* decided in favor of the school; *Goldman v. Weinberger* decided, upholding Air Force regulations against wearing of a skull cap on duty; *Bowen v. Roy* decided.

1987   *Edwards v. Aguillard* "creationism" ruling by the Supreme Court; *Corporation of the Presiding Bishop of the Church of Jesus Christ of Latter-day Saints v. Amos* decided.

1988   Congress enacts Indian Gaming Regulatory Act. Court decides *Bowen v. Kendrick* and *Lyng v. Northwest Indian Cemetery Protection Association*.

1989   *County of Allegheny v. ACLU of Greater Pittsburgh Chapter* decision handed down by the Supreme Court banning a nativity scene placed alone in a courthouse staircase as unconstitutional; delivers its opinion in *Texas Monthly, Inc. v. Bullock*.

1990   Congress passes Native American Graves Protection and Repatriation Act. Court renders its opinion in *Board of Education of the Westside Community Schools v. Mergens*, requiring public schools to provide equal access to religious groups as to secular groups; in *Employment Division v. Smith*, it allowed Oregon to fire employee for smoking peyote during a religious ceremony.

1992   *Lee v. Weisman* decided by Supreme Court: an officially sanctioned prayer at graduation was unconstitutional but the school could provide a sign language interpreter to a deaf child at a religious school; *R.A. V. v. City of St. Paul* decided.

1993   Court announces in *Lamb's Chapel v. Center Moriches Union Free School District* and *Church of Lukumi Babalu Aye v. City of Hialeah*.

1994   *Zobrest v. Catalina Foothills School District* case decided, as is *Board of Education of Kiryas Joel Village School v. Grumet* that overturns New York law benefiting a single religious group, a special school for disabled Orthodox Jewish children.

1994   Congress enacts Religious Freedom Restoration Act to ensure that interest in religious freedom is protected. Government must show compelling state interest to restrict religious freedom. Court decides *Rosenberger v. University of Virginia*; in *Capitol Square Review and Advisory Board v. Pinette*, it allowed for a cross by a private group in a public forum to the state house as the space was open to all on equal terms.

1997   Court rules in *Agostini V. Felton* and *City of Boerne v. Flores*.

2000   Supreme Court decides case of *Santa Fe Independent School District v. Doe*, strikes down use of prayer voted on by students to be read at football games as subtle religious coercion of the minority by the majority; in *Mitchell v. Helms*, it rules the federal government could provide computer equipment to all schools under the Elementary and Secondary Education Act.

2001   Terrorists attack Twin Towers in New York and the Pentagon in Washington, D.C., and down plane in Pennsylvania headed for Capitol Hill and the Congress to set off Islamic Terrorism threat; as does an Anthrax contamination threat. Supreme Court decides religious clubs allowed to meet in public schools in *Good News Club v. Milford Central School*.

2002   Court approves voucher system for private schools in *Zelman v. Simmons-Harris* decision. Court decides *Elk Grove Unified School District v. Newdow* ruling on narrow "standing to sue" technical grounds; in *Locke v. Davey*, it allows state to refuse scholarship funds to college students pursuing divinity degrees.

2005   *McCreary County v. ACLU of Kentucky*; *Van Ordern v. Perry*; and *Cutter v. Wilkinson* decisions announced by the Supreme Court regarding monuments displaying Ten Commandments on capitol grounds or in Kentucky courthouses.

2006   Court renders its decision in *Gonzales v. O Centro Espirita Beneficente Uniao do Vegetal* allowing small religious sect to use a hallucinogenic herbal tea in religious ceremonies.

2007   Mitt Romney runs for president on the Republican Party ticket. Court rules taxpayers cannot bring Establishment Clause cases against Office of Faith-Based and Community Initiatives created by the President George W. Bush administration in the case of *Hein v. Freedom from Religion Foundation*.

2010   In *Christian Legal Society v. Martinez*, the Court ruled that student organization at a public university could not limit their membership to those who shared their belief system if doing so resulted in discrimination on the basis of sexual orientation.

2011   *Arizona Christian School Tuition Organization v. Winn* decided.

2012   *Hosanna-Tabor Evangelical Lutheran Church and School v. E.E.O.C.* decides for the Church and against the Equal Employment Opportunity Commission.

2014   *Town of Greece v. Galloway* opinion rendered by Court.

2016   In the waning months of his administration, President Obama directed his Department of Education to issue a "guidance" to state local schools to allow transgender students the right of access to bathrooms that match their gender identity as Title IX, which prohibits sex discrimination in education, applies also to gender identity. President Obama did so despite opposition from the religious right organizations, which argued that such policy should be up to the discretion of local schools. In February 2017, newly appointed Secretary of Education

DeVos, under direction of the President Trump White House, as her first act as secretary of education rescinded the Obama "guidance." Newly appointed Attorney General Jeff Sessions endorsed the policy change. President Trump and Attorney General Sessions also announced the administration would rescind the Johnson Amendment rules that ban religious organizations from political endorsements from the pulpit. The White House announced a flurry of Executive Orders that rescinded Obamacare rules and DACA and DAPA executive actions on Dreamers and fired Acting Attorney General Sally Yates for her refusal to defend the constitutionality of the travel ban for those from seven predominantly Muslim countries. A district court and two appellate courts place a stay order on the travel bans. Trump announced a rewrite of the travel ban to clarify it was not a Muslim ban, which would be unconstitutional on its face, and vows to appeal to Supreme Court.

Amish are a traditionalist Christian fellowship arising in 18th-century Europe, named after Jakob Amman, who share with Mennonites an origin in the Swiss Anabaptist movement, known for simple living, plain dress, and a reluctance to adopt modern technology and lifestyle.

Anabaptists is a Christian movement arising out of the radical reformation, known as Rebaptizers. It was an offshoot of Protestantism in 16th-century Europe that advocated the separation of church and state.

Antinomianism is the belief in faith and divine grace means that the "saved" are not bound to follow the law of Moses.

Apostate is a person who renounces a religious or political belief or principle, from the Greek word "apostasies."

Appellant/Appellee are the two parties to an appeal case. An appeal is a procedure by which an appellant (a person or entity) seeks review of a lower court's ruling. Appellee is the respondent to an appeal.

Arguendo is Latin and sometimes used in Supreme Court opinions, meaning "for the sake of argument."

Arminianism refers to the theological ideas of Dutch reformed theologian Jacabus Arminius, 1560–1609.

Bigamy means to be married to two persons at the same time; it is a crime to do so.

Bill of Rights   are the first 10 amendments to the Constitution of the United States, 1789.

Black Muslims   is the common name for members of the Nation of Islam.

Celestial marriage,   a doctrine of the Church of Jesus Christ of Latter-day Saints, is a marriage performed in the temple for time and eternity and remains a central doctrine of the Latter-day Saints. While it is a concept separate from plural marriage, it was a doctrine associated with the justification of polygamy.

Certiorari   is a writ seeking judicial review. It is issued by a superior court, directing an inferior court, tribunal, or other public authority to send the record of a proceeding for review.

Common schools   was the term used in the 19th century to refer to public schools.

Communitarian   is a philosophy stressing the connection between the individual and the community, a collection of interactions among a community of people in a given place who share interests and a history.

Creationism   is the religious belief that the universe and life originated "from specific acts of divine creation." Literalist creationists base their belief on a literal reading of Genesis, that creation occurred over six 24-hour days.

Creche   is a model or tableau representing the scene of Jesus Christ's birth, displayed in homes or public places at Christmas time.

Cult   is a system of belief and religious veneration directed toward a particular figure or object, usually a small group having beliefs and practices that others see as heretical, strange, or sinister.

Decalogue   is the statement of the Ten Commandments as in the laws of Moses.

Denomination   is a recognized, autonomous branch of the Christian church.

Dicta (plural for dictum) is legal terminology, a statement of opinion considered to be authoritative, although not binding, given the recognized authoritativeness of the person who pronounced it.

Disfellowshipping is the practice among Jehovah's Witnesses to maintain congregational discipline and unity by expulsion and shunning those members who break with established doctrine and practices.

Doctrine of incorporation is the legal theory allowing the Supreme Court to apply the Bill of Rights to the states under the Fourteenth Amendment.

Dunkers is a term referring to the Old German Baptist Brethren, a conservative, plain church emerging from the Anabaptist movement and Pietism. They stressed adult baptism (often rebaptizing) using full immersion, usually in a river.

Emolument is a salary, fee, or profit from employment or office. Article 1, Section 9, clause 8 of the Constitution states: "no Title of Nobility, shall be granted by the United States, and no Person holding any Office of Profit or Trust, under them, Shall, without the consent of Congress, accept any present, Emolument, Office, or Title, of any kind whatever, from any King, Prince or foreign state."

Evangelicals/evangelism or Evangelical Protestantism, is a worldwide, trans-denominational movement that emphasizes the essence of the gospel and doctrine of salvation by grace through faith and personal experience of Christ's atonement.

Federal abstention doctrine is any of several doctrines that a court of law in the United States may (and in some cases, must) apply to refuse to hear a case if doing so would potentially intrude upon the powers of another court.

Forced assimilation is the process of forced cultural assimilation of religious or ethnic minority groups into the larger society by enforcement of new language, education, literature, and worship services. It was used in particular to suppress Native American Indian religion and culture by Indian boarding schools.

Ghetto   is a part of a city, usually in a slum-like neighborhood or area occupied by a minority group or groups, typically a religious minority like Jews or Muslims.

Great Awakening   refers to several periods of religious revival in American history, in three or four waves, mostly during the 18th and 19th centuries.

Great Depression   is the severe, worldwide economic depression during the 1930s that began with the 1929 collapse of the stock market. It was the longest, widest, and deepest depression (economic downturn) of the 20th century.

Hallucinogen   is a drug or substance capable of causing hallucinations when smoked or ingested.

Hierarchical church   is a church that is formally organized into levels of authority: for example, archbishop, bishop, pope, priest, board of elders, laity, and so on.

Hoasca   is a herbal plant used to make hallucinogenic tea used in religious ceremonies by a religious sect of the Santeria religion. Its use is prohibited by the Controlled Substance Act (1970).

Huguenots   are French Protestants of the 16th and 17th centuries, inspired by John Calvin, in 1530, who endorsed the reform tradition of Protestantism.

Injunctive relief   is a writ or court order stopping an agency or governmental official from taking actions that petitioners argue before a court would be harmful.

Invocation   is a prayer to or calling upon God to bless an event, such as the opening of a session of the U.S. Congress or a state legislature.

Jurisprudence   is taking legal action in courts of law or the system of applying judicial judgment (reviews, for example).

Kosher foods are those that conform to the regulations (dietary laws) of kashrut. Food that may be consumed according to halakha is termed kosher in English, from the Ashkenazi pronunciation of the Hebrew term "kasher."

Landmark decision is a Supreme Court decision that sets a precedent, establishes tests or other guidelines that determine subsequent court cases on a legal matter.

Magna Carta (signed in 1215) is the first written document presented to King John of England (1166–1216). It forced the king to sign the document limiting the monarch's powers. It was the basis of English citizens' rights.

Mennonites are a Christian group of the Anabaptist movement named after Menno Simons of Friesland, who articulated and formalized the religious ideas of its early Swiss founders. It strongly emphasized pacificism. The term refers to an ethnic group as well as a religious one.

Millennial movement is the belief by a religious, social, or political group or movement, meaning "containing a thousand."

Ministerial exception rule is a court or congressional rule that exempts ministers of churches from suing their church in civil court, for example, on personnel matters, rights to unemployment compensation, hiring, and firing.

Moravian Brethren is one of the oldest Protestant denominations of the 15th-century Bohemian Reformation, and spread from Saxony to Moravia to escape religious persecution.

Mormon Manifesto is the 1890 statement that advised against any future plural marriage in the Church of Jesus Christ of Latter-day Saints, issued by the Mormon president Wilford Woodruff in September 1890. It was promulgated primarily to clear the way for accepting the Utah territory into the Union.

Ordnung   refers to the set of rules for living of the Amish, Old Order Mennonite, and Conservative Mennonites; it is from the old German word for order, discipline, or rule. It includes shunning to enforce discipline of members.

Papist   is the pejorative term used by Protestants for the Roman Catholic Church, its teachings, practices, and adherents.

Pennsylvania Dutch   is the old German dialect used by the Amish and Mennonite people. It is *not* Dutch, but comes from the mispronunciation by outsiders (non-Amish or Mennonites) of the German word "Deutsch."

Per curiam   decision in law is a ruling issued by an appellate court of multiple judges in which the decision is rendered by the court (or at least, a majority of the court) acting collectively and unanimously.

Peyote   is a mushroom that is ingested or smoked in Native American Indian religious ceremonies that is a powerful hallucinogenic drug made illegal by the Controlled Substance Act of 1970.

Pietist   is an influential movement of Lutheranism emphasizing Biblical doctrine, Reformed Christianity, with an emphasis on piety and the living of a vigorous Christian life.

Polygamy   is marriage involving more than three partners: polygny (a man having two or more wives) and polyandry (a woman having two or more husbands).

Popery   is a Protestant pejorative term used to refer to the Roman Catholic Church and to Catholics and Catholic rites and practices.

Premillennialists   believe that Jesus will physically return to earth before the Millennium—his Second Coming—prior to the start of the Millennium.

Proselytize   is the conversion or attempted conversion of someone from one religion, belief, or opinion to another.

Pull factor   is a social or environmental benefit that draws people from one region or country to another.

Quakers   refers to the Religious Society of Friends, the priesthood of all believers. It avoids creeds and hierarchical structures. In 2007, an estimated 359,000 adults in the United States self-identified as Quakers.

Rebbe   is the Yiddish word from the Hebrew word "rabbi," meaning master, teacher, or mentor. It refers to teachers of Torah or leaders of Jewry, especially Hasidic.

Religious symbol   is found or used in a religion (Christianity, Buddhism, Hinduism, Judaism, etc.) to teach people about beliefs and ideas of that particular religion and to inculcate certain values in them.

Remand   is an action taken by a higher court reviewing the decision of a lower court by which the case is sent back to the lower court for new action following the dicta or guidance of the higher court as to some point of law, often involving a constitutional question or issue.

Sabbatarianism   is a Protestant movement advocating the observance and code of law, delineating how to keep Sunday holy, in observance of the Sabbath commandment or principle. Catholics, Orthodox Christians, and most mainline Protestant denominations follow it with regard to Sunday. Seventh Day Baptists, Seventh-day Adventists, the Church of God, and Judaism hold the Sabbath (Shabbat in Judaism) on Saturday as the holy day.

Sandemanianism   is an aspect of Christian theology regarding the nature of faith as promoted by Robert Sandeman (1718–1781) and John Glas (1695–1773) in Scotland and England in the mid-18th century. Its followers were celebate, communal, pacifist Protestant Christians.

Scapegoat   in the Bible is a goat sent out into the wilderness after the Jewish chief priest had symbolically laid the sins of the people on it. To make a scapegoat of someone or group is to blame that person for the sins of others.

Schism   is a split or division between strongly opposed sectarians or parties caused by differences of opinion or beliefs.

Sect　is a group of people with somewhat different religious beliefs (typically regarded as heretical) from those of a larger group to which they belong.

Shakers　is the common name or term for the United Society of Believers in Christ's Second Appearing, a religious sect founded in 18th-century England. It is a branch of Quakers, or Shaking Quakers, so named because of their ecstatic behavior during worship services.

Shtetls　are small towns with large Jewish population, in central and eastern Europe (especially Poland) before the Holocaust, from the Middle German word "stetel."

Socinianism　was a non-trinitarian Christian doctrine of Fausto Sozzini, held among Polish Brethren in the minor Reformed Church of Poland in the 15th to 17th centuries.

Stakeholder　is a person with an interest or concern in something, especially in a business or political organization; a shareholder or participant.

Sunday laws　were local ordinances that required the cessation of keeping open stores and similar retail operations and especially the closing of alcoholic sales establishments on Sunday.

Swing vote　is a term used to refer to the vote of an associate justice of the U.S. Supreme Court who provides in a Court evenly divided 4–4 along liberal and conservative lines the fifth vote to tip the decision.

Tax exemption　is a rule of a tax code legally excusing a person or group from having to pay a tax, for example, exempting churches from property taxes.

Theistic evolution　is the theory that reconciles religion with science.

Trinitarianism　is the belief in One God (monotheism) who is constituted as three personalities—Father, Son, and Holy Spirit.

Unitarianism　is the liberal religion characterized by free and responsible search for truth and meaning.

United Society of Believers in Christ's Second Coming refers to Shakers or Shaker Quakers and is a millennial restorationist Christian sect founded in 18th-century England, characterized by their ecstatic behavior during worship service. It allowed women spiritual leadership roles in the sect, for example, Mother Ann Lee, Mother Lacy Wright, and Jane Wardley.

Universalism or Christian universalism is a school of Christian theology believing in universal reconciliation, that all human beings are already reconciled to God even if they are unaware of it.

Utopia is an imagined community or society with highly desirable or nearly perfect qualities for its citizens; it stresses egalitarian principles in economics, government, and justice.

Voucher is a small piece of paper that entitles the holder to a discount or that may be exchanged for goods or services.

Voucher system is a system of accounting in which vouchers (as for an amount payable) are prepared with supporting documents attached for each transaction or a series of transactions affecting a single account and entered into a voucher registry. In education, it is used by some state and local governments to help fund education to nonpublic schools.

Wall of separation doctrine is the language of Thomas Jefferson echoing Roger Williams, between the garden of the church and the wilderness of the world; it refers to the American Constitutional principle of the separation of church and state.

Wicca is Pagan (or neo-pagan) witchcraft; contemporary Paganism as a religious movement that began in England in the early 20th century and was introduced and popularized in 1954 by Gerald Gardner.

Writ is a form of legal command in the name of a court or other legal authority to act or to abstain from acting in some way.

Xenophobia   is an intense or irrational dislike or fear of people from other countries—a "fear of the foreign."

Yarmulke   is a skull cap worn by devout Jews.

Yeshiva   is a Jewish institution focusing on the study of traditional religious texts, primarily the Talmud and Torah study, given in daily shivrum (lectures) that are presented in chavruta style (pairings).

Index

Note: page numbers followed by *f* indicate figures and *t* indicate tables.

About the Author

Dr. Michael C. LeMay is professor emeritus from California State University-San Bernardino, where he served as director of the National Security Studies program, an interdisciplinary master's degree program, and as chair of the Department of Political Science and assistant dean for student affairs of the College of Social and Behavioral Sciences. He has frequently written and presented papers at professional conferences on the topic of immigration. He has also written numerous journal articles, book chapters, published essays, and book reviews. He has published in *The International Migration Review, In Defense of the Alien, Journal of American Ethnic History, Southeastern Political Science Review, Teaching Political Science*, and the *National Civic Review*. He is author of more than a dozen academic volumes dealing with immigration history and policy. His prior books on the subject are *Illegal Immigration: A Reference Handbook*, 2nd ed. (2015: ABC-CLIO); *Doctors at the Borders: Immigration and the Rise of Public Health* (2015: Praeger), editor of the three-volume set *Transforming America: Perspectives on Immigration* (2013: ABC-CLIO); *Illegal Immigration: A Reference Handbook* (2007: ABC-CLIO); *Guarding the Gates: Immigration and National Security* (2006: Praeger Security International); *U.S. Immigration: A Reference Handbook* (2004: ABC-CLIO); *U.S. Immigration and Naturalization Laws and Issues: A Documentary History*, edited with Elliott Barkan (1999: Greenwood); *Anatomy of a Public Policy: The Reform of Contemporary Immigration Law* (1994: Praeger); *The Gatekeepers: Comparative Immigration Policy* (1989: Praeger); *From*

Open Door to Dutch Door: An Analysis of U.S. Immigration Policy Since 1820 (1987: Praeger); and *The Struggle for Influence* (1985). Professor LeMay has written two textbooks that have considerable material related to these topics: *Public Administration: Clashing Values in the Administration of Public Policy*, 2nd ed. (2006); *The Perennial Struggle: Race, Ethnicity and Minority Group Relations in the United States*, 3rd ed. (2009). He frequently lecturers on topics related to immigration history and policy. He loves to travel and has lectured around the world and visited more than 100 cities in 40 countries. He has two works in progress: *Winning Office and Making a Nation: Immigration and the American Political Party System* (under review, coauthored with Scot Zentner), and *From Open Door to Storm Door: The Cycles of Immigration Policymaking* (under review).